LEGAL TENDER

D1738749

signale
modern german letters, cultures, and thought

Series editor: Peter Uwe Hohendahl, Cornell University

Signale: Modern German Letters, Cultures, and Thought publishes new English-language books in literary studies, criticism, cultural studies, and intellectual history pertaining to the German-speaking world, as well as translations of important German-language works. *Signale* construes "modern" in the broadest terms: the series covers topics ranging from the early modern period to the present. *Signale* books are published under a joint imprint of Cornell University Press and Cornell University Library in electronic and print formats. Please see http://signale.cornell.edu/.

LEGAL TENDER

Love and Legitimacy in the East German Cultural Imagination

JOHN GRIFFITH URANG

A Signale Book

CORNELL UNIVERSITY PRESS AND CORNELL UNIVERSITY LIBRARY
ITHACA, NEW YORK

Cornell University Press and Cornell University Library gratefully acknowledge the support of The Andrew W. Mellon Foundation for the publication of this volume.

First published 2010 by Cornell University Press and Cornell University Library

Printed in the United States of America

Library of Congress Cataloging-in-Publication Data

Urang, John Griffith, 1975–
   Legal tender : love and legitimacy in the East German cultural imagination / John Griffith Urang.
         p. cm. — (Signale : modern German letters, cultures, and thought)
   Includes bibliographical references and index.
   ISBN 978-0-8014-7653-2 (pbk. : alk. paper)
  1. Love stories, German—Germany (East)—History and criticism.
2. German fiction—Germany (East)—History and criticism.   3. Romance films—Germany (East)—History.   4. Love in literature.   5. Love in motion pictures.   6. Love—Social aspects—Germany (East)
7. Germany (East)—Civilization.   I. Title.   II. Series: Signale (Ithaca, N.Y.)
 √ PT3723.5.L6U73   2010
   843'.085090914—dc22   2010009971

Paperback printing   10   9   8   7   6   5   4   3   2   1

For Jenn and Griffith

Contents

ACKNOWLEDGMENTS

Research for this book was made possible by the generous financial support of the Deutscher Akademischer Austauschdienst (DAAD), the Franke Institute for the Humanities, the University of Chicago, and Reed College.

Parts of chapter 1 appeared as "Realism and Romance in the East German Cinema, 1952–1962" in *Film History* 18.1 (2006). I have presented portions of other chapters at the University of California, Berkeley; the University of Oregon, Eugene; Reed College; and the Midwest MLA convention in Chicago. I am grateful for the productive comments and suggestions I received on those occasions.

Many thanks to Ute Klawitter at the Bundesarchiv Filmarchiv, Manja Meister at defa-spektrum, Elke Jung-Wolff at Fotografie Jung-Wolff, and Bettina Erlenkamp at Deutsche Fotothek Dresden for their assistance in acquiring images for this book. Stills and photographs are reproduced with the kind permission of defa-spektrum and the Staats- und Universitätsbibliothek Dresden.

I owe a debt of gratitude to readers of chapters and drafts, including Hunter Bivens, Matt Hunter, Jennifer Schuberth, Rob Slifkin, Gunnar Urang, and the Franke Fellows. Thanks are due to Marc Silberman, who put together the DEFA issue of *Film History*, for his keen editorial eye. My thanks as well to Kizer Walker, Peter Hohendahl, the *Signale* editorial board, and the two thoughtful, exacting, and generous anonymous readers for Cornell University Press. I am extremely grateful to Marian Rogers, who edited the manuscript with astonishing discernment and thoroughness.

I'm particularly indebted to several members of the faculty in the Department of Germanic Studies at the University of Chicago for their guidance, support, and encouragement of the ideas and research that culminated in this book. Many thanks to Katie Trumpener, whose work as a scholar and a teacher has always been an inspiration; to David Levin, for his careful readings, incisive comments, and delightful conversation; and to Eric Santner, for the depth of his questions and the breadth of his vision.

Thanks to all the friends, teachers, students, and colleagues who have accompanied me on my academic journey. Particular thanks to Catherine Baumann, Andreas Gailus, John Humler, Loren Kruger, Leslie Morris, Moishe Postone, Malynne Sternstein, and David Wellbery for their inspiring teaching and academic work. I am thankful for the friendship and encouragement of my colleagues at Reed College, especially Mark Burford, Katja Garloff, Ülker Gökberk, Ben Lazier, Jan Mieszkowski, Tahir Naqvi, Joel Revill, Paul Silverstein, and Rob Slifkin. I would also like to thank my students at Reed for their invigorating curiosity, insightfulness, and enthusiasm.

Much love to family and friends here and far away. Love and gratitude to my parents, Sarah and Gunnar, for their constant support.

This book is dedicated to Jenn, my partner in everything, and to Gus: cat fancier, cornflake fanatic, bird spotter, pumpkin enthusiast.

Legal Tender

INTRODUCTION

Eros and Exchange

At the end of Leander Haußmann's 1999 film, *Sonnenallee,* a light romantic comedy set in East Germany in the 1970s, the camera pulls back through the open border to the West, and the color fades to black and white. On the sound track, Nina Hagen sings: "Du hast den Farbfilm vergessen, mein Michael" (You forgot the color film, my Michael). In suddenly—and polemically—remembering to forget its own "color film," *Sonnenallee* anticipates and satirizes the reactions of a Western audience. As in the scene where the hero and his best friend sarcastically pantomime "oppression" for a West German tour bus, *Sonnenallee* here assumes it knows what is expected of it, and adjusts accordingly. As Christiane Kuehl remarks in a review of the film for Berlin's *Tageszeitung,*

> Whoever came back from there [the GDR] reported one thing above all, and it was the same thing that dominated every report made by curious newly united Germans after '89: that it was damned gray over there. The GDR was gray. Gray walls, gray streets, gray air, ashen faces. Always the same sentence, sometimes an additional one: over there you felt like you were driving through a black-and-white movie from the '50s.

With mock astonishment, Kuehl describes the overturning of this image in *Sonnenallee:* "Leander Haußmann made a color film. About the GDR. The GDR gleams."

As many of its reviewers were quick to point out, *Sonnenallee*'s colors were rendered particularly bright by the lens of *Ostalgie,* or "nostalgia for the former East Germany." In the words of a review of *Sonnenallee* in *Der Spiegel,*

> Nostalgia is shorthand for "how lovely it was back then," and Ostalgia for "we really had it good in the GDR," even if, yeah, yeah, under further consideration a few things were not so nice back then. Ten years after the fall of the Wall, former East Germans (*Ossis*) remember above all the pleasant things....Sadness sinks into the depths of memory, details blur. (Wellershoff)

Reveling in its gleeful forgetfulness, *Sonnenallee* caused a minor scandal—even before its release. In their review of Haußmann's film, Kerstin and Gunnar Decker make note of some of this negative press:

> The film wasn't even in cinemas yet, and already it met with antipathy. A Berlin city magazine worked itself up to the absurd and intentionally malicious opinion that *Sonnenallee* reminded one of "Nazi comedies" and of the "West German schoolroom- and barracks-comedies of the '50s and '60s." Overall assessment: "a lack of political instinct." (277)

In January 2000 the organization HELP, which advocates for the victims of political persecution, sued Haußmann on the basis of Germany's Paragraph 194, which forbids the insulting of victims of state persecution. HELP objected to Haußmann's creation of a GDR where people "dance in front of the murderous Wall—but not after the fall of the Wall, but rather at a time when this wall was a bloody everyday reality." Even worse, in the film an "escapee who has been shot down" cries, "but not because of the attempted murder, not because of the pain, not on account of fear in the face of upcoming Stasi-imprisonment, but rather because the bullets shattered his Rolling Stones records" ("Strafanzeige gegen Film *Sonnenallee*").[1]

As if anticipating such negative reactions, *Sonnenallee* unloads its most biting satire on the tourists who peer over the Wall from a platform on the Western side. For these caricatured "Wessis," the existence of joy or pleasure on the other side of the Wall is unthinkable: "We're doing great," one sneers down at Michael, the film's hero, near the beginning of the film. "And you?" The others laugh. In another scene the tourists watch Michael dancing on an outdoor ping-pong table. "Hey, a happy commie!" scoffs one of the spectators. Thus, as much as *Sonnenallee* represents an exercise in nostalgic re-membering for the citizens of the former

---

1. All translations of German texts are mine unless otherwise indicated. Actually, Wuschel is not trying to escape when he gets shot down; he is running to avoid confiscation of his newly bought copy of *Exile on Main Street.*

GDR, it is also a performance for a potentially hostile—or worse yet, humorless—Western audience.

In the face of this audience, however, *Sonnenallee*'s *Ostalgie* is not entirely un-repentant. During the film's final tracking shot, speaking over the opening piano chords of "Du hast den Farbfilm vergessen," the hero observes in a voice-over: "Once upon a time there was a country. And I lived there. And when someone asks me, how it was—It was the most beautiful time of my life, because I was young and in love." As the last word on this riot of ostalgic exuberance, the final clause in this statement seems conciliatory, even apologetic: "because I was young and in love" provides a retroactive explanation for the film's redemptive reminiscence—as though such an account were necessary. This explanation would be less psychological than generic: in case we had forgotten to do so, Michael's final voice-over reminds us to read this film as a love story—more specifically, as a story of young love.

In this way, Michael begs the question posed to Haußmann by the *Süddeutsche Zeitung*'s Astrid Becker: "At the end of your film the GDR is described as the most beautiful country in the world for those who were young and in love. Could one really mask the political reality that much?" With a few exceptions, *Sonnenallee*'s audience seemed to think one could. Reviewers dutifully recorded that *Sonnenallee* was a work of fiction and that certain facts had been left out, but most viewers seemed to get it. Even HELP eventually withdrew the charges against Haußmann. As the film's last line reminds us, "getting it," in the case of *Sonnenallee,* is less a question of judging the film's historical accuracy than of recognizing its genre: this is a romantic comedy, and as such it *can be expected* to mask or fade out (*ausblenden*) its "political reality."

This assumption seems fairly intuitive to a modern moviegoer or reader. A love story solicits a certain credulity, a suspension of disbelief stretching from start to finish. Love can set a plot in motion; it can provoke all manner of action and senti-ment; it can mean the protagonists' life or death, joy or undoing. In the love story, all's well that ends well, and all loose ends are tied in the lovers' final embrace. Yet the conditions of love, its grounds and purpose, appear unquestionable, even if its limits are probed and its depths tested. In one of the short "figures" that comprise *A Lover's Discourse,* Roland Barthes's "amorous subject" declares: "There exists a higher value for me: my love. I never say to myself: 'What's the use?' I am not nihil-istic. I do not ask myself the question of ends" (186).[2] Nor do we as observers tend to audit the love story's account: the balance of reasons is always the same. The follow-ing analysis explores these intuitions, taking a closer look at some of the love story's

---

2. Barthes is characteristically cagey about the reliability of the narrator(s) in *A Lover's Discourse:* "[These] reminders of reading, of listening, have been left in the frequently uncertain, incompleted state suitable to a discourse whose occasion is indeed the memory of the sites (books, encounters) where such and such a thing has been read, spoken, heard. For if the author here lends his 'culture' to the amorous subject, in exchange the amorous subject affords him the innocence of his image-repertoire, indifferent to the proprieties of knowledge" (9).

traditional perquisites: its capacity to act as an unmotivated motivator, its primacy in the text's hierarchy of values, its privileged relationship to narrative closure.

Such characteristics stand out in particularly stark relief within the public culture of the GDR, where the "realistic" depiction of cause and effect was mandatory, and the standard of realism dogmatically defined.[3] In Günter de Bruyn's 1972 novel, *Preisverleihung* (The Award Ceremony), an East German university student complains:

> Our literature is supposed to be realistic, but we write about love as though we were in the Middle Ages.... Everything's submerged in mystical darkness.... You can never tell why these two people in particular love each other. Even if they don't know, the author could at least make some speculations.... Political development and love appear in every book. On the first question—which really isn't a question for me, since it's clear—I get a thousand answers. On the second, none or a half. (44–45)

This character asks a question much like the one that set my own inquiry in motion. Why is it that in so many East German novels and films—or better yet, *even* in East German novels and films—the terms of the romantic plot are more or less taken for granted, and the grounds of the lovers' affection left unexplored? Given the tendency—indeed requirement—of East German cultural products to narrativize political economy, a corresponding reflection on the "political economy" of love, the implicit laws governing the distribution of romantic attachments within the text, is conspicuous in its absence. Why did love seem to be a self-evident exception to the rule? Why did what Northrop Frye calls the "communism of convention" (98)—the communal pool of tropes and traditions available to writers within a given culture (for instance, the topoi of romance)—trump the conventions of communism? The answer, I believe, has to do with the unique functionality of the love story, the services that it alone could render, and that were urgently needed within the public culture of the GDR.

Much of the theoretical impetus and infrastructure for this project is provided by Niklas Luhmann's extraordinary study of the origins and history of modern romance: *Love as Passion: The Codification of Intimacy.* In this systems-theoretical history of what he calls the "semantics of love" (8), Luhmann analyzes love as a medium—that is, "not itself a feeling, but rather a code of communication, according to the rules of which one can express, form and simulate feelings, deny them, impute them to others, and be prepared to face up to all the consequences which enacting such a communication may bring with it" (20). By asking not "What is love?" but rather "What is love supposed to *do*?" Luhmann is able to explore the

---

3. Officially, the doctrine of "socialist realism," the mutable and imprecise blueprint of political correctness for East German public culture, held sway at least until 1971, when Eric Honecker declared that there should be "no taboos" in the art and culture of the GDR.

role of the romantic code in the evolution of modern understandings of subjectivity and the individual.

Modern love, according to Luhmann, carries with it a unique set of rules, assumptions, and potentialities. Among the most salient of these capacities is the ability to help organize the illogical and paradoxical into a socially acceptable form. Love thus becomes a means by which the social body can assimilate the unassimilable contradictions of modern life. As Luhmann puts it, "The task of semantics, and in our case, of the semantics of love, would seem to be to sublate these contradictions, to reveal them in controversies, to relate them to one another and to mediate between them" (46). Love does this by providing a discursive structure in which paradox does not endanger but rather constitutes the system as a whole: "The unity of love becomes the framework in which paradoxy that has a practical function in life can be portrayed" (62). In its role as mediator, the "semantics of love" became paramount in negotiating the contradictions and dilemmas accompanying the rise of the modern conception of the individual, hollowing out the necessary space of autonomy within the rigid stratification of the social network.

Proceeding in part from Luhmann's insights, I pose a question he leaves unasked: How might we understand the ideological stakes of the conventions of romantic love? More specifically, how do romantic codes interact with the operation of power, the machinery of persuasion and control?

In using the notoriously elusive concept of "ideology," I hope to address several aspects of the discursive networks commonly associated with this term. The most immediate level would correspond to what Terry Eagleton calls "the single most widely accepted definition of ideology," namely a set of ideas that have to do with "*legitimating* the power of a dominant social group or class" (5). As Eagleton points out, this definition is insufficient to account for many of the characteristics and functions associated with ideology, or for the fact that many beliefs and behaviors considered "ideological" actually run counter to the prevailing disposition of political influence. What this narrower understanding of ideology lacks in agility and sweep, however, it makes up for in directness. Its stakes are fairly clear, its implications explicit: ideology in this sense oils the wheels of power, ensuring acquiescence prior to coercion. This, then, is the sense of "ideology" first intended by Marx and Engels in *The German Ideology:* the "ideas of the ruling class [that] are in every epoch the ruling ideas"; for the "class which has the means of material production at its disposal, has control at the same time over the means of mental production, so that thereby, generally speaking, the ideas of those who lack the means of mental production are subject to it" (64).

Though it may be true that all culture is ideological, I would argue that romance is particularly and uniquely so. It is my contention that this factor—what might be called the ideological use-value of romance—is indispensable in accounting for the love story's ubiquity in modern Western culture. If love stories predominate, it is partly because they do something—ideologically—that few other narrative tropes can. Proceeding from Luhmann's argument, we can see how love, referring to an always-unknowable motivating force, acts within a narrative as a kind of wildcard, rendering the improbable believable, the injudicious justifiable. The romantic plot does not need to appeal to an outside legitimation: it is itself an authorizing force in the narrative. In a hypothetical "conventional" love story, questions about the characters' actions or behaviors could always be answered "because they love each other." If ideology is defined (at least in part) as the way society attempts to vindicate itself to itself, then the explanatory carte blanche that love provides has tremendous ideological potential. The love plot offers an enticingly simple solution to gaps or weaknesses in the narrative's ideological infrastructure: staged as a romantic scenario, ideological conflict can be resolved according to the terms of the romance. Even the most irreconcilable positions can be subjected to the mysterious laws of elective affinity, and the most fundamental conflicts conjured away with a kiss. Thus the semantics of love picks up where politics is forced to leave off, lending a provisional legitimacy to the bankrupt claims of ideology. It renders these claims, one might say, legal tender.

The importance of this argument would be found less in its utility as a political-historical "explanation" of love stories than in the approach it suggests for critical work on romance. It helps direct our investigation of the romantic plot, calling our attention to the cracks and flaws beneath the love story's polished veneer. In fact, as we will see, this surface is not so smooth after all. For the ideological disappearing act wrought by the love story always leaves a trace: the romantic plot itself takes on the tension it was mobilized to alleviate. This tension appears in the narrative as that which cannot be metabolized within the terms of the love story. It creates loose ends and rough edges, the unresolved questions that trip up the reader and cause him or her to ask, "But what about...?" and "What now?" The gambit of this book is that an examination of incongruities in a given love plot will uncover aporias in the ideological framework of the text. What I propose, then, might be called an etiology of the romance, a search for the irritating pebble of ideological self-contradiction coated by the love story's pearl.

Impermanent Revolution, or the Political Economy of Legitimacy in the GDR

We could choose no better case study for the mechanisms and breakdowns of the process of generating legitimacy than the public culture of the GDR. Throughout its forty-year existence, East Germany was plagued with an ongoing problem of legitimacy. Its very validity as a state, for instance, was not generally acknowledged until 1973, when the GDR was granted a seat in the United Nations. Internally, the East German state's most potent machinery of legitimation was found in the appeal to its immediate prehistory: from the first, East Germany was defined as an antifascist state. The Socialist Unity Party, or SED, could then justify its monolithic rule with the claim—in equal parts valid and misleading—to be the inheritor of the German antifascist tradition.[4] In her remarkable book *Post-Fascist Fantasies,* Julia Hell shows how the cultural imagination of the GDR was marked by what she calls an "antifascist myth," the organization of personal and national identity around an imagined legacy of antifascist resistance. In this cultural configuration, a disproportionate amount of attention was paid to the mythologized history of the heroic antifascists, to the detriment of a real coming-to-terms with individual and national culpability.

Yet, without diminishing the significance of the cultural-historical dynamic Hell has so convincingly brought to light, I would suggest that it is possible to overestimate the effectiveness and penetration of the antifascist myth in the ongoing cultural life of the GDR. Though the party insisted on the inviolability and immutability of its antifascist discourse, even this ideological stronghold was subject to the degradations of time. Eventually, as we will see especially in chapter 3, the GDR had to stop saying what it was *not,* and decide what it *was.* The reluctance or inability to do so led to an enduring legitimacy crisis, an evacuation of meaning that could be felt from the most trivial practices of everyday life to the grandest formulations of East German self-understanding.

At a colloquium held at East Berlin's Akademie der Wissenschaften in December 1989 and January 1990, historians reevaluated East German history as a sequence of "Brüche, Krisen, Wendepünkte" (breaks, crises, turning points) culminating in the most recent and decisive upheaval, the Herbstrevolution of 1989. The incidents chosen for discussion at the colloquium amount to a succession of legitimacy crises, moments of breakdown pertaining not just to the surface effects of East German society, but to the foundations of the GDR's ideological self-understanding. For the most part, this series includes fairly predictable entries: the June 17 uprising in 1953, the building of the Wall in 1961, the cultural "freeze" effected by the SED's Eleventh Plenum in 1965, the economic crisis of the early 1970s, and finally the Herbstrevolution of 1989 (Cerny). The sequence of events chosen by the Akademie colloquium exemplifies what I take to be a distinctive teleology toward which histories of the GDR gravitate, one that describes the gradual, inexorable evacuation of the SED's legitimacy claim, until all that remained was to collapse its hollow shell with the assertion "WIR sind das Volk."

Indeed, after hindsight has made historical contingency into inevitability, such a teleological account provides a compelling narrative with which to explain the GDR's peculiar last days, its collapse not with a bang but a whimper. As we will see, the importance of these moments of crisis can hardly be exaggerated. They will return again and again, in explicit and enciphered forms, in the public imagination of the GDR. Yet, I argue, the most profound threat to the ideological legitimacy of

---

4. Valid because many of the SED's members were indeed heroes of the antifascist resistance, returning from exile or imprisonment to government posts at every level. Spurious insofar as party members' self-stylization as the sole representatives of antifascist activity—and sole victims of fascist persecution—was an egregious act of historical revisionism. See Meuschel, 60–70.

East German socialism arose less from these explosive crisis points than from an ongoing and deepening problem throughout the history of the GDR, a problem to which nearly all of the individual crises were intrinsically related.

I follow historian Charles Maier in locating the primary engine of East Germany's slow demise in the increasing unsustainability of its economic base. In *Dissolution: The Crisis of Communism and the End of East Germany,* Maier describes the steady decline of an economy doomed by massive foreign debt and a hopelessly obsolete industrial base. The consumer-side problems engendered by this economic free fall, especially shortages of consumer goods, intensified and accelerated the second catalyst for the Herbstrevolution, namely the growing reluctance of East German citizens to tolerate the repression and restrictions of the SED regime. Sapped by nationwide economic fiasco and essentially abandoned by the Soviet Union, which was caught up in financial troubles of its own, the SED simply gave up the ghost.

On one important point, however, Maier's thesis resists absorption into my line of argument. Maier polemicizes against the use of the term "legitimacy" in connection with the SED regime, taking for granted that the yoke of communist rule could never be considered legitimate, at least according to the terms of Western civil society: "If the possibility of force is never renounced and organized opposition is never sanctioned, the concept of 'legitimacy,' I believe, will not serve any historical or social science analysis. The question must be reformulated: what quality of acceptance was at stake under communism?" (52). Maier's point, that even popular acceptance does not necessarily confer legitimacy on a state, is well taken. Yet the criteria by which he determines legitimacy—majority-ratified accession to power, the ability to maintain power without coercion alone, a use of power in accordance with the standards of international public opinion (51)—which may be useful, for instance, within the context of international diplomacy, have little to tell us about the system-internal struggles of the GDR. Maier's logic would demonstrate that the socialist East German state was illegitimate, but only according to the standards of Western (capitalist) legitimacy. All in all, a fairly predictable result. As I hope to show, a more compelling claim may be formulated not by appealing to the criteria of Western liberal consensus, but by considering the question of the GDR's legitimacy according to the terms of its own ideological infrastructure. The question we will explore, then, is how the GDR measured up to its own goals and aspirations—and what happened when it failed to do so.

The ongoing crisis of legitimacy with which my argument is most concerned consists not just in the SED-state's failure to meet the standards of civil society, nor solely in a quantitative economic crisis, the fatal accumulation of foreign debt and disastrous mismanagement of production and distribution. Far more, this analysis deals with what might be called the GDR's *qualitative* economic crisis, a problem inhering in the nature of economic developments in East Germany from the 1950s on. The trajectory we will follow describes a consistent trend toward economic decentralization, a shift in focus from the sphere of production toward that of consumption, and an ever-greater class divide. In short, the economic landscape of East

German socialism begins to look more and more like that of a market economy, with all its attendant inequalities.

In particular, we will see how the GDR's gravitation toward a market model brought with it the logic of what Marx calls the "commodity fetish," a misrecognition whereby the "definite social relation between men themselves…assumes…the fantastic form of a relation between things" (*Capital,* 165). By this process, Marx claims, the obscured social character of an object—the conditions of its production—is taken to be a quality of the object itself: its intrinsic "value." As Slavoj Žižek reminds us in *The Sublime Object of Ideology,* commodity fetishism is not just a belief, but also a practice. "The illusion is not on the side of knowledge," he points out,

> it is on the side of reality itself, of what the people are doing. What they do not know is that their social reality itself, their activity, is guided by an illusion, by a fetishistic inversion. What they overlook, what they misrecognize, is not the reality but the illusion which is structuring their reality, their real social activity. They know very well how things really are, but still they are doing it as if they did not know. The illusion is therefore double: it consists in overlooking the illusion which is structuring our real, effective relationship to reality. And this overlooked, unconscious illusion is what may be called the *ideological fantasy.* (32)[5]

What I call the "socialist commodity fetish," however, reverses the Marxist dynamic. According to party rhetoric, commodities would not obscure but rather reveal the social relations that produced them—and in so doing, would attest to the triumph of socialist production. The "ideological fantasy" at work in the GDR commodity fetish, then, does not uncouple the commodity from the social network that produced it, but rather erroneously believes consumer goods to be ideologically *inseparable* from this network. Ideological *belief,* in other words, would draw a straight line from the socialist factory to the socialist consumer: the socialist subject would produce and consume with the same intent. In her panoramic history of East German consumer culture, *Utopie und Bedürfnis,* Ina Merkel identifies this logic as a central strategy of GDR *Konsumpolitik:*

> The discourse paradigm of displacing responsibility onto the consumers as producers had an important function, both in terms of defining the community and mobilizing the masses. The fundamental idea was that the working people, as co-owners of production, were no longer working in the interest of exploiters, but rather would themselves benefit—along with the whole population—from their work. To buy and use goods, they had to work for them. (122)

---

5. Terry Eagleton also sees the commodity fetish as the point where ideology becomes "real": "[Whereas] in the *German Ideology* ideology was a matter of not seeing things as they really were, it is a question in *Capital* of reality itself being duplicitous and deceitful" (87).

Yet, as we will see in chapters 1 and 2, the *practice* of consumption in the GDR—and thus, by the logic of "consumers as producers," the practice of production—was a long way from proving the superiority of socialism. If anything, it testified to the opposite.

Breaking It Down: Romantic Economies

The friction generated by the contradiction between the party's lofty hopes and loftier promises on the one hand, and the sad state of GDR factories and showrooms on the other, may be found behind much of the tension and anxiety in the cultural objects discussed here. To put a finer point on it, it is this contradiction in particular against which the romantic plot is so often rallied. The love story, I argue, is uniquely positioned to intervene in the economic logic—that is, the logic that determines the allocation of value, the flow of attraction, the exchange of desire—of a given text. Romance does this by appealing to its own exclusive economy, a circulation of desire that, at least in principle, flouts the laws of economic exchange writ large. This point is made incisively by Lydia Davis in her short story "Break It Down," in which the main character systematically—and literally—puts a price on a brief love affair:

> He's sitting there staring at a piece of paper in front of him. He's trying to break it down. He says:
> I'm breaking it all down. The ticket was $600 and then after that there was more for the hotel and food and so on, for just ten days. Say $80 a day, no, more like $100 a day. And we made love, say once a day on the average. That's $100 a shot. And each time it lasted maybe two or three hours so that would be anywhere from $33 to $50 an hour, which is expensive.
> Though of course that wasn't all that went on, because we were together almost all day long. She would keep looking at me and every time she looked at me it was worth something. (20)

Once he has turned over all the events of their short time together and factored in the time spent thinking about her after the fact, the hourly rate has dropped: "So when you add up all that, you've only spent maybe $3 an hour on it" (27). Finally, he turns his attention to the "bad times" of the relationship, especially the moment of parting:

> Walking away I looked back once and the door was still open, I could see her standing far back in the dark of the room, I could only really see her white face still looking out at me, and her white arms.
> I guess you get to a point where you look at that pain as if it were there in front of you three feet away lying in a box, an open box, in a window somewhere. It's hard

and cold, like a bar of metal. You just look at it there and say, All right, I'll take it, I'll buy it. That's what it is. Because you know all about it before you even go into this thing. You know the pain is part of the whole thing. And it isn't that you can say afterwards the pleasure was greater than the pain and that's why you would do it again. That has nothing to do with it. You can't measure it, because the pain comes after and it lasts longer. So the question really is, Why doesn't that pain make you say, I won't do it again? When the pain is so bad that you have to say that, but you don't.

So I'm thinking about it, how you can go in with $600, more like $1000, and how you can come out with an old shirt. (29–30)

Why, the story's "I" asks, do we let ourselves into this apparently unfavorable exchange again and again? Why does no amount of money or suffering seem to tip the scales away from love? The incommensurability of such calculations with the logic of romantic love lends Davis's story its wry poignancy. The protagonist will never know if his relationship was "worth it," because the code of love explodes the concept of worth itself.

In his preface to *The American,* Henry James captures this quality of romantic plots with characteristic precision and finesse:

The only general attribute of projected romance that I can see, the only one that fits all its cases, is the fact of the kind of experience with which it deals—experience liberated, so to speak; experience disengaged, disembroiled, disencumbered, exempt from the conditions that we usually know to attach to it and, if we wish so to put the matter, drag upon it, and operating in a medium which relieves it, in a particular interest, of the inconvenience of a related, a measurable state, a state subject to all our vulgar communities. (33)

Extending the metaphor, James imagines romance as an attempt to "cut the cable" between the "balloon of experience" and the earth—that is, the "vulgar communities" of economic logic, of "measurable states" (33). Perhaps more than any writer's, James's work shows the resilience of this cable, this taut tether between romantic flight and worldly concerns.

Luhmann, as well, comes to the conclusion that love precludes any kind of cost-benefit analysis, especially of an economic nature:

Paradoxicalization and particularly the incorporation of effort, worry and pain into love further result in a differentiation of love and interest, i.e. love and economy (in the broadest sense, i.e. including the household economy). In contrast to what is true of one's interests, it is impossible in love to calculate the costs or weigh up the accounts, because both one's profits and one's losses are enjoyed, indeed, they serve to make one aware of love and to keep it alive. (66–67)

Indeed, love stories seem to exult in spurning considerations of profit and loss, leading the protagonists to renounce power, status, fortune, and sometimes even life itself in the pursuit of romantic fulfillment. How, despite the general trend toward ever greater rationalization in the modern age, does romance—at least in its cultural articulations—continue to resist economic rationalization?

One framework within which to begin constructing an answer to this question may be found in the so-called numismatics of Freudian-Marxist theorist Jean-Joseph Goux. In *Symbolic Economies: After Marx and Freud,* Goux presents a sweeping system of convergences and equivalences, tracing the outline of a general theory of social exchange. Yet in the whole series of symbolic substitutions that constitutes the numismatic system, love never makes an appearance. In this sense, Goux seems to follow Freud in his tendency to treat love more as a psychic and biological phenomenon than as a social or cultural one—that is, to subsume romantic love into sexuality.

That the "love" of Freud's libido theory often represents an object quite different from the one under consideration in this project may be seen in the "economic" element introduced in the opening passage of *Beyond the Pleasure Principle:*

> In the theory of psycho-analysis we have no hesitation in assuming that the course taken by mental events is automatically regulated by the pleasure principle. We believe, that is to say, that the course of those events is invariably set in motion by an unpleasurable tension, and that it takes a direction such that its final outcome coincides with a lowering of that tension—that is, with an avoidance of unpleasure or a production of pleasure. *In taking that course into account in our consideration of the mental processes which are the subject of our study, we are introducing an 'economic' point of view into our work;* and if, in describing those processes, we try to estimate this "economic" factor in addition to the "topographical" and "dynamic" ones, we shall, I think, be giving the most complete description of them of which we can at present conceive, and one which deserves to be distinguished by the term "metapsychological." (3, italics mine)

As Davis's story in particular teaches us, it is precisely such "economic" considerations that the cultural topos of romantic love works so hard to resist. The individual psyche may hedge its bets, weighing the yield of pleasure against that of unpleasure, but in the romantic plot, love is always all-in. As mentioned above, the disparity here does not arise from incommensurable theories, but rather from nonidentical objects of study: love as a psychic phenomenon versus love in its conventionalized cultural articulation.

From this latter point of view, we can speculate why Goux must exclude love from his numismatic chain. Goux's system identifies a number of "general equivalents" that anchor various social organizations: money, language, the state. Within these symbolic economies, general equivalents serve to make comparable the values of dissimilar objects. Just as one commodity, gold, became the standard by which all others were evaluated, such general equivalents as the father, the phallus, the monarch, and the spoken word came to unify their various symbolic networks, rendering the elements of those networks assimilable into a hierarchy of value. Yet romantic love, as we have seen, insists on the *incomparability* of its object, locating all value within the closed system of the lovers' union.

Shakespeare's twenty-first sonnet calls our attention to the paradoxical implications of this injunction for romantic literature—in particular, for the sonnet's traditional use of metaphor to communicate the incommunicable:

> So is it not with me as with that Muse
> Stirred by a painted beauty to his verse,
> Who heaven itself for ornament doth use
> And every fair with his fair doth rehearse
> Making a couplement of proud compare,
> With sun and moon, with earth and sea's rich gems,
> With April's first-born flowers, and all things rare
> That heaven's air in this huge rondure hems.
> O let me, true in love, but truly write,
> And then believe me, my love is as fair
> As any mother's child, though not so bright
> As those gold candles fixed in heaven's air:
> Let them say more that like of hearsay well;
> I will not praise that purpose not to sell.[6]

As it is characterized here, metaphor would function like Goux's general equivalent, translating disparate qualities into "marketable" value. As the sonnet's concluding couplet points out, the poet should in fact want the opposite: that the beloved's charms remain inscrutable, inestimable, invaluable in the eyes of the world. Insofar as romantic love claims to resist such systems of exchange, it also defies economic rationalization. It demands exclusion, in other words, from the symbolic economies described by Goux.

Yet if love were, indeed, only in the eye of the beholder, few love stories would be of interest to anyone but the participants. And even these participants would always be uncertain of each other's affections. According to Luhmann, this paradox, which he formulates at one point as "the incommunicability of genuineness" (45–46), necessitated the creation of the romantic code in the first place. Luhmann remarks: "[Precisely] the irrationality of passion makes it improbable that two people are seized by it at the same time with respect to one another. Cupid does

---

6. Shakespeare, "Sonnet XXI," ed. Wells and Taylor, 781.

not, after all, shoot off two arrows at once; love may well occur by coincidence, but normally not as a double coincidence" (62). The radical doubt generated by this state of affairs demanded a semantic codification of passion, a shared language with which to encourage, express, compare, and evaluate these experiences. Thus Luhmann notes: "Love as a communicative medium refers not to the psychic but to the social system" (63).

In this sense, we can call the love story's bluff: love may be an ineffable experience, and the virtues of the beloved incomparable—this may be, in other words, an economy without a proper general equivalent—but the love story is forced, for the sake of communicability, to establish a more universal arrangement. Striving to get its point across, the romantic plot enters into dialogue with the symbolic economies of its social and cultural context: it may, for instance, cross the no-man's-land between warring families, proving the characters' love stronger than the prohibition of father or clan; love may trump money when a fortune or a fortunate marriage is sacrificed for its sake; worldly passions may get the better of religious faith and sacred commitments. In each of these cases, the introduction of love into a symbolic economy neutralizes the ruling term of that system, rendering father, money, or God merely a foil to demonstrate the supremacy of romantic passion.

Yet the love plot is equally likely to incorporate elements of these neighboring economies into its own semantic framework and value structure. In the interest of intelligibility, the love story collects and redeploys whichever symbolic configurations will best complement or accentuate it. By this mechanism, certain characteristics or behaviors that in fact belong to other sign systems entirely become "romantic." Such qualities as "good breeding," for instance, or virtue and piety or material wealth may come to signify the desirability of a romantic partner. At the same time as it insists on its primacy and autonomy, romance becomes entangled in symbolic structures that threaten its narrative privilege. It is here, as we will see, that the love story becomes harnessed to ideology, and its romantic economy begins to look like the political economy of the society from which it springs.

Within the romantic mode, the temporality of love is as self-referential as its semantic content: entirely self-sustaining, love would escape the demands of time, persisting immutably in the face of fate and circumstance. The notion of "everlasting love," however, owes its poignancy in large part to the fact that it is the direct inverse of what is happening at the narrative level: as soon as we can be assured that the couple's love is eternal, the story ends and we are released from its libidinal economy. Sometimes this release is brought about by the lovers' deaths, sometimes by the promise of their living "happily ever after." The precipitous tragic or happy ending of the romance testifies to the extraordinary narrative exertion required to sustain this temporary utopia. Before the inevitable realities—the economic realities, broadly defined—of coexistence catch up with the lovers, we must part company with them and return to our own everyday lives. The love story's utopia is thus less a revolution than a state of exception: it does not negate the laws of political economy; it only suspends them.

Even so, this provisional rearrangement of the hierarchies of value within a given symbolic structure represents a significant threat to the hegemony of that order. Indeed, the same functions that render it so effective an instrument of ideological persuasion also constitute the subversive pleasure of the romantic text: in insisting on its narrative prerogatives, romance invokes a world beyond the tyranny of political economy, a private utopia shared by the lovers and their empathetic audience. In this way, the couple's intractable self-involvement undermines the totalizing claims of any given social network or institution in the narrative: even the most law-abiding citizen roots for Bonnie and Clyde. The love plot, in other words, always presents an *alternative* regime to the one(s) that claim primacy in the text—it holds the promise of what James Baldwin calls "another country."[7] For this reason, it is a dangerous proposition to borrow legitimacy from the love plot. "For love is so created," the narrator of Goethe's *Wahlverwandschaften* tells us, "that it itself alone claims to be right and all other claims disappear before it" (86). Or, in the words of Marie von Ebner-Eschenbach's aphorism, "Love does not just have rights, love is always right" (15).

German Democratic Love Stories

The love story's unique and unpredictable mix of stabilizing and subversive effects helps illuminate its peculiar status within the East German cultural sphere. While traditional romance presented a potent challenge to the aesthetic and ideological orthodoxy demanded by East German cultural policy, it could also bypass some of the unavoidable and insoluble contradictions of the GDR's ideological infrastructure—and, perhaps more importantly, it could provide a welcome respite from the onerous polemicism of East German public culture.

East German love stories were the inheritors of a fraught and ambivalent tradition: on the one hand, East German writers had recourse to the age-old history (discontinuous and heterogeneous though it may be) of what Denis de Rougemont calls "love in the Western world." Romantic texts and tropes made up a good deal of the so-called *Kulturerbe* (cultural heritage), that part of the Western cultural tradition that the party deemed acceptable for inclusion in the East German canon. Thus classic love stories such as *The Sorrows of Young Werther, Anna Karenina,* and *Madame Bovary* played as important a role in shaping the romantic imagination in the East as they did in the West.

At the same time, however, the East German love story was heir to a long history of suspicion regarding the institutions and practices of romantic love, from

---

7. Baldwin's novel *Another Country* follows several romantic couples in their search for love's alternate reality, for a union that transcends the constraints of class, sex, and race. Whether this state is attained—or attainable—within the terms of the novel is a question for another forum.

the critiques of bourgeois familialism put forward by Marx, Engels, Bebel, and Zetkin to the rearrangement of traditional gender roles and relations effected by the Russian Revolution. The latter was particularly significant in this regard, since it seemed destined to implement the changes its architects had only theorized. As Sheila Rowbotham notes in an intriguing chapter on sexual politics during this era in her book *Women, Resistance, and Revolution,* "In the early years of the revolution it was generally assumed that the family would wither along with other institutions which had persisted from capitalist society" (145).

Perhaps no one was more attuned to the psychosexual consequences of the Russian Revolution than Alexandra Kollontai, whose writings—and biography—attest to the transformed erotic potential of the revolutionary period. In the chapter "Love and the New Morality" in her book *Sexual Relations and the Class Struggle,* for instance, Kollontai uses a then-recent book by German writer Grete Meisel-Hess, *The Sexual Crisis,* to put forward a program of sexual liberation for the new socialist society:

> Society must above all learn to accept all forms of personal relationships however unusual they may seem, provided they comply with two conditions. Provided that they do not affect the physical health of the human race and provided they are not determined by the economic factor. The monogamous union based on "great love" still remains the ideal. But this is not a permanent or set relationship. The more complicated the individual psyche the more inevitable are the changes. "A succession of monogamous relationships" is the basic structure of personal relationships. But side by side there are a whole range of possible forms of "erotic friendship" between the sexes. (25)

Other cultural producers as well articulated the turbulent status of erotic relationships in the years following the revolution. Abram Room's 1927 film, *Bed and Sofa,* for instance, depicts a complicated love triangle between three young people who are forced by the housing crisis to share an apartment. They live together in a number of amorous permutations before the woman finally decides to seek fulfillment on her own. Dasha, a character in F. V. Gladkov's 1928 novel, *Cement,* reaches a similar decision, finding marriage incompatible with her new role in socialist society. "I don't know, Gleb," she tells her husband. "Perhaps I don't love any man. And perhaps I love—. I love you, Gleb; that's true—but perhaps I love others, too? I don't know, Gleb; everything is broken up and changed and become confused. Somehow love will have to be arranged differently" (292).

As these examples suggest, it seemed for a time that Soviet revolutionary culture would indeed arrange love differently. The conservative social policies of the Stalinist era, however, systematically stifled such challenges to gender roles and sexual norms. In *The Great Retreat,* Nicholas Timasheff describes some of the radical changes brought about by Soviet social policy, then outlines the process by which these developments were reversed in the 1930s: marriage was reemphasized, divorce made more difficult, abortion declared illegal, and parental (paternal) authority strengthened through propaganda and legislation (192–203).[8] When socialist realism was adopted as official doctrine at the First Soviet Writers' Congress in 1934, it bore the marks of Stalinist social conservatism in its suspicion of the love story, a genre prone to irrationality, individualism, and excess. In the end, love plots were to be warily tolerated, as long as they remained subordinate to the overall ideological template of the work.

In many ways, however, socialist realism has a great deal in common with the bourgeois romance. Considering how little romance actually appears in these texts, it is remarkable how romantic socialist realism tends to be, retaining such elements as the ideal hero, the binary organization of good and bad characters, the utopian tendency, and the predictable happy ending. Indeed, as Andre Zdanov observed at the First Soviet Writers' Congress, "Our literature, which stands with both feet firmly planted on a materialist basis, cannot be hostile to romanticism, but it must be a romanticism of a new type, revolutionary romanticism" (Scott, 21). In terms of the above analysis, we might say that revolutionary romanticism wanted to retain the ideologically stabilizing effect of the traditional love story, but without the destabilizing tendencies of passion and desire. Referring to this propensity for stabilization, Régine Robin calls socialist realism "an aesthetics of the return to order" (7).

Along with the rest of socialist-realist doctrine, this socially conservative prototype of the love plot was carried over into the cultural policy of the fledgling East German state. From the outset, however, doctrinal socialist realism had an uphill struggle in East Germany. As commentators such as David Bathrick have pointed out, a significant challenge came from countercurrents within the East German public sphere, especially in the form of what Bathrick calls a "return of the repressed," a reappearance of the modernist and avant-garde traditions of the early revolutionary period in the works of artists like Bertolt Brecht and Hanns Eisler (89).

Even more, however, socialist realism's aesthetic hegemony was threatened by the entertainment superpower to the west. Before the building of the Berlin Wall in 1961, "imperialist propaganda" was only as far away as the nearest border-cinema.[9] As we will see in chapter 1, the influence of the Western culture industry was particularly noticeable in what might be called the "romantic imagination" of the East German audience—their assumptions and expectations regarding the structure and mechanics of the love story—for romance, from the comic to the melodramatic, was what Hollywood and its imitators did best.

---

8. See also Robin, 6–7.
9. For a fascinating discussion of border cinemas in divided Berlin, see "Border Cinemas: Mediascapes of the Cold War," in Katie Trumpener's *The Divided Screen: The Cold War and the Cinemas of Postwar Germany.*

David Bordwell, Kristin Thompson, and Janet Staiger claim in *The Classical Hollywood Cinema* that 95 of the 100 films they surveyed include a romantic plot, and 85 have romance as their primary plot.[10] "Screenplay manuals," they write, "stress love as the theme with greatest human appeal" (16). Love has always been the bread and butter of Hollywood, and from the beginning the film industry set out to refine and redefine the genre, capitalizing on both its commercial and its ideological potential. Film became an extremely effective means of organizing and disseminating changing practices of courtship and romance. The larger-than-life images on the screen were a far more efficient romantic primer than theater or literature had been, as a 1933 study by Herbert Blumer makes clear.[11] Based on interviews, questionnaires, and direct observation, Blumer concludes that both children and young adults are highly susceptible to the influence of motion pictures and tend to imitate the attitudes and behaviors they see on screen. Romantic love, Blumer claims, is particularly significant in this regard: "From the earlier discussion of love pictures and imitation and of the influence of love pictures in stimulating emotions, one would expect young men and young women to derive from these pictures ideas of love and of the behavior associated with it" (153).[12]

The movies were especially instructive in one particular area. Virginia Wright Wexman observes: "If close-up photography has influenced the subtlety with which emotions and information are signified through performance, it has also privileged a particular element associated with romantic attraction: the kiss" (18). The long-deferred kiss, the terminus of countless romantic movies, represented a powerful new technology in the semantics of love: all the anticipation of courtship, all the promise of happiness to come, could now be distilled into one moment, one gesture.

Just as the screen kiss taught audiences how love's fulfillment was supposed to look, the development and cultivation of Hollywood's star system gave romance a recognizable face. The star system took the love story's traditional machinery of projection and identification to a new level: instead of a particular character, the moviegoer could now identify with or idealize a "real" person. As Edgar Morin expresses it,

> Henceforth we embark upon the stellar dialectic. The star's beauty and youth magnify her roles as lover and heroine. Her love and heroism magnify in turn the young and beautiful star. In the movies she incarnates a private life. In private she must incarnate

---

10. I am indebted to Virginia Wright Wexman's book *Creating the Couple: Love, Marriage, and Hollywood Performance* for alerting me to this quantification (3).

11. Eva Illouz's *Consuming the Romantic Utopia* (44–45) pointed me toward Blumer's study.

12. In Buster Keaton's *Sherlock Jr.*, an inexperienced young projectionist woos his girlfriend in the projection booth while a romantic movie is playing. Unsure how to proceed, he simply imitates everything he sees on screen.

a movie life: by means of each of her film characterizations the star interprets herself;
by revealing her own character, she interprets the heroines of her films.

What is a film if not a "romance," i.e., a personal story destined for the public?
The star's personal life must be public. (58)

In this way, the movies' glamorous fantasies were brought into the "real world,"
hypostatized in an offscreen lifestyle as romantic as any the actor portrayed in his
or her films.

The nature and content of this romance constitute Hollywood's most significant
reorganization of the romantic code. Borrowing a phrase from Leo Lowenthal,
Richard Dyer has called American movie stars "idols of consumption," glorified
not for their social productivity, but for their activities in the sphere of leisure (Lowenthal, 115; qtd. in Dyer, 39). Living advertisements for the life of luxury, movie
stars helped cement the bond between romance and consumption in the cultural
imagination of the United States and beyond. In her remarkable analysis of modern American romance, *Consuming the Romantic Utopia: Love and the Cultural
Contradictions of Capitalism,* Eva Illouz offers a useful terminology with which to
approach the connection between romance and consumption. She juxtaposes what
she calls the "romanticization of commodities," the romantic aura attached to
commodities in films and advertising, and the "commodification of romance," the
intertwining of romantic practices with the consumption of consumer goods and
leisure technologies (26). As we will see, both of these developments took root in the
East, notwithstanding the many obstacles to their transplantation.

East German romance, then, may be seen as a unique combination of four distinct strands: first, the romantic tradition of the *Kulturerbe*'s classic love stories, with
the accumulated tropes and tendencies of its venerable pedigree; then, in almost di-
ametrical opposition, the radical challenge of revolutionary socialism, the attempt
to realign Eros with the new social ties of the coming order. Such restructuring was
cut short by the socially conservative hard line of Stalinism, with its cultural corollary in the doctrine of socialist realism, which projected its own romantic vision
onto the socialist tradition. Finally, to the vexation of ideologues and functionaries, the GDR's amorous imagination bore the unmistakable stamp of Hollywood's
commodified romance, especially by way of West German imports and imitations.
We will see these strands interweave and intersect in the public culture of the GDR,
as writers, filmmakers, functionaries, and audiences searched for a model of love
appropriate to the demands and achievements of East German socialism.

The first chapter of this book explores the collision between two of these romantic
paradigms: the Westernized template of glamorous, commodified romance on
the one hand, and the rigorously ideological couplings of 1950s socialist realism on
the other. Tracking the gradual loss of ground by hyperpoliticized socialist-realist
love plots to a romantic model more Lubitsch than Lenin, we will gain insight into
not only the characteristic tendencies of modern romance, but also the mechanisms

by which ideological friction became encoded in the East German romantic imagination. This drift does not just represent a capitulation to the West or a concession to the demands of East German audiences, but rather marks a rift internal to the self-understanding of the SED state. Within the changing fortunes of East German romance, in other words, we will see the inconsistency and ambivalence of an uncharacteristically erratic party line. In the early part of this decade, East German cultural policy underwent an extensive revision, essentially reversing the mandate of cultural producers overnight while insisting that the underlying principles remained the same.

Chapter 1 examines these shifts through the lens of film policy, specifically the debates around the proper role of romance in the East German cinema. As we will see, the increasingly volatile dissatisfaction of the GDR's citizenry made the need for distracting "light entertainment"—comedy and romance—greater than any scruples the champions of socialist realism might have about the films' political content, or lack thereof. This cultural concession, however, was just the surface effect of a deeper and more radical transformation in the GDR's political economy. Scrambling to find a brake to its accelerating labor crisis, the SED was putting policies into effect that would bring the East German economy closer to that of its neighbor to the west. This was, in short, the start of an East German consumer culture. It is this change, then, that is reflected in—and was fostered by—the ever-greater role of commodities and consumption in the libidinal economy of 1950s East German public culture.

If love stories were harbingers of East German consumer culture, however, they were also mobilized in the nascent opposition to this trend. The second part of chapter 1 takes a close look at two important DEFA films from the late 1950s, emphasizing their shared concern with the eager participation of East German youth in the attitudes and practices of Westernized, commodified romance.[13] Though the stance of these films represents a significant challenge to the course of East German public policy at the time, they fail to present a viable alternative to the glamorous promises—whether from the West or from the East—that lead the young protagonists astray.

In this respect, we can say that the novels described in chapter 2 pick up where these films leave off. Both novels, which belong to a genre known as the *Ankunftsroman,* or "novel of arrival," set themselves the task of forging the bonds that would connect young East Germans to their socialist homeland. The *Ankunftsroman* attempts to do so not through the allure of conspicuous consumption, but rather through the satisfactions of industrial production. This objective, I argue, is structured, supported, and often brought about by the *Ankunftsroman*'s central love story.

---

13. The Deutsche Film Aktiengesellschaft, or DEFA, was the state film studio of East Germany.

The first part of chapter 2, a reading of Brigitte Reimann's *Ankunft im Alltag* (Arrival in the Everyday), identifies two competing modes of romance in the text: the idealistic "neue Romantik," which finds erotic charge in the rigors and rewards of the production process; and the Americanized romance of conspicuous consumption. Wavering between these poles, the heroine's romantic decision comes to stand in for the choice—or desired choice—of her generation. As we will see in the second half of chapter 2, a "neue Romantik" also seems to fuel the irrepressible optimism of the young protagonists of Karl Heinz Jakobs's *Beschreibung eines Sommers* (Description of a Summer). Yet it is precisely this enthusiasm, this "anticipatory consciousness," that necessitates the scenario of correction and control that concludes the novel, for although the young workers' productive zeal is indispensable to the socialist project, their uncompromising vision also presents a threat to the stability of the East German state.

Chapter 3 considers the situation created by the economic developments outlined in the first two chapters. In particular, the works analyzed in chapter 3 respond to the ideological friction created by the emergence of salient class divisions within "real existing socialism." In my readings of these works—novels and films spanning the years 1968–1978—I show how their love stories mediate the problem of class in the GDR, providing a language with which to discuss the experience of class antagonism without undermining the legitimacy of the SED's claim to preside over a society in which such dynamics had been overcome. In these novels and films, the love relationship becomes the space in which the protagonists experience—and often resolve—immanent class tensions. Each of the texts analyzed here discovers the same "solution" to the problem of class (though the authors approach this solution with differing amounts of credulity or irony): a bourgeois protagonist rediscovers his or her dormant penchant for the "neue Romantik" and begins a love affair with a member of the working class. The course and outcome of this cross-class romance, then, become ciphers for a negotiation of the increasingly stratified society of "real existing socialism."

The first part of chapter 4 sketches the priorities and horizons of East German gender discourse by investigating a fascinating anthology published in 1975: *Blitz aus heiterm Himmel* (Bolt from the Blue), a volume of short stories envisioning magical or scientific sex-reversals. Whereas *Blitz aus heiterm Himmel* makes a strong case for what might now be called a postmodern conception of gender as performative, fluid, socially constructed, and universally disseminated, the following decade saw a reconsideration of these assumptions; works from the 1980s tend to portray gender as an inherent and essential component of one's identity—especially women's identity. Chapter 4 tracks the significance and consequences of this shift through close readings of two key novels by Irmtraud Morgner: the 1974 pastiche picaresque *Leben und Abenteuer der Trobadora Beatriz* (Life and Adventures of Trobadora Beatrice) and the 1983 epic *Amanda: Ein Hexenroman* (Amanda: A Witch Novel). Read together, these novels constitute a radical interrogation of the conditions of possibility for real love between equals—even in the allegedly egalitarian society of "real existing socialism." The final section of the chapter speculates about how romantic love might have fared in the bleak, postutopian landscape of Morgner's ambitious, unfinished novel, *Das heroische Testament* (The Heroic Testament), the third work in the planned trilogy.

The ideological arc described by the first four chapters is that of a state increasingly at odds with its foundational and guiding principles (the ideals of socialist equality) and ever more out of touch with its own populace, especially its nominal "ruling" (that is, working) class. By the 1980s the SED state was effectively out of control, reduced to helpless (but not harmless) watching and waiting. This condition is epitomized in the metastasis of the state surveillance apparatus: the notorious *Staatssicherheitsdienst* grew ever larger the weaker its masters became. Chapter 5 focuses on three "Stasi novels," one written before unification and two after, all sharing a concern with what could be called the psychosexual dimension of surveillance work: the conscious or unconscious desires and fantasies that motivate the professional snoop. These are not love stories, but rather stories of not-love: more specifically, I argue, stories of perversion. In the perverse fantasy-lives of three Stasi men—and, more importantly, in the novels' fantasies of these fantasies—we can see reflected both the necrotic condition of the East German state in the 1980s and the retrospective reevaluation of life in the East from the vantage point of a newly unified Germany.

1

WARES OF LOVE

Socialist Romance and the Commodity

Wann lernen Sie, daß Liebe ... auch ihre Grenzen hat?

When will you learn that love also has its borders?

> — WILLI, factory-militia captain, stopping East German call girls
> from crossing the newly closed border to the West, in Gerhard
> Klein's 1966 film, *Geschichten jener Nacht* (Stories from That Night)

The problem is summed up by a pair of juxtaposed photographs in the May 1954 issue of the East German entertainment magazine *Das Magazin*. The first looks outward from a bookshop at a young couple window-shopping arm in arm (fig. 1). Both are gazing intently at a book entitled *Verliebte Welt,* (World in Love). The caption reads: "wahre Liebe" (True Love). On the facing page is a photograph of another couple, from the waist down (fig. 2). He is wearing a wrinkled sportscoat and pointed shoes; she a tight sweater, a short floral-print skirt, and stockings. On a billboard behind them we can see most of the words "St. Pauli," a reference to the red-light district of Hamburg. The caption reads: "Liebesware" (Wares of Love).

At first, the intended moral of the story seems fairly clear. Against the Cold War backdrop of the early 1950s, "Wares of Love" seems to point to the decadent West, where love is for sale, literally and figuratively. The couple's clothes suggest that they are *Halbstarken* (literally, "half-strong"), the German version of the rebels-without-a-cause who appeared all over Europe and the United States in the 1950s.[1] In consuming the latest fashion trends, in buying the products that are supposed to make them more desirable, these young West Germans are in fact selling themselves.

---

1. For a contemporary account of the *Halbstarken* epidemic, see Curt Bondy et al., *Jugendliche stören die Ordnung: Bericht und Stellungnahme zu den Halbstarkenkrawallen.*

wahre Liebe

Figure 1. "True Love." A young couple window-shops at a bookstore. Source: *Das Magazin*, May 1954, 38.

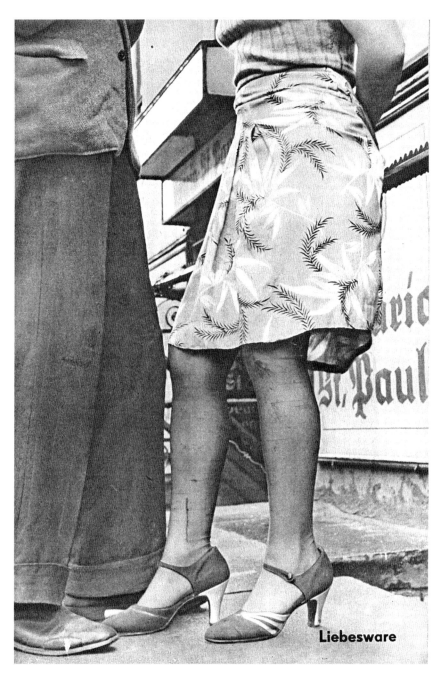

Liebesware

Figure 2. "Wares of Love." Behind this pair we can see the words "St. Pauli," a reference to the red-light district of Hamburg. Source: *Das Magazin,* May 1954, 39.

The East, we may infer, is the land of "True Love," where young lovers are brought together by culture and ideas, rather than fashion. The pair in the bookstore, however, are not *not* consuming: their romantic moment is created and defined by commodities—in this case, books. In fact, the books are not even products of the socialist bloc: one title, faintly visible, identifies a translation of British author David Severn's 1946 children's novel *Forest Holiday,* while *Verliebte Welt* is a picture book by the popular French cartoonist Raymond Peynet. Both "true love" and "love-for-sale," it seems, may involve the act of consumption—even of Western products. The determining difference seems to lie in the intention behind the consumption. Perhaps this need for qualitative discernment explains the third figure in the "wahre Liebe" photograph, a man wearing a trenchcoat, hat, and glasses, standing behind the couple and watching them. Implicit or explicit supervision appears frequently in East German love stories from this period. With such a thin line between "true love" and "love-for-sale," only constant vigilance could prevent the former from giving way to the latter.

This chapter will examine the ideological friction generated at the intersection of romance and consumer culture. In particular, my analysis will focus on the ways in which commodities become imbricated in the ideals and practices of romantic love, the subtle or conspicuous ways in which commodities come to mediate even—indeed, especially—this, the most intimate of interpersonal relationships. In the case of the GDR, this scandal (for, as we will see, the threat of scandal is never far from the commodified relationship) is doubled: within the East German context, a love affair with the commodity implies a deeper betrayal, a refutation of the system's most basic commitments and principles. Yet, by the end of the 1950s, the East's flirtation with consumer culture had given way to a deeper and more permanent attachment—and the party, for its part, seemed content to help its rival move in. The following analysis will unpack the grounds and terms of these developments and explore their broader implications for the history of romantic narratives in East German culture. The guiding question of this chapter might be phrased as follows: How did socialist East Germany end up with a capitalist libidinal economy?

As the "Liebesware" photograph reminds us, the limit-case of commodity-mediated romance would be prostitution, the direct exchange of money for sex. If, as I have argued in the introduction, one of the primary elements of modern romance is a suspension of the prevailing economies (political, financial) in favor of a temporary and unique *libidinal* economy, then prostitution would represent the opposite: the incursion of market conditions into the purview of romance, the sphere of sexual intimacy.[2] A number of social critics from Marx on have argued that capitalist conditions render prostitution not the exception, but the norm: Engels's famous cri-

---

2. If this reversal implies a challenge to romantic love, then the riposte would be found in the plotline, from *La Traviata* to *Pretty Woman* (and, as we will see, *Der Kinnhaken* [see p. 59]), wherein the unromantic exchange of prostitution becomes resupplanted by romantic love.

tique of marriage, for instance, claims that bourgeois marriage "turns often enough into the crassest prostitution—sometimes of both partners, but far more commonly of the woman, who only differs from the ordinary courtesan in that she does not let out her body on piecework as a wage worker, but sells it once and for all into slavery" (134). Engels uses prostitution both literally and rhetorically here: he has in mind not only the exchange of sex for money, but also the mediation of any relationship through material calculation or necessity. Engels's polemical strategy calls attention to the inconsistency of a system that encourages commodity-mediated relationships in some contexts (from fashion to marriage) while condemning—in fact criminalizing—them in others.

As I have argued in the introduction, such ideological contradictions are the stuff of romance, and this case is no exception. Particularly in the eighteenth and nineteenth centuries, a great number of love plots go out of their way to assure the protagonists—and the reader—that there are no covert material interests informing their romantic destiny. Thus in Lessing's *Minna von Barnhelm* Tellheim marries Minna only when it seems that she has lost her considerable fortune, Elizabeth refuses Darcy's first proposal in Austen's *Pride and Prejudice,* and Ferdinand and Luise follow their star-crossed love to its tragic end in Schiller's *Kabale und Liebe* (Cabal and Love). In such narratives, the possibility that interpersonal relationships might be subject to economic conditions is held at a distance from the central romantic pair, instead projected wholesale or piecemeal onto the society surrounding them. Often the specter of material interest is foisted onto a few straw men (or women), whose only affinities are those from which they are likely to profit. The romantic code prohibits an attraction to wealth as such, reserving such undignified, unromantic behavior for gold diggers and social climbers. At the same time, however, the habitus of wealth—the manners, style, education, and taste of the upper classes—are the very objects of romantic desire: thus, in the end, the love-object, chosen for every trait besides wealth, usually happens to be rich as well.[3] In this sense, romantic plots can have it both ways: they insist on the possibility of a "pure," materially disinterested relationship without denying the desirability of wealth and status. The forced choice of economic dependency—and thus by no means coincidentally a "choice" usually given to a female protagonist—is recast as a real choice from a position of romantic independence.[4] These love stories, we might say, mediate the social fact of commodity mediation.

In the twentieth century, the role of commodities in romantic ideals and practices became both more diffuse and more pronounced: more diffuse as buying

---

3. As the old saying has it, "Love not for money, love where money is." Or, in Pierre Bourdieu's somewhat more cryptic phrasing, "Taste is the form par excellence of *amor fati*" (244).

4. For more on love and choice, see Luhmann, 50–57. Luhmann outlines the importance of what he calls "double contingency" in the romantic code: "the freedom each partner has to decide whether or not to become involved in a love relationship" (50).

power dispersed somewhat more evenly across lines of gender and class (a "good match" being no longer a matter of survival for middle-class women, nor "romantic" practices reserved only for the upper classes), yet more pronounced with the ever-greater imbrication of consumer goods into daily life.[5] In *Consuming the Romantic Utopia: Love and the Cultural Contradictions of Capitalism,* Eva Illouz argues that twentieth-century romantic tropes are inseparable from consumption—that romance, despite its antimaterialist precepts, has become the commodity-mediated relationship par excellence. Illouz analyzes the development of modern "romantic" imagery, especially in advertising, and traces the gradual replacement of such courtship practices as "calling" with modern forms such as "dating." The culture of dating, according to Illouz, is the quintessential form of "commodified" romance:

> In modern dating…the consumption of commodities becomes an end in itself.…[The] dating period is often one of intense consumerist activity whereby two people interact with the surrounding public culture and come to know each other within this framework. In the modern romantic ideal it is the very act of consumption that constitutes and creates the romantic moment. (76)

The notion that capitalist romance is fueled by commodity consumption is unlikely to shock anyone: similar arguments have been made in a number of forums.[6] It would be more surprising, however, to see the same dynamics playing out in socialist East Germany. And more astonishing still to find the SED (East Germany's ruling Socialist Unity Party) actively encouraging policies and rhetoric that legitimated, even promoted, both the commodification of romance and the romanticization of commodities.[7] As we will see, in the course of the GDR's first decade both situations came to pass. In the East German cultural imagination from the late 1950s on, "wahre Liebe" (true love) and "Liebesware" (wares of love) were not as far apart as one might expect.

Aufbau or *Wirtschaftswunder:* Reconstruction and Legitimation

The state of East Germany's cultural landscape at the beginning of the 1950s makes such a correlation between romance and commodities appear highly improbable. For one thing, there was not yet a consumer culture to romanticize. One of

---

5. The relative economic independence of working women in the nineteenth century inspires Engels's remark that disinterested love—what he calls sex love—"becomes and can only become the real rule among the oppressed classes, which means today among the proletariat" (135).

6. Erich Fromm's quasi-self-help bestseller *The Art of Loving,* for instance, identifies capitalist consumer culture as one of the main impediments to modern love: "Our whole culture is based on the appetite for buying, on the idea of a mutually favorable exchange. Modern man's happiness consists in the thrill of looking at the shop windows, and in buying all that he can afford to buy, either for cash or on installments. He (or she) looks at people in a similar way" (2).

7. This is Illouz's chiasmus (26).

the most significant differences between the postwar Germanys was the fact that a *Wirtschaftswunder* (economic miracle) never happened in the East. While Western Europe was rebuilding industry and infrastructure with capital from the Marshall Plan, large-scale démontage in the Soviet Occupied Zone was slowing down the already devastated economy. Though the citizens of the GDR were working just as hard as their neighbors to the west, less material enjoyment was to be had in the fruits of their labor. Where the *Wirtschaftswunder* made itself felt in high wages and a market flush with consumer goods, the GDR's *Aufbau* (reconstruction) was primarily concerned with building up the infrastructure of heavy industry. And as impressive as the construction sites in Stalinstadt or Hoyerswerda may have been, they could not promise gratification like that offered by the resplendent shop windows of West Berlin's Kurfürstendamm.

The symbolic order of the fledgling GDR, however, did offer compensation for its sluggish economic growth. While the literal and libidinal economies of the Federal Republic coalesced around the new Deutschmark, East Germans were given a new object of cathexis and ego-identification in the personality cult around the figure of Stalin.[8] Despite his importance as a political focal point, there is a

---

8. Wolf Biermann's poem "Deutschland: Ein Wintermärchen" (Germany: A Winter's Tale) (Berlin: K. Wagenbach, 1972) explores the parallel structure of the postwar libidinal economies of East and West Germany. In Biermann's poem, history becomes the "excrement" of Germany, the "ass of the world." Each half of the divided Germany has its own way of dealing with the "German shit":

So that it won't embarrass us	Die deutschen Exkremente sind
The German excrement,	Daß es uns nicht geniert
With good West German diligence	In Westdeutschland mit deutschem
Is given shine and scent	Fleiß Poliert und parfümiert
What alchemists could never do	Was nie ein Alchemist erreicht
—they've managed there (I'm told)	—sie haben es geschafft
They've taken all the German shit	Aus deutscher Scheiße haben sie
And made it into gold	Sich hartes Gold gemacht
The GDR, my fatherland	Die DDR, mein Vaterland
Is clean in any case	Ist sauber immerhin
A relapse of the Nazi-time	Die Wiederkehr der Nazizeit
Could never now take place	Ist absolut nicht drin
With Stalin's broom so thoroughly	So gründlich haben wir geschrubbt
We scrubbed everything down	Mit Stalins hartem Besen
That red and scarred the backside is	Daß rot verschrammt der Hintern
Which earlier was brown	ist Der vorher braun gewesen

Biermann's poem, which revisits Heine's raucously sarcastic cycle from 1844, identifies two divergent mechanisms for processing the sediment—the excreta—of German history. By Biermann's account, both the manic industriousness of the FRG's *Wirtschaftswunder* and the rigor and violence of East German Stalinism are attempts to deal with the trace of National Socialism: while the West perfumes and polishes the "German shit" until it turns to gold, the East scrubs Nazi brown into Stalinist red. To conceal this historical remnant, the two Germanys in Biermann's poem reach for tangible objects, the materiality of which is emphasized by the reduplication of the word *hard*: the "hard gold" (*hartes Gold*) in the West and the "hard broom" (*harte[r] Besen*) in the East. In Biermann's somewhat formulaic

danger in overstating the importance of Stalin himself in the symbolic machinery known as "Stalinism." To judge from official cultural artifacts of the time—state-sanctioned literature, films, posters, and so on—the Soviet premier occupied a central place in the GDR's collective imagination. Yet it is hard to say how thoroughly the personality cult penetrated GDR society as a whole. Peter Skyba, for instance, suggests that among GDR youth in the early 1950s "the Stalin cult had a far smaller effect outside of functionary circles than party and youth organizations expected" (163). Since it is beyond the scope of this inquiry to speculate on the actual depth and breadth of the Stalin cult, I will assert only that the figure of Stalin provided a "good-enough" legitimating object. Good enough, that is, to anchor a symbolic mechanism whereby the legitimacy of socialism—or more precisely, of socialism's claim to represent best the interests of the working class—was grounded not in the horizontal conditions of production, but in the vertical relations of authority.

A glance at the GDR workplace during the *Aufbau* period will make it clear that the East German worker did not experience an improvement in working conditions corresponding to his or her promotion to the ruling class. The hours were as long as ever, the labor as menial and dangerous, the pay as low as or lower than it had been before the founding of the GDR. In short, the assurance that they now owned the means of production did not change the lived experience of workers in the GDR. The proof of socialism's superiority over capitalism, and in turn the proof of the party's mandate to represent the working class, had to be sought elsewhere. When it was functioning effectively, the Stalinist symbolic machinery provided this "proof": Stalin's all-seeing gaze, his all-encompassing concern, was visible assurance that the party was literally looking out for all of its citizens. And where these specular bonds failed to take hold, their negative guarantee remained: Stalin's loving gaze gave way to the suspicious eyes of the secret police, the vengeful stare of the show trial.

In this sense, we may describe many *Aufbau*-era cultural products as "Stalinist," not because they necessarily exhibit the brutal rigor of the Stalinist party line, but because they anchor ideological legitimacy in the hierarchies of state power and Soviet hegemony. If, in these works, the party is always right, it is because it has a privileged relationship to the coming social order: tautologically, the SED's monopoly on power is legitimated in relation to a future that it alone has the power to determine. The aesthetic category correlative to this legitimatory strategy is that of socialist realism, which, by definition, "evaluates the individual, particular phenomena of reality from the standpoint of the coming society" ("Sozialistischer Realismus," 791).

---

account, postwar Germany divides itself under the signs of competing objects, what psychoanalysis might call fetish objects: the "hard gold" of the commodity or the "hard broom" of Stalinism.

"Dismal Expectations for Amour": Socialist-Realist Love Stories and the 1953 Film Debate

The cultural imperative of socialist realism would have a chilling effect on the growth of the love story in the GDR, for where West German film largely adopted the tried-and-true Hollywood template of commodified romance, filmmakers in the East had a harder time finding a viable romantic model.[9] As we will see, one of the goals of *Aufbau*-era cultural policy was the transformation, if not the elimination, of traditional romance. Which is not to say that there were no love plots in this period. As a March 1953 editorial in *Neues Deutschland* pointed out, "There is hardly a film produced by [the state film production company] DEFA in which people's love relationships do not play a thematic role" (Reinecke).[10] Yet these early DEFA love stories do not *feel* particularly romantic. The grounds for this intuition, I would argue, have to do with the structure and mechanism of the traditional romantic code, the demanding logic of love-as-topos. If prostitution represents the limit-case of capitalist romance, the point where consumption necessarily becomes unromantic, then the socialist equivalent would be found in the politicization of any and all intimate interpersonal ties, the cutting of passion to the measure of politics. This tendency might best be summed up by one character's dismissal of DEFA love stories in Gerhard Klein and Wolfgang Kohlhaase's 1965 film, *Berlin um die Ecke* (Berlin around the Corner). Asked about DEFA films, Horst (Kaspar Eichel) simply sneers: "Liebespaar macht Selbstkritik" (Lovers do self-critique). This three-word sentence captures a sense felt by many audiences of East German public culture that there is something de facto unromantic about its tendency to instrumentalize love for propaganda. I would hasten to point out, however, that this unromantic quality lies not in the content of the propaganda—for there are many undeniably romantic, profoundly propagandistic love stories to be found all over the political spectrum—but rather in its denial of romance's right to self-determination. In the idiom of this book, we can characterize the problem here as that of an imposition of the socialist symbolic economy—that is, of socialist ideology's self-understanding and ordering of the world—onto the love story's erotic economy. As Piotr Fast claims in a short but evocative chapter on romantic conventions in Soviet socialist realism in his book *Ideology, Aesthetics, Literary History,*

> In spite of the "uselessness" of the theme [of love], socialist realism tries to adopt it by depriving it of its characteristic autotelicity and subjecting it to its ideological

---

9. For more on West German consumerist romance, see Erica Carter's compelling book *How German Is She? Postwar West German Reconstruction and the Consuming Woman,* esp. chap. 5, "Film, Melodrama, and the Consuming Woman as Cultural Deviant."

10. A 1953 article in the West German newspaper *Die Zeit* claims otherwise: "A statistician calculated that love had appeared in only 3 percent of DEFA films hitherto" ("Glück—groß und klein"). This discrepancy may be explained by conflicting definitions of the love story.

objectives in two different ways. First, it uses "romance" as a testing ground of morality, smuggling into novels postulates of the so-called socialist morality; second, it embeds the theme in the story of the ideological formation of the protagonists, making of love a teleological motivation of their behavior or a reward for their good deeds or attitudes. (64)

This dynamic is exemplified in the film *Roman einer jungen Ehe* (Story of a Young Couple), directed by Kurt Maetzig and written by Maetzig with Bodo Uhse. The "young couple" in the title are Jochen (Hans-Peter Thielen) and Agnes (Yvonne Merin), struggling actors in postwar Berlin. Where Jochen drifts into the not-so-successfully-denazified West German theater scene, Agnes inclines toward the East, working on a highly political—and, in Jochen's eyes, shamelessly propagandistic—film project. Eventually, the political divisions between Agnes and Jochen become too great, and they file for divorce. A last-minute courtroom reconciliation, however, saves their marriage—just in time for the celebration of the opening of Berlin's new Stalinallee, "Stalin Boulevard."

In comparing *Roman einer jungen Ehe* with an earlier film by Maetzig, *Ehe im Schatten* (Marriage in the Shadows), Heinz Kersten alerts us—perhaps inadvertently—to the fundamental difference between these two love stories. In Kersten's view, *Roman einer jungen Ehe* reveals

the transformation of an otherwise talented director under the party's increasingly dictatorial film policy. Where in the 1947 film *Ehe im Schatten* [Marriage in the Shadows] Kurt Maetzig depicted the fate of a marriage between an "Aryan" and a Jew under National Socialism—a story in which both husband and wife would rather seek death than let themselves be separated by the inhuman laws of a criminal political order—he would assert five years later in *Roman einer jungen Ehe* the impossibility of marital harmony between partners whose "political progress" was unequal. (69)

In one sense, the point that Kersten seems to want to make here is highly problematic. Presented as a logical apposition, the two halves of this sentence would appear to argue that the challenge facing the couple in *Roman einer jungen Ehe* is equivalent to that faced by the couple in *Ehe im Schatten*. Maetzig, it seems, is somehow aesthetically and morally negligent in his failure to allow Agnes and Jochen to resist the oppressive demands of political polarization, a resistance that would be akin to Hans and Elisabeth's fatal stand in *Ehe im Schatten*. If, however, we put aside the politico-moral aspect, the question of relative dictatorships and modes of resistance, and ask instead about the status of these two love stories *as* love stories, then we find a telling structural difference.

Ehe im Schatten relies on the love story to resolve its tragic plot, reaching back into the Romantic tradition to portray a love that is greater than, but ends in, death. *Roman einer jungen Ehe,* on the other hand, refuses to use romance to bring the characters into an ideologically suitable formation (a lovelorn Jochen, for instance, might suddenly see the error of his ways), and instead makes the protagonists' love contingent upon their politics: Jochen returns to Agnes only after he has been convinced—through unemployment and a thrashing by West German rowdies, among other arguments—of the superiority of socialism. When he reaches this political position, he finds Agnes waiting for him. In *Roman einer jungen Ehe,* the force that reunites this young couple is not love, but it has a name. With her husband proudly looking on, Agnes reads a poem by Kuba (Kurt Barthel) at the Stalinallee ceremony: "Stalin himself took us by the hand / and told us to hold our heads high." Where Andrew Marvell had once imagined true love as a pair of parallel lines that, "though infinite, can never meet," Kuba names the point where Jochen and Agnes will come together: "Straight to Stalin leads the path / On which the friends have come."[11]

It is this narrative subordination, more than the film's clumsy propaganda, that makes *Roman einer jungen Ehe* a fundamentally unromantic movie. In this sense, we can speak of a "transformation...under the party's increasingly dictatorial film policy"—less of Maetzig himself (for any shift in ideological content between these films probably owes more to the difference in their settings than to a change in Maetzig's own thinking) than of the love story as a genre. As the following outline of East German cultural policy—more specifically, film policy—will reveal, this was precisely the transformation that GDR cultural functionaries were trying to bring about. The trade-off for such political rigor, however, is that romance is thereby prevented from doing what it does best, namely ameliorating the tension caused by ideological self-contradiction. Rather than obeying its own self-contained logic, romantic passion becomes subject to political doctrine: its internal structure and overall trajectory must correspond to the ambitions of socialist social engineering. This would not present a problem, except that the ideological fabric of East Germany in the 1950s was riddled with holes. As we will see, the Workers' and Peasants' State was unable to decide whether it was a producer's or a consumer's paradise. In fact, it was emphatically neither. Films and literature from this period needed desperately the narrative patch that the love story could provide, and audiences clamored for its uncomplicated satisfactions.

In his history of early East German cinema, Thomas Heimann sums up the state of romance in DEFA films of the early 1950s: "Given the sterility of the subject [of love], the *bonmot* made the rounds that 'DEFA' stood for '*D*ismal *E*xpectations

---

11. Marvell, "The Definition of Love," ed. Donno, 49–50. The seventh stanza of the poem (published posthumously in 1681) reads:

As lines, so loves oblique may well
Themselves in every angle greet;
But ours so truly parallel,
Though infinite, can never meet.

for Amour' [Dürre Ernte für Amor]" (130). Such "sterility" was the product of a cultural line that was characterized on the one hand by the demand for relentless agitation and propaganda from cultural producers, and on the other by an almost paranoiac suspicion of any cultural product with an air of Western "kitsch" or "pornography."[12] *Kabale und Liebe* was acceptable, but without the stamp of *Kulturerbe* (cultural heritage), a love story had to prove its merits by its political content. Walter Ulbricht's address to the Second Party Conference of the SED in July 1952 draws attention to the propagandistic importance of film for the *Aufbau* effort:

> Artists should be aware that what the people want, above all, is more films. The struggle for the new Germany presents so many dramatic conflicts that one cannot speak of a lack of material. DEFA should switch over to making films about the struggle to build the groundwork of socialism; it should pay more attention to the questions of village life; and it should make more films that depict the works of great figures in the history of our people. Our authors should also learn to use the weapon of comedy in the fight against backwardness, mocking and ridiculing backwardness in order to help overcome it. (Schubbe, 240)

By this account, even comedies must be brought to bear in the "fight against backwardness": films exist to enlighten, not to entertain. A conference of East German filmmakers in September 1952 solidified this rule into doctrine.[13] Hermann Axen's keynote address lamented the lack of feature-length films addressing the important issues of the day. Predictably, he discovered the root of this problem in "ideological ambiguity," specifically "insufficient application of the methods of socialist realism" (Zentralkomitee, "Für den Aufschwung," 28). Other speeches continued along these lines: "In the name of the people," Gustav Müller, head of the Machine-Lending Station (MAS) in Possek said, "I want to ask you for cultural support. We have no need for fluff like *Das Flutenkonzert* [*The Flute Concerto,* a

---

12. See, for instance, the resolution of the Central Committee of the SED at the Fifth Party Congress, March15–17, 1951: "To poison the consciousness and corrupt the taste of the masses, the imperialist culture-destroyers deploy the weapon of kitsch. Kitsch is pseudo-art. Kitsch is also artistic form with false content. This can be seen in the mass distribution of pornographic magazines, detective stories, and pulp fiction of the most wretched kind and in the production of kitsch- and crime-films. Cosmopolitanism in popular music is also an important means to corrupt the human being and likewise to destroy the national cultural heritage of the people" (Schubbe, 181–82).

13. Most of the presentations at the 1952 film conference essentially elaborated and restated the tenets of the Politburo directive "For the Improvement of Progressive German Filmmaking," adopted a few months earlier. In the Politburo resolution, as in Ulbricht's speech, the emphasis is on film's didactic potential: "The progressive German cinema fulfills a key national duty in that it imparts the ideas necessary to defend freedom, democracy, national independence, and humanism as well as cultivating and developing the national cultural heritage of our people" (Zentralkomitee, "Für den Aufschwung," 5). For more on the Politburo resolution, see Heimann, 134–37.

popular costume-drama made in 1930]....We want to see films that address our ways, our work, and our mission" ("Für den Aufschwung," 60).

One of the few exceptions to this socialist-realist consensus was Horst Ilgen, a guest from the Wismut uranium mine near Chemnitz. As reported in *Neues Deutschland*'s account of the conference (but not recorded in the conference protocol), Ilgen brought greetings and a request: the Wismut miners wanted more film comedies ("Die DEFA zu einem schöpferischen Kollektiv entwickeln!" 6). Ilgen's cameo at the film conference accords with a pattern visible throughout the early 1950s. Where cultural functionaries decried the not-yet-didactic-enough efforts of DEFA, the target audience had a very different set of complaints: the East German workers were tired of being edified and agitated; they wanted to be entertained.

Thus, while the feuilleton pages of newspapers and magazines thrashed out the political viability of the previous year's film production, readers' letters spoke to the films' entertainment value, or lack thereof.[14] In a letter to the *Neue Filmwelt* (New World of Film) from June 1952, Werner Pfeifer of Chemnitz criticizes the tendency of cultural functionaries to focus on films' "values and content" without paying any attention to the demands and reactions of the audience. This short-sightedness, he argues, has led to a worrisome attendance-gap between films imported from the West and DEFA films: where the former are nearly always sold out, the latter can scarcely scrape together an audience at all. In the following issue of *Neue Filmwelt,* a letter from Rolf Behrends of Meißenfels puts a finer point on the problem: "I think we're getting to the root of the problem....DEFA doesn't quite understand yet how to make really good comic and romantic movies." Similar letters appeared in the SED's central organ *Neues Deutschland* (New Germany). Lilo Hübner of Klein-Machnow, for instance, writes: "Especially now, as we build socialism according to plan, we need more films that make us laugh and be happy."

By the next year, the message was starting to get through. In the spring of 1953, *Neues Deutschland* asked a number of prominent DEFA directors and writers to submit editorials in response to three questions: "1. Do they consider our DEFA films exciting, i.e., enthralling, and where in their opinion does the excitement lie? 2. Why is there no love in our films? 3. Why are no comedies being made here?" These pointed questions are an obvious invitation to self-critique, and the guiding lights of East German film did not disappoint. In the ensuing months, DEFA

---

14. It is uncertain whether these "letters to the editor" are bona fide readers' opinions or ventriloquized editorials. Here I've chosen to treat them as real letters from actual readers, but it might be even more interesting to conceptualize them as the projected viewpoint of an imaginary ideal readership. If this were the case, they would represent an articulation by cultural functionaries of opinions they could not yet officially hold.

engaged in a public spectacle of hand-wringing and self-recrimination. Readers' letters as well stated and restated the same demands: "Why not for once put love at the center?" (Klemm and Klemm). "Always the same question: Why doesn't DEFA make comedies?" (Eyck). The consensus seemed to be that East German films were neither fun nor romantic. The thornier questions were why, and what to do about it.[15]

Director Kurt Maetzig opens the discussion with a lengthy defense of love as a theme in progressive socialist art. He asks: "Why does a simple love story that comes to us from abroad, such as *One Summer of Happiness,* bring in millions of viewers who only rarely go to our films?" ("Warum gibt es keine Liebe?" 4).[16] The task of socialist film, Maetzig argues, is to reach the greatest number of viewers with the message of socialism. If DEFA cannot provide the love stories they desire, East German viewers will turn to the "often bad and kitschy" films from the West. Socialist filmmakers, he claims, should not underestimate this genre, for love stories are uniquely suited to portray the struggle for and realization of human happiness—the goal, ultimately, of all socialist society. Maetzig blames the dearth of romance on socialist writers' mistrust of love as a theme. It is a misplaced wariness, according to Maetzig: "Many just want to see in love a flight from the struggles of our time into the four walls of the bedroom. And so they mistrust all love stories in literature or in film, or want at most to throw a little love into art like a pinch of salt into a nutritious soup....But they are wrong!" Love is only unproductive and escapist, Maetzig claims, within capitalist culture: "Under dying capitalism, love is doomed to unfruitfulness." He elaborates this position with a quote from Thomas Mann's *Dr. Faustus;* the devil says to Adrian: "You shall not love! Love is forbidden to you, in that it warms. Your life should be cold—thus you must not love another person. We want you cold—the fires of production should barely be hot enough to warm yourself in. You'll retreat into them from the coldness of your life."[17]

In the next paragraph, however, Maetzig turns this quote on its head, applying it to life in the East: "But our life must not be a retreat, neither a flight from the struggles of the day and from production into the bedroom nor a flight from cold lovelessness and isolation into the fires of production. The complete human being is the ideal of our epoch." The aptly chosen Mann quote thus performs a double duty here: initially describing cultural production under "dying capitalism," it then becomes a sidelong critique of socialist realism's one-sidedness, its sole reliance on the "fires of production" to warm the cold lives of its heroes (and readers). This risky ambivalence—potentially aligning socialist realism with the devil—might be one of the reasons why, in their concluding comments on the

---

15. For a brief analysis of the *Neues Deutschland* film discussion, see also Heimann, 130.

16. *Sie tanzte nur einen Sommer* (She Danced Only One Summer), a Swedish film, brought two million viewers to GDR cinemas in 1952. See Heimann, 223.

17. This is Lowe-Porter's translation in Mann, 249.

film discussion, *Neues Deutschland*'s editorial board criticizes Maetzig's article as "ambivalent, to some extent erroneously argued" (Redaktionskollegium *Neues Deutschland*). Maetzig's subtle challenge to socialist-realist doctrine contains a revealing assumption. Here, love is represented as existing outside of the sphere of production; it provides a crucial narrative counterbalance, without which one cannot portray "the complete human being." For the next four months, DEFA's loyal socialist-realists would endeavor to prod love back into the fires of production.

The first step in this effort was to reiterate the subordination of romantic love to the broader social sphere. Along these lines, scriptwriter Ehm Welk attributes DEFA's wariness of love stories to a misinterpretation of the social role of love:

> Why are there so few films about love here…? I think because the pressing task of settling our political, economic, and governmental concerns has led our [cultural] functionaries to a misapprehension of the meaning of Eros in the fight for a better social order: at least publicly they view love as an entirely personal, indeed, private affair and consider addressing or embracing it to be outdated, bourgeois backwardness that distracts us from the political struggle.

Kurt Stern, another DEFA author, takes a similar line, refuting those who would say: "Today we have to deal with more important things, with peace, with the unification of Germany, with the construction of socialism. We have no time for love." For the sake of realism, Stern says, love cannot be left out: "Doesn't everything that plays an important role in the lives of our people belong in the realm of realistic art? Why not love?" As author Hedda Zinner succinctly puts it, "A film without love (with a few exceptions) is not only not realistic; it is also not at all socialist-realist."

For dramaturge Horst Reinecke, "realism" also plays a decisive role. Reinecke sees the problem less as a lack of love stories than as a lack of "convincing" love stories—a failure to convince due to insufficient realism: "Whether the portrayal of interpersonal relationships at work, in love, and in conflict is convincing or not depends on the artist's ability to show life realistically, universally, and in its typical development. Ideological clarity and artistic mastery cannot be separated."

Here, the magic word "typical" indicates that the discussion has come full circle. Despite efforts like Maetzig's to dig out the roots of the problem, the party line does not budge: love is to remain *typisch*—that is, socialist-realist—in DEFA films. *Neues Deutschland*'s editorial board drives this nail deeper with a stinging critique of Maetzig's contribution to the discussion:

> Dr. Maetzig wrote: "Our viewers do not mean a film 'about village life' in which a love story also plays a role, they are not talking about the story of an activist brigade

that ends happily with a young couple coming together; no, they mean love itself, as strong and grand as that of Romeo and Juliet, of Ferdinand and Louisa." And that is precisely the wrong standpoint in that it separates the story of an activist brigade from the story of love between two people.

Of course, love stories in our films are only conceivable when they develop out of real life. But why exactly do we want to see an activist brigade, why exactly the new village life? Because we want to lead people forward with the medium of film as well. The typical love-conflicts of our time play out precisely in the activist brigades, in the new villages. (Redaktionskollegium *Neues Deutschland*)

And with that, *Neues Deutschland* considered the matter settled: DEFA artists would have to find a way to make a new dish from the old recipe.

The conversation, however, was far from over. With *Neues Deutschland*'s film discussion stuck in a cultural-political cul-de-sac, the topic passed to a forum better equipped to handle such "hot potatoes" (*heiße Eisen*): satire.[18] *Eine Liebesgeschichte* (A Love Story), one of the first of the *Stacheltier* (Hedgehog) series, satirical film shorts that accompanied DEFA's weekly newsreel *Der Wochenschau*, lampoons the clumsy efforts of cultural functionaries to find a place for romance in the cultural universe of 1950s East Germany.[19] In this 6 1/2-minute short, written by Richard Groschopp and Günter Kunert in the late summer of 1953, a writer brings his latest work—a love story—to the office of the "Art Experts" (*Kunstsachverständigen*), two nearly identical men in grey suits and dark glasses.[20] They are eager to hear it. Schmidt, the writer, begins reading his story aloud. As he reads, we see the scene he is narrating: a man and a woman, both young and fashionably dressed, share a tender moment in a forest glade while romantic music plays quietly in the background. "He pulls her along," Schmidt's voice-over narrates, "but they only go a few steps and then stop to entwine and embrace. The loving couple give themselves over to breathless, wordless joy." The film cuts back to the office, where the Art Experts register their unease:

> AE1: Great, really well written, but I think the question of the happy life of our youth isn't emphasized enough.
> AE2: That's right. And the role of the emancipation of women is insufficiently addressed. And why?

---

18. See Sylvia Klötzer's discussion of the East German satire magazine *Eulenspiegel:* "Under 'distinguishing characteristics,' the 'ID card' of its title figure reads: 'incorruptibly clear vision, sharp tongue,…long arms (reach from high to low), brave heart,' and, underlined: *'seizes hot potatoes!'* ('*Packt heiße Eisen an!'*)" ("Über den Umgang mit heißen Eisen," 105).

19. I am indebted to Bill Martin for pointing me toward *Eine Liebesgeschichte.*

20. For an insightful and comprehensive analysis of *Eine Liebesgeschichte*, see Sylvia Klötzer's *Satire und Macht: Film, Zeitung, Kabarett in der DDR*, 53–59.

AE1: Because the writer hasn't yet understood how to develop the central problem of collective unity.

AE2: And therefore the writer should revise his work self-critically.

AE1 and AE2 (*in unison*): Yes, revise.

With hanging head, Schmidt takes his hat and leaves.

Schmidt returns later, enthusiastic about his revised love story: "Your criticisms helped me a lot!" he tells the Art Experts and begins reading once again: "Hanno, the young steelworker, and Irmgard, the tractor driver, sit on a wooden bench." Fade to a crudely built stage-set of an industrial landscape with an enormous sickle moon hanging over silos and smokestacks. "The birds chirp a song of the happy life of our youth. On the horizon, the towering smokestacks spread their mighty arms." Cardboard smokestacks rise on strings. Hanno stands stiffly, turns to Irmgard, raises his sledgehammer to his chest, and intones: "Beloved comrade, how my heart, which otherwise beats only in time with my hammer, has longed for you" (see fig. 3). Irmgard, outfitted in ill-fitting overalls and carrying an enormous wrench, replies: "Oh Hanno, I long for the day when we can begin a happy married life. On an emancipated basis, of course."

> HANNO: Irmgard, I love you like—like my riveting hammer. No stepmother's backwardness will ever sabotage us.
>
> IRMGARD: No, together we will stride toward the radiant morning.
>
> HANNO (*reaching into the pocket of his uniform*): Yes. I brought you something: a piece of steel from the latest production.

"Hanno's eyes glowed," Schmidt concludes, "like coke in a blast furnace." Looking up, he expects accolades from the Art Experts, but they have not been listening at all. Both are leaning out the window, watching the scene below. In the park across the street a man and a woman are sharing a tender moment—it is, in fact, a scene identical to the first version of Schmidt's story. "Yes," exclaims one of the Art Experts. "That's life. That's what you have to describe. That's real. We recommend you revise your story." Schmidt snatches up his hat and snarls: "No, I'll write a new story: about true-to-life Art Experts!" The camera freezes on the surprised Art Experts, and the still image becomes a photograph, which is placed among others in a folder. As the folder closes, we see its title: "Superfluous Contemporaries." When it comes to romance, *Eine Liebesgeschichte* suggests, the GDR's Art Experts—*Neues Deutschland*'s editorial board, for instance—should leave well enough alone. The meddling, hairsplitting cultural politics of the early 1950s seems to have become "superfluous."

"Der Alptraum" (The Nightmare), a comic sketch published in the popular monthly *Das Magazin* in 1954, tells a similar story. The narrator runs into

Figure 3. Hanno and Irmgard pledge to "stride into the radiant morning" in Richard Groschopp's 1953 satirical sketch, "A Love Story," from the Stacheltier (Hedgehog) series. Source: Bundesarchiv [FilmSG1/BArch/26065 Eine Liebesgeschichte].

his friend Paul, a dramaturge for the DEFA studios. Paul looks terrible: sunken cheeks, bloodshot eyes, gnawed fingernails, and a nervous tic. We then learn why: Paul is just returning from a meeting of the DEFA board, where his latest script, "There Is Only One Happiness," was "nearly" accepted. "Just a few things have to be changed," he says.

> The hero can't go under at the end. That's not typical for us. He should be decorated instead. His girlfriend shouldn't cheat on him—that's not typical. She should be a DFD functionary. And the union meeting should be more earnest, not so silly—that's not typical here. And the title has to change. Suggestion: *DFD and Love.* Then the film can be made. (T.N., 48)

The pointed reference to the DFD (Democratic Women's Federation of Germany) suggests a real-life corollary to Paul's tribulations in "Der Alptraum." A year earlier, the DFD had singled out Slatan Dudow's 1952 film, *Frauenschicksale* (Destinies of Women), for harsh public criticism. Dudow's film tells the story of four women in Berlin, all of whom are in love with the same man: a con and ladies' man named, appropriately enough, Conny (Hanns Groth). By the end of the film, Renate (Sonja Sutter), Barbara (Anneliese Book), and Anni (Susanne Düllmann) all see the light and turn away from Conny toward a new life in the East.[21] Even with its abundance of ungainly propaganda, *Frauenschicksale* did not pass ideological muster easily. In an editorial on August 29, 1952, in *Neues Deutschland,* the DFD's board of directors had written: "This film shows the destinies of women…destinies that do exist in real life. But are these destinies really typical for the women of the German Democratic Republic? No, because they pertain only to the smallest percentage of our women." The film, in short, is not positive enough:

> The new aspects of our life are not expressed convincingly enough, while the criticisms of the old ways succeed. The figure of a young German woman is missing whose development does not follow the path of a "Conny," but rather the path taken by thousands of women in the Republic and the Democratic Sector of Berlin, the path of work—at first to support themselves and their families, and then because our social transformation allows them to find a new relationship to work. (Bundesvorstand des DFD)

Rather than the "path of a 'Conny'"—rather, in other words, than the narrative logic of romance, whereby the changing fortunes of love determine the lover's fate—the DFD demands a more "realistic" approach: the "path of work." As the satire of "Der Alptraum" brings out, such relentless politicization—which would add even more ideological certainty to Dudow's already unsubtle moral tale—hardly sounds like a formula for gripping cinema. The insistence on "typical"—read: ideal—characters and content would leave little possibility for drama, humor, or romance.

Between 1952, the year *Frauenschicksale* was released, and 1954, the year "Der Alptraum" was written, massive changes were underway in the GDR's cultural and political environment. Thus in "Der Alptraum" the narrator's second encounter with Paul reflects a radical turnaround. The revised *DFD and Love,* Paul says, has been accepted. Just a few changes have to be made:

> It should be called *There Is Only One Happiness.* The union meeting is too earnest and dry. It's sometimes like that here, but the average isn't the typical. The meeting should be funnier. And the girl. She shouldn't be a DFD functionary. Why not just a plain, nice, happy girl for once? And the hero doesn't necessarily need to be decorated at the end—better at the beginning or in the middle, or perhaps not at all. (T.N., 49)

Here, as in *Eine Liebesgeschichte,* the second revision of the love story restores the original version nearly point for point. Whereas Schmidt is infuriated by this reversal, Paul is just relieved: "This'll be a film," he says (49).

---

21. The decadent Isa von Trautwald, however, stays with Conny. Not to leave virtue unrewarded, Renate, Anni, and Barbara all end up with more suitable partners by the end of the film.

In both of these sketches, the repeated demand to rework the love story according to a changing standard of "realism" leads to two very different products: first, a politically correct (if ham-fisted) piece of agitprop, then a relatively apolitical (and somewhat kitschy) "traditional" love story. In both cases, the satire draws on the audience's preexisting understanding of how a love story is "supposed" to look. Against this backdrop, the first revision seems ridiculous. The second comes as a relief. This relief marks the restitution of the love story's customary prerogatives, its traditional narrative and ideological autonomy, over the extreme politicization demanded by the Art Experts and by the DEFA board in "Der Alptraum."

These coinciding satirical accounts of the trials of writing DEFA love stories signal a significant change in the cultural climate of the GDR. As if overnight, DEFA's commitment to the primacy of politics, even in love, seems to have become laughable. To have credibility as a mass medium, the GDR cinema would have to learn to produce "real"—that is, nonrealist—love stories. In the meantime they outsourced this task to the experts. In 1954 East Germany's Film Office (Hauptverwaltung Film) bought the rights to more than a dozen West German features, most of which, as Heimann notes, had a "noncommittal" quality: *"Fanfares of Love, Hocuspocus, I and You, A Lovesick Ride on the Moselle, As Long as You're Near Me, Don't Forget Love"* (52, 226). The sudden appearance of such titles on East German cinema marquees must have been startling for moviegoers; less than a year earlier, they would have been considered proof of the "decline of art and culture in West Germany," as a June 23, 1953, editorial in *Neues Deutschland* described it. "As far as artistic merit is concerned," the editorial sneers,

> we can illustrate the general level of the repertoire ... with the following: the two cinemas in Bad Hersfeld, Hessen, were recently playing simultaneously *The Hostess from Worthersee, Rose of the Mountain, When the Heath Dreams at Night, Roses Bloom on the Grave in the Meadow.* If one understands anything about capitalist film production, one knows that such titles conceal the most vulgar, mawkish, and dishonest kitsch. ("Vom Verfall der Kunst und Kultur in Westdeutschland")

First pillorying sentimental Western love stories, then importing them by the dozen, the party made the U-turn parodied in *Eine Liebesgeschichte* and "Der Alptraum." Given the vehemence with which cultural functionaries fought to ward off the influence of Western entertainment films in early 1953, it is striking how self-evident the opposite position had become by 1954.

"How life laughs and loves today": *Das Magazin* and the New Course

The immediate cause of this cultural-political turnaround is not hard to identify. The sudden escalation of workers' disgruntlement into a full-blown general strike on June 17, 1953, necessitated decisive action on the part of the party, not just in the workplace, but in every aspect of public life in the GDR. Scrambling to placate a citizenry not only seething with the resentment that sent them into the streets in the first place, but now also traumatized by the violent suppression of the demonstrations by Soviet tanks and troops, the SED availed itself of a time-tested strategy. As Heimann describes it,

> At first the state reacted…pragmatically, in accordance with the motto "Bread and Circuses." At the end of July, steps were taken to increase the number of purely entertaining films in the program.…While the proportion of East German or Soviet political "thematic films" had until June 1953 exceeded "entertainment" films by a ratio of 60% to 40%, the proportion of the latter now increased to 75%. "Thematic films" would now only make up a quarter (!) of the moviehouses' schedules.
>
> The lack of films in this rather vague category of "entertainment" was offset by the increased purchase of Western films in the second half of the year. (223–24)

If films, especially love stories, were the "circuses" of post–June 17 East Germany, the "bread" was to be supplied by the "New Course," as the economic and social reforms introduced in the second half of 1953 were called. Essentially the New Course marked the emergence of an East German consumer culture: from now on, commodities and consumption would play an increasingly significant role in the GDR's ideological self-understanding. The death of Stalin was not incidental to these developments. In the face of a society boiling over with rage and frustration, and suddenly deprived of the potent political fetish represented by the figure of Stalin, SED officials put their faith in a new fetish object (one close to hand, if in the wrong hands); the policies and rhetoric of the mid- to late 1950s evince an increasing appeal to the logic of the commodity fetish in the official culture of the GDR.

As I outlined in the introduction, this particular commodity fetish has a socialist-utopian flavor. According to the SED's rhetoric, the material existence of the domestic commodity would prove the ascendancy of the socialist system. It is this legitimatory burden that lends the East German commodity its characteristic fetish quality; it was deliberately cast as a reification of socialist social relations, a materialization of Marxist-Leninist ideals. In *Utopie und Bedürfnis,* Ina Merkel draws attention to the increasing symbolic significance of commodities and consumption for East German ideological self-understanding:

> The sphere of consumer culture was to a large degree symbolically freighted. The new department stores, as "display-windows of socialism," were to demonstrate the success and even the superiority of the new social order. They were to reflect the new standard of living. In the end the contest between the [capitalist and socialist] systems would be held on the field of consumption. (164)

Or as Walter Ulbricht observed in 1959, "[We will] prove the superiority of social-ism…not with any old durable goods, with trash, with surplus product, but in-stead with commodities which possess a high use-value, which are beautiful and tasteful, which the working person can buy and use with pleasure."[22] Summing up her argument, Merkel connects these developments to the SED-state's ongoing cri-sis of legitimacy:

> The real problem lay not in the fact that the East did not succeed in becoming like the West, but rather that the East tried to become like the West. It had to do this be-cause it had not earned the legitimacy of its rule, but rather had ended up in power as a result of World War II. By means of the history of consumption one can show that the social history of the GDR was defined by the effort of the rulers to acquire the people's mandate. Instead of attaining this endorsement in the actual sphere of politi-cal power (democracy, legal security, freedom of speech, and travel), they displaced it onto the sphere of consumption, the area of immediate need. (416)

The danger inherent in this policy—pegging socialism's success and the party's mandate to the availability of consumer goods in the GDR—was that the East Ger-man manufacturing sector could not produce enough of these goods to back up the party's promises, let alone outpace the West. The *Aufbau* period's exclusive emphasis on heavy industry had led to a critical shortage even of basic consumer goods, and luxury items were out of the question. Nonetheless, the SED continued to promise satisfaction through commodities under the aegis of the New Course, thus lending official sanction to East Germans' dalliance with the consumerist lifestyle. In this way the fetish character of the commodity—of consumer goods in particular—was deliberately cultivated by the policies and rhetoric of the SED, even though the ob-ject of fetish was noticeably absent from East German homes and stores. The SED attempted to offset this jarring discrepancy through an institutionalized *promesse de bonheur,* whereby present hardships were mortgaged against the promise of future prosperity. As the famous SED slogan expressed it, "As we work today, so shall we live tomorrow" (Wie wir heute arbeiten, werden wir morgen leben).

As this future prosperity drifted further and further away, the effort to keep the party's legitimacy afloat called for all the ideological legerdemain that GDR public culture could summon. The love story would have an important role to play in this effort. Though there were scant commodities to romanticize, there would at least be romance to commodify.[23] This necessity helps to explain the policy change re-flected in *Eine Liebesgeschichte* and "Der Alptraum" and the explosion of imported

---

22. *Der Handel im Siebenjahrplan der DDR und seine Aufgaben zur weiteren Verbesserung der Ver-sorgung der Bevölkerung,* 105; qtd. in Kaminsky, 50.
23. Here I am alluding to Illouz's distinction, as elaborated in the introduction, between the "romanticization of commodities" and the "commodification of romance" (27).

romantic films in 1954. The cultural face of the New Course combined entertainment, romance, consumer culture, and socialist optimism. All of these elements can be seen in the genesis of the GDR's first entertainment magazine, *Das Magazin*. In the verses introducing *Das Magazin* to its readers in January 1954, it is explicitly cast as a child of the New Course:

The Birth of the Magazine	*Die Geburt des Magazins*
The compass points a bold New Course	Der Kompaß steht auf Neuen Kurs
And has for many weeks.	Nun schon seit vielen Wochen.
There's sausage on our buttered bread	Es gibt mehr Wurst aufs Butterbrot,
And lots for us to eat.	Und Mutter hat gut kochen.
Coffee, even, from the south	Selbst Kaffee kommt aus fernem Süd,
From China silk and tea,	Aus China Tee und Seide;
And pretty ribbons for your dress	Vom Böhmerwald bis Samarkand
From Prague to far Qarshi.	Kommt Schmuck zum neuen Kleide.
"Man does not live by bread alone"	"Der Mensch lebt nicht von Brot allein."
The Bible somewhere states,	Das steht schon in der Bibel,
Which is why a clever chap	Weshalb ein Mann mit Köpfchen sagt:
Said: "Wouldn't it be great	"Es wäre gar nicht übel,
If with the *Bockwurst* we could find	Wenn zu der Bockwurst der HO
A flower at the store,	Uns noch ein Blümlein blühte,
Half rosey-red, half violet-blue	Halb rosenrot—halb veilchenblau
To make the spirit soar."	So recht was fürs Gemüte."
And lo, a board of editors	Ein Redaktionskollegium
Was piece by piece compiled	Ward Stück für Stück erkoren
And through its labor, day and night,	Und hat in Tag- und Nachtarbeit
United bore a child.	Vereint das Kind geboren.
....	....
Go forth, my child, to East and West	Zieh' hin, mein Kind, nach Ost und West
To women and to men,	Zu Mädchen und zu Knaben,
And when you're all grown up you'll find	Und wenn du gut gewachsen bist,
You draw both parties in.	Dann woll'n dich beide haben.
Show how life laughs and loves today	Zeig', wie das Leben lacht und liebt
And on the "New Course" makes its way.	Und sich auf "Neuen Kurs" begibt.
And show as well the toil and fuss,	Und zeig' auch, wie wir schuften,
How after we have worked all week	Wie nach des Tages Arbeitsmühn
The flowers' scent is twice as sweet	Die Blumen doppelt schön uns blühn,
Because they bloom for us.	Weil für uns selbst sie duften.[24]

---

24. Schmidt, 1.

Just as the New Course was to offer coffee and silk alongside sausage and bread, *Das Magazin* would add humor and romance to the uniformly political bent of the East German press. As Manfred Gebhardt notes in his history of this periodical, "*Das Magazin* was given an eminent political task, which it fulfilled until the end of the GDR: socialism should be fun" (12–13). As emphasized by the above verses, penned by the magazine's first managing editor, Heinz H. Schmidt, *Das Magazin* was intended for young and old, men and women, committed socialists and the apolitical. Its contents covered travel, sports, adventure, fashion, humor, and, above all, romance. The cover of every issue promised the latter with a colorful, often humorous image of a romantic couple engaged in a seasonally appropriate activity—lounging on the beach, celebrating New Year's Eve, costumed for carnival, and so on. After 1955, *Das Magazin*'s covers were drawn exclusively by one artist: Werner Klemke (see fig. 4). As another East German graphic artist, Axel Bertram, remarked, "Werner Klemke had just one theme, well suited to the *Magazin,* namely love: heavenly love, earthly love, instant love, and eternal love" (Gebhardt, 38).

Of particular importance here is the *kind* of romance propagated by *Das Magazin.* Like the love stories revised and restored in *Eine Liebesgeschichte* and "Der Alptraum," *Das Magazin*'s New Course romance can be seen as a return to a previous romantic mode, one harking back to a prewar, presocialist order. In precisely this sense, Gebhardt refers to the magazine's first years as those of an "anachronism with a future" (25). Gebhardt relates how Arnold Zweig, speaking at the magazine's ten-year anniversary party in 1964, unpacked the word *Magazin* from the Arabic *machazin,* meaning "a warehouse or department store":

> He recalled the burgeoning of [printed] magazines in the 1920s, which coincided with the boom of the great department stores, the *machazins,* in Berlin. Both magazines, the department stores and the periodicals, were expressions of a new attitude toward life, a mass mood: the emporiums with their constantly growing selection, where anyone could buy anything any time, quickly, cheaply, and conveniently.... And the periodicals of the same name, which with their multifarious offerings of short, easy-to-read articles, from literary fiction to trivial stories, tried to give something to everyone in every issue. Colorful pictures and brief texts seduced the reader to open it. (15)

As this comparison attests, the lifestyle endorsed by *Das Magazin* was unapologetically consumerist: this was the new attitude of the department-store boom, a time when "anyone could buy anything any time." The mode of romance found in *Das Magazin* might best be understood in terms of a concept that had its origins in the Hollywood star-system of the 1930s: glamour. In his article "Hollywood Glamour and Mass Consumption in Postwar Italy," Stephen Gundle analyzes how postwar economic and ideological reconstruction in Italy brought with it a new set of practices, aspirations, and ideals, an Americanized "way of

Figure 4. *Das Magazin* covers by Werner Klemke. Source: *Das Magazin,* March 1959, June 1962, August 1965, July 1971.

life" conforming to the dictates of American capitalism. The thin end of this wedge was glamour:

> Glamour, it may be said, is the language of allure and desirability of capitalist society. Its forms change but it is always available to be consumed vicariously by the masses who see in glamour an image of life writ large according to the criteria of a market society. As a language it is a hybrid, in that it mixes luxury, class, exclusivity, and privilege with the sexuality and seduction of prostitution, entertainment, and the commercial world. (339)

This seductive mix of old and new, Gundle argues, was inseparable from the Hollywood star-system:

> Glamour as it is understood today, as a structure of enchantment deployed by cultural industries, was first developed by Hollywood. In the 1930s, the major studios, having consolidated their domination of the industry, developed a star system in which dozens of young men and women were groomed and molded into glittering ideal-types whose fortune, beauty, spending power, and exciting lives dazzled the film-going public. Writing in 1939 about American film stars, Margaret Thorp defined glamour as "sex appeal plus luxury plus elegance plus romance."[25]
>
> "The place to study glamour today is the fan magazines" [she noted]. "Fan magazines are distilled as stimulants of the most exhilarating kind. Everything is superlative, surprising, exciting…Nothing ever stands still, nothing ever rests, least of all the sentences…Clothes of course are endlessly pictured and described usually with marble fountains, private swimming pools or limousines in the background…Every aspect of life, trivial and important, should be bathed in the purple glow of publicity."[26] (Gundle, 338)

Das Magazin found its inspiration in this era, the heyday of classic Hollywood glamour. Thus it is no coincidence that an article in the April 1954 issue of *Das Magazin* argues for the creation of an East German star-system. Shuttling back and forth between the astronomical and colloquial definitions of "star"—or, in the article's tongue-in-cheek acronym, "ST-ate A-pproved entertaine-R" (ST-aatlich A-nerkannter R-ahmenkulturarbeiter)—the author ("Klaus" [Klaus Bartho]) scolds DEFA for having neglected this important aspect of movie culture. Sometimes, he says, stars fail to appear at all. "Astronomically, this can be observed in the 'black

---

25. Thorp, 65. Thorp also calls attention to the peculiar spelling of glamour in the American context: "The natural American spelling of glamour would be g-l-á-m-o-r, with the accent on the first syllable. Hollywood spells it with a *u,* accenting the last syllable and drawing it out as long as possible, whether in derision or enthusiasm—glamour" (65).

26. Thorp, 69–74; qtd. in Gundle.

hole' of the starry sky at night, artistically it can be observed in DEFA" (36). "When you see a shooting star," he concludes, "you can wish for something. I wish for a star. Not an engineered, subsidized, dollar-made one, but a real one, a great and shining DEFA-star" (37). In a sense, then, *Das Magazin* is a fan magazine in reverse: in contrast to the magazines of the '30s, which sprang up to document the lifestyles of Hollywood stars, *Das Magazin* positions itself here as a harbinger of the GDR star-system—a glamour magazine in advance of the glamour.

Countercurrents: *Eine Berliner Romanze* and *Berlin, Ecke Schönhauser*

Yet not all of East Germany's cultural producers accepted the burnished promises of the New Course. For many, East German commodity culture represented not an "anachronism with a future," but rather a betrayal of the German socialist experiment. Some of the strongest critiques of consumer culture in the 1950s were made by Gerhard Klein and Wolfgang Kohlhaase in the first two of their so-called Berlin films: *Eine Berliner Romanze* (A Berlin Romance, 1956) and *Berlin, Ecke Schönhauser* (Berlin, Schönhauser Corner, 1957). Both of these films resist the New Course ethos by disavowing consumerism in the East, portraying it as a Westernized habit that must be overcome before real socialist relationships can be constructed. Where we earlier saw the glamorous gratifications of traditional romance contravening socialist realism's rigid politicization of social bonds, love here has the opposite valence: within Klein and Kohlhaase's films, the romantic plot offers a means to circumvent the mediation of interpersonal relationships by commodities.

In deploying the love story to this purpose, however, the films jump over their own ideological shadow: though they reject the insinuation of commodities into interpersonal relationships, they also fail to suggest an alternate source of social cohesion. The process begun by these love stories is left unfinished. As we will see in chapters 2 and 3, GDR culture in the 1960s and 1970s is characterized by an ongoing search for the broad and deep social ties that might bind East Germans to the socialist experiment.

Eine Berliner Romanze tells the story of Hans (Ulrich Thein), a young, unemployed auto mechanic from West Berlin, and Uschi (Annekathrin Bürger), a salesgirl and would-be model from the Eastern half of the city. Their relationship has an unpropitious start: when they meet, Uschi is on a date with Hans's friend Lord (Uwe-Jens Pape), a fashionable West Berlin ladies' man. Lord had spotted Uschi window-shopping on the Kurfürstendamm, West Berlin's golden shopping street, and asked her to a movie: *Lockende Sünde* (Tempting Sin). Although she had earlier that day turned down a friend's invitation to see *Lockende Sünde,* declaring it "too dumb," Uschi is willing to go to the film with Lord.

Lord, we may infer, is the embodiment of the "tempting sin" of West Berlin. Uschi gravitates toward his charm, his good looks, and, perhaps above all, toward the transistor radio he wears around his neck: "I love transistor radios," she explains. The *Kofferradio* was an important piece of iconography in DEFA films from this period. The object itself, as well as the "hot jazz" that usually blared out of it, identified its owner as a rock-and-roll rebel, a *Halbstarker.* The symbolic valence of the *Kofferradio* is owed also to its status as a reminder of the failures of the GDR's system of production and distribution: GDR transistor technology lagged behind that of the FRG, and when an East German model was finally developed, it fell victim to the sluggish reactions of the command economy. In the early 1960s, 80 percent of GDR radio production was still devoted to vacuum-tubed giants (Kaminsky, 113). To own a *Kofferradio,* then, generally signified that one had the means to secure one in the West. Uschi's "love" of *Kofferradios* thus carries with it a number of implications: what attracts her to Lord is his affluence, his rebelliousness, and, above all, his Westernness.

Uschi has little time, however, for Hans. When Hans tags along on her date with Lord, she makes it clear that three's a crowd. And after Hans drops ice cream on her dress, her impatience gives way to open contempt. "I hate you," she tells him and frets about the stain. Hans refuses to take the hint and cleverly manages to take Lord's place on a second date, but it is a disaster. Eventually, Uschi insults him: "I think you're fresh, ugly, and mean"; and he responds: "I think you're dumb." She pours her coffee on him. Though angry and humiliated, Hans pays for their coffee and buys their ferry tickets home. This display of chivalry seems to win Uschi over. She helps Hans clean his shirt, and from then on the two are a pair.

From the first, then, consumer goods—especially clothing, which, in light of Uschi's work as a model in East and West, takes on particular significance in the film's rendition of the Cold War commodity race—frame and mediate Uschi and Hans's relationship. Her hostility toward him begins with the accidental staining of her dress and ends with the deliberate staining of his shirt. An uncharitable reading might note that her affection is secured only by his dogged willingness to pay for her entertainment. Their relationship seems to continue in this vein: on their third date (or first intentional one), Hans gives Uschi a transistor radio, which he has bought on credit. He also pays for her courses at a West Berlin modeling school and borrows a friend's apartment to impress her with his independent lifestyle.

This is not the story of a gold digger and her prey, however. This, the film would have us believe, is a typical courtship under capitalist conditions. Uschi and Hans are simply participating in the exchange economy of the date, the ultimate expression of Illouz's "commodified romance" (53–54).[27] If romance is coextensive with

---

27. As Illouz reminds us, the consumer economy of the date is not just a matter of the man's footing the bill, nor is it dependent entirely on his buying power: "Men were expected to pay for the date, and women had to spend money for 'grooming.' The market constructed and reinforced definitions of masculinity and femininity that made *both* men and women depend on different practices of consumption" (74).

spending money, then West Berlin had an incontestable advantage over East Berlin in the 1950s. It is thus perhaps inevitable that Uschi and Hans's courtship takes place entirely on ground that Klein's film cedes to the West: the "romantic" settings of movie theaters, dance halls, and cocktail bars. The problem faced by the film narrative, then, is how to counter the West's advantage, how to coax Uschi, Hans, and the viewer away from a commodity-based model of romance.

Eine Berliner Romanze mobilizes both narrative and form in this effort. As the plot's unfolding gives the lie to an untenable standard of romance, the increasingly stark contours of the film's neorealist aesthetic present the viewer with a compelling visual argument: beyond the smoke and mirrors of Hollywood romance, love must still take place in the real world. It requires more than attraction and affection to keep it alive and is endangered by more than petty misunderstandings. This young couple, we might say, must find their way in the world of the *Bicycle Thief,* and not in that of the film posters its hero Ricci has been employed to hang.[28] In Klein's depictions of the West a gulf yawns between the daydream of romance and the day-to-day struggles of life as a working-class West Berliner. Visual and audio cues distinctly mark this gap. A world away from the bright lights and glossy sheen of the Kurfürstendamm and the amusement park, the apartment where Hans lives with his mother is cramped and dark. A streetlight flickers from time to time through the window, a faint, gloomy echo of the shopping street's neon promises. Rather than the up-tempo, Dixieland-inspired jazz of the soundtrack hitherto, the scenes in Hans's mother's apartment are characterized only by diegetic, "real world" sound, including the roar of a train going by overhead.

In these scenes at home with Hans and his mother, we can see and hear the influence of Italian neorealism on Klein and his cinematographer, Wolf Göthe. The film's scriptwriter, Wolfgang Kohlhaase, commented in 1996: "For us and some of our friends neo-realism was a revelation. We were fascinated by the themes and the methods, the social commentary, the way they relied on the poetry of everyday life, the sober tone which [fit] well with the post-war era" (128). Both the film's aesthetic sensibility and its plot take a neorealist turn when Hans and Uschi's Hollywood romance becomes an everyday affair. Hounded by creditors and working only intermittently, Hans finds it harder and harder to make ends meet. He joins the throngs of men looking for work, eventually taking a job doing demolition at a construction site. Hans and his coworkers are paid for speed and not held to safety standards. After Hans is injured by a falling beam, he is forced to quit his job and suddenly finds it impossible to keep the illusion of prosperity going. He explains this to Uschi with a telling cinematic reference: "You just have to imagine you're at the movies. The boy rents a cozy room, the girl becomes a model because she's

---

28. Both Stephen Gundle and Peter Bondanella point out the significance of the fact that Ricci, the main character of De Sica's *Bicycle Thief,* has been hired to post advertisements for a Rita Hayworth film (Gundle, 341; Bondanella, 57).

so pretty. But it isn't true. The boy can't pay the rent. The radio isn't paid for, either…Does that matter to you?" More to the point, did it matter to young East German moviegoers? Did they want pretty illusions, or real life? Here, as in the film debate in the early part of the decade, realism is juxtaposed to Hollywood's shimmering phantasmagoria. Yet whereas East German filmmakers had earlier tried to counter the charms of Western commodity culture with the rigid certainties of socialist realism, Klein and Kohlhaase now used neorealist techniques to expose the shadow side of West Berlin's opulence (see fig. 5).

To the same degree that these techniques successfully disarm Western, capitalist tropes of romance, the film's skepticism vis-à-vis consumer culture also flies in the face of New Course optimism. When so much had been staked on consumer satisfaction in the East, the film's sharp turn away from consumption would have rankled some officials, even if few would have admitted to this objection. Compared with the flashy promises of the New Course, the conclusion of *Eine Berliner Romanze* seems all too mundane. Hans and Uschi decide to move to East Berlin in the end, but their reasons are more practical than romantic: Hans needs a job. The final voice-over sums up the film's message: "Now the two are a couple, one of thousands in Berlin.… And together they will find their place, Uschi und Hans, in the middle of our life, in which there is work, struggle, and love."

Love has a heavy burden in this trinity of life in the GDR. If Uschi's earlier statement that "you're always supposed to work over here" is to be proved wrong, love must offer compensation for the glamour and adventure left behind in the West—not just to Uschi and Hans, but more importantly to the film's viewership—for as the public's distaste for 1950s socialist realism made clear, "work" and "struggle" were not the box-office draws the party had hoped they would be. Though unwilling simply to furnish a pipe dream knocked off from the capitalist culture industry, Klein and Kohlhaase still had to find a generically satisfying conclusion to their Berlin romance. That love is considered adequate to this task attests to the potency of the romantic code. In (literally) giving love the last word, however, *Eine Berliner Romanze* undermines its own critique of Hollywood's modus operandi. Ultimately, it is forced to drop its critical-realistic perspective and rely on a compensatory machinery, the narrative catholicon of the romantic happy ending. This fallback is not simply a narrative strategy among many, but rather symptomatic of a larger structural problem. The film's reliance on generic means to achieve social integration attests to the critical attenuation of East Germans' affective ties to their homeland.

A year after *Eine Berliner Romanze,* Klein and Kohlhaase released the second in what was to become a trilogy of "Berlin films": *Berlin, Ecke Schönhauser.* In many ways, *Berlin, Ecke Schönhauser* continues the work begun in *Eine Berliner Romanze,* employing many of the same narrative and formal techniques to tell the story of a young man's choice between life in the East and in the West. Here, however, the neorealist style that had remained largely circumscribed in *Eine Berliner Romanze*

Figure 5. Promotional flyer for the film *A Berlin Romance.* The text reads: "Berliners fall in love everywhere. And love does not stop at the sector borders. Yet the ruinous division of our city often puts the love of young Berliners to the test. And Uschi and Hans don't have it easy with their first love, until they learn to differentiate between real values and false luster. This DEFA film tells of the fate of these two [lovers] as they make their way from tender flirtation to solid companionship in the great divided city." Source: Bundesarchiv [FilmSG1/BArch/1454 *Eine Berliner Romanze*].

to a specific function—that of debunking Hollywood romantic conventions and the empty promises of Western consumer culture—becomes the dominant aesthetic throughout. *Berlin, Ecke Schönhauser* shines on the East the same harsh light its predecessor had shone on the West. As several commentators have pointed out, this feature ensured the film a starkly split reception: accolades from the public and many reviewers, rebukes from the side of the party and the high priests of socialist realism.[29]

As in *Eine Berliner Romanze,* one of the central problems in *Berlin, Ecke Schönhauser* is that of the interlacing of commodities into the fabric of society. Where in the former film such commodity mediation had been assumed to be confined to the West, we now see that it has crept over to the East. *Berlin, Ecke Schönhauser* takes us into a milieu where the ideals of socialism have little cachet. For these young East Germans, Westernized attitudes and behaviors set the standard for social interaction and personal ambitions. Thus, as in *Eine Berliner Romanze,* the ideological mission of *Berlin, Ecke Schönhauser* entails breaking these bonds with

---

29. See Claus, 109–10.

the West and replacing them with corresponding attachments to the East. As we will see, the film is adequate to the former task. The latter, however, will prove more difficult.

The opening sequence of *Berlin, Ecke Schönhauser,* which actually occurs last in the film's plot time, may be understood as a literalization of such a turning away from the West. After the credits, the camera follows a young man as he runs through the streets of Berlin. It pauses on a sign announcing the beginning of the "Democratic Sector": East Berlin. We then learn who is running, and where, when the film's protagonist, Dieter, bursts into an East German police station and announces: "Kohle is dead." These words begin the film's framing device: Dieter's confession to a kind but severe *Volkspolizei* commissioner. Dieter asks about "a girl" and insists that she has "nothing to do with it," then starts the story from the beginning. We follow Angela from her mother's apartment down to the street corner where Dieter and the neighborhood boys used to gather. They are dancing boogie to their own accompaniment, singing and clapping the time.

For this milieu, the coveted *Kofferradio* of *Eine Berliner Romanze* is out of the question: West-marks are precious and hard to come by, as we learn when Karl-Heinz dares Kohle to break a streetlight with a stone. For one Mark East, Kohle refuses to take the bet; for one Mark West, worth several times as much, he steps up to the challenge. After he breaks the light on the first throw, irate passersby call the police, who round up a few of the boys and take them to the station. There, the same police commissioner to whom Dieter will later make his confession interrogates the boys. He chides them for wasting their strength and wants to know why Karl-Heinz and Kohle are not working. The former, it turns out, is living off his bourgeois parents; the latter cannot find a suitable job. The commissioner promises to secure an apprenticeship for Kohle. At this point Dieter speaks up: "You can't do anything for me," he says. "I have a steady job and feed myself." Throughout the film, Dieter's excellent—even, at one point, heroic—work performance is a sticking point for the representatives of the party. From their perspective, it seems impossible that such a good worker could be so unreliable politically. As the secretary of the factory's youth organization puts it, "I don't understand you: you do your work, you're a good man, but evenings you play the tough guy." Dieter's social integration, it seems, is only half-complete: he is well established at work but otherwise has no strong emotional attachments to his society. During his interrogation, the commissioner asks him: "What are you interested in, anyway?" Dieter replies:

"Motorcycles."
"And other than that?"
"Soccer."
"And what else?"
"Nothing else."

A review of Klein's film in the FDJ newspaper *Junge Welt* suggests that the real origin of the "youth problem" (*Halbstarkenproblem*) lies in this paucity of extravocational ties, in the fact that "many young people are left to their own devices after work" (M.P., 8).[30]

Berlin, Ecke Schönhauser's neorealist aesthetic highlights the inhospitable atmosphere that surrounds these young East Germans, taking us into their cramped homes and broken families. The strongest visual correlative to the social position of Dieter and his friends can be found in the setting that gives the film its name: the corner of Schönhauser Boulevard, to which we are introduced in the film's establishing title shot. This small triangular patch of concrete under the elevated-train tracks is utterly public, wedged between several well-traveled streets, and yet the only autonomous space available to Dieter and his friends.

The danger presented by this state of affairs is captured in a statement made by the commissioner at the end of the film, a phrase that gave the film its working title: "Where we are not, there are our enemies" (Wo wir nicht sind, sind unsere Feinde). Although Schönhauser corner is in the heart of East Berlin, the party has no positive influence there at all and is able to intervene only negatively, through the police. The party's enemies, however, are all too present. Dieter and his friends are united by a shared taste for Western music, movies, and fashion. Their relationships, in other words, are shot through with commodities. It is the promise of a West-mark, we recall, that sets the whole story in motion. For Kohle, this prize means the price of a movie ticket. He brags to the commissioner that he has seen at least a hundred films "drüben" (over there). Angela is equally impressed by Hollywood, informing Dieter at one point that she likes men who look like Marlon Brando. The most Westernized member of the group is Karl-Heinz, who begins trafficking in currency and identity-papers to earn the money for, among other things, a new leather jacket.

As might be expected, such consumerist proclivities turn out to have higher stakes than these young rebels first imagine. When Dieter and Kohle try to collect on the promised West-mark, Karl-Heinz pulls a gun, and Kohle hits him on the head. Dieter and Kohle assume they have killed Karl-Heinz and flee to a refugee camp in West Berlin. When it seems that he will be separated from Dieter, Kohle drinks coffee mixed with cigar tobacco to bring on a fever, a trick he claims to have learned from the movies. Kohle dies from the poisonous mixture—a victim, literally, of too many Hollywood movies. By the middle of the film, Angela seems also to have been betrayed by her Westernized tastes: her preference for rebels, for Marlon Brando types, leaves her pregnant by a man who has fled to the West.

---

30. The Freie Deutsche Jugend (Free German Youth), or FDJ, was East Germany's equivalent of the Boy Scouts (though girls were encouraged to join the FDJ).

In this way the film's main characters are forced to live out their Hollywood-inspired fantasies of romance, gunplay, and crime. These elements of *Berlin, Ecke Schönhauser*'s plot seem cut to the party's official line on the consequences of receptivity to Western popular culture. The capitalists, according to SED rhetoric, used music and movies to lead East German youth into rebellion and crime:

> In this way it became easier for the pied pipers of the RIAS [Radio in the American Sector] and the always-outdated relics of the capitalist age in our own Republic to use their temptations and traducements to lure our youth into idleness, in some cases into hostile activities and even into forsaking our Republic for the land of yesterday, where there is no future, where the old powers rule, those powers that entice today and tomorrow come with the whip, with terror and murder. ("An euch alle, die ihr Jung seid")

This turgid sentence captures the party's official position on the origins of the "youth problem": it is not that the East German *halbstark* rebels turn to Western popular culture to express their restlessness and discontent, but rather that the incursion of Western popular culture into the GDR creates the *Halbstarken* in the first place. "Hot" jazz and Hollywood movies, according to the East German authorities, were simply two more weapons in the Cold War.

Although *Berlin, Ecke Schönhauser* takes a more nuanced view of this matter, partially exposing the domestic roots of the East German youth problem, it is faced with a conundrum similar to that faced by the party and the Politburo: how to disrupt the ties of East German youth to West German commodity culture. And here the film has recourse to a stratagem far less tractable this side of a movie script: Dieter returns to the East not because he likes his job, nor because of a newfound appreciation for the socialist order, nor even on account of his unpleasant experiences in the West German refugee camp. Rather, he returns because of his love for Angela. In her book *Jazz, Rock, and Rebels: Cold War Politics and American Culture in a Divided Germany,* Uta Poiger points out that this resolution parallels those prevalent in the West German discourse on the youth problem:

> *Berlin, Schönhauser Corner,* like the West German liberal discourse on adolescence, also focused on a heterosexual relationship to resolve overdrawn East German rebelliousness. As the East German program flyer said, Dieter's girlfriend Angela was the only one who gave him support. Dieter returned to East Berlin to "create a meaningful life together with Angela." (128)

Though Poiger is right to stress the importance of the film's love plot, a crucial aspect of this story line must be added here: by the end of the film, Angela and Dieter's relationship is no longer simply a bond of mutual affection or of shared interests, but rather a relationship sanctioned and mediated by the party, as represented by Dieter's brother and the commissioner.[31] When Dieter flees to the West, his brother, having learned his lesson from Dieter's delinquency, offers to let Angela move in with him. That Dieter's brother is a party-loyal policeman, however, gives this arrangement a further significance. In a way, the policeman's role as boyfriend ersatz is a literalization of the film's motto. Rather than letting Angela fall victim once again to her taste for rebels, Dieter's brother moves bodily into the space of her desire. The commissioner as well plays a role in reuniting the young couple. When Dieter returns from the West, the commissioner tells him that Angela is expecting a child, and urges him to "go to her."

In this sense, the resolution of the love story in *Berlin, Ecke Schönhauser* modifies the strategy of legitimation found in *Eine Berliner Romanze.* Where the latter relies on romantic love alone to draw the protagonists together and toward better prospects in the East, the former adds a pair of policemen to the equation—for romantic attraction, as we have seen, is a hazardous undertaking. It is as likely, and perhaps more so, to turn to the West as to the East—away from the "work and struggle" of building socialism and toward the glamour of commodified romance. These two policemen guarantee that this volatile force remains contained and directed. They perform, in other words, the function I ascribed to the man in the bookstore photograph from *Das Magazin,* ensuring in this case that what finally brings Dieter and Angela together is "true love" (*wahre Liebe*), and not another Hollywood fantasy. Such romantic oversight is one component of what could be called the Stalinist mode of romance, a phenomenon that will be examined in more detail in the next chapter.

In one important respect, however, *Berlin, Ecke Schönhauser* fails to solve the problem it sets out for itself in the beginning. Although by the end of the film Dieter and Angela have seen the error of their Westernized ways, their positive ties to East German society are no more substantial than they were at the start. The film does not—perhaps cannot—suggest how the Western attachments of East German youth could be countered and compensated. The romantic scenario offers a provisional solution, but only insofar as it is mediated by agents of the state: "where we are not," after all, is the enemy. The enemy's bid was clear. What East Germany's "we" had to offer was still under negotiation. Thus the film ends with the commissioner's exhortation "Start over, young man" (Fang neu an, Jung!). At least with regard to the question of social attachment, we end where we began.

---

31. The heterosexual relationship of West German liberal discourse, on the other hand, is a reaction *against* this kind of authoritarian mediation: "In such personal relationships the *Halbstarken* can build their own world and feel that they can show themselves as they really are and still be taken seriously" (Bondy, 92). The therapeutic value of "building one's own world" would not have received much support in the GDR at this time. Instead, the focus was on assimilating into the shared world of socialism.

"Like in a film, until you get used to me": *Der Kinnhaken* and the Wall

In the early 1960s, the party took drastic measures to prevent young people from selling or seeking the "wares of love" in the West. Almost overnight on August 13, 1961, the "Antifascist Wall of Protection," or Berlin Wall, was built.[32] In light of the reading outlined here the Wall's bold belligerence in fact signals a broad acquiescence. With this gesture the party admitted to the GDR's inability (temporary, it hoped) to surpass the West as a consumer power, and consequently also capitulated to the overarching logic of commodity culture, the promises and betrayals of the consumer economy. When the inter-German border closed, such decisions as those made by Hans, Uschi, and Dieter became moot. East German officials hoped to recompense this drastic curtailment with increased consumer choice. To this end, the New Course was extended and amplified into the New Economic System (NÖS), a wide-ranging set of initiatives designed to make good on the promises of the 1950s reforms.

As Charles Maier points out in his book *Dissolution: The Crisis of Communism and the End of East Germany,* the New Economic System gave the GDR a firm push in the direction of a decentralized market economy:

> Between December 1962 and early 1963, the SED thrashed out major proposals for economic decentralization along the lines envisaged by the Soviet and Czech reformers.... As did similar reforms elsewhere, the New Economic System (NÖS) deemphasized central planning and placed more power in the associations (VVB) of socialized industries (VEB). Profits were to serve as measurements of firm performance and could be retained to cover reinvestment and finance.... The logic of reform in the late 1960s was to free prices, which alone might reliably communicate social preferences, allow supply and demand to converge, and reconcile the needs of the present with ambitions for the future. (87–88)

Annette Kaminsky draws attention to the significance of these economic reforms for the East German consumer:

> The "New Economic System of Planning and Leadership" (NÖSPL [or NÖS]) was supposed to modernize the GDR economy within a few years and give new impetus to the production of consumer goods. The Sixth Party Congress in 1963 announced that a new era had begun, and blamed all previous problems on the "imperialist class enemy." For years, the enemy had been drawing massive profits through the open border, at the cost of the East German people. Now the promised improvements

---

32. "Antifascist Wall of Protection" (Antifaschistischer Schutzwall) was the official name for the Berlin Wall in the East.

would be implemented without further disturbance. In particular, the people would be able to satisfy their increased demands for consumer goods. (72)

The New Economic System, like the New Course, relied on the promise of future enjoyment to compensate present inconvenience—an enjoyment with a distinctly consumerist character. The problem, then, was how to convince East German consumers that GDR commodities would be worth the wait.

This seems to be one of the motivations behind Heinz Thiel's 1962 DEFA film, *Der Kinnhaken* (The Uppercut). The film opens with a radio report breaking the news of the border closure. Carolin (Dietlinde Greiff) panics and heads to the newly built Wall in an effort to find a way into the West. As she explains to Georg (Manfred Krug), the kindhearted factory-militia soldier who stops her at the border, she has a good job in West Berlin and needs to get across. He temporizes, offering to smuggle her over at a later date. When she visits him at home to discuss the plan, he reveals that he has no intention of taking her across. "What should I do?" she asks him. "You can come visit me," he replies, handing her a set of keys to his apartment. "Tomorrow, the day after tomorrow, more and more, like in a film, until you get used to me." Georg's invitation to Carolin, to keep coming back until she learns to like him, parallels the film's implicit (and rather cynical) message to the citizens of the GDR: "Since you can't leave, you might as well learn to like it here." In line with this effort *Der Kinnhaken* is a veritable advertisement for the products and attractions of East Germany. Just after this conversation between George and Carolin, for instance, the film cuts to footage of the bright lights of East Berlin's nightlife and the neon signs of stores reading "His" and "Hers."

The GDR of Thiel's film is a consumer paradise, even if, as the characters point out in a number of scenes, a few of the products aren't quite up to Western standards yet. In one exchange Georg jokes about the poor quality of GDR whisky, in another about the unavailability of seamless stockings in the East. In the grocery store where Carolin gets a job there is a shortage of apples, much to the annoyance of one customer. Yet just as Georg's patience will pay off eventually in Carolin's love, the frustrated East German consumer is assured that, as the banner above Georg's workplace proclaims, "As we work today, so shall we live tomorrow" (Wie wir heute arbeiten, werden wir morgen leben). Consumption is acceptable, *Der Kinnhaken* tells the viewer, as long as the socialist commodity is consumed. And the film does depict the alternative: it turns out that Carolin's lucrative job in the West was nothing short of prostitution, as we learn when her pimp, Bubi, comes to the East to blackmail her into going to Switzerland to be with her "boyfriend," "Uncle Franz." Having learned of Carolin's unseemly past, Georg's friend Hübner (Horst Bastian) puts it bluntly: "She did it for money. That's a fact." The patient and forgiving Georg, however, decides to give Carolin another chance, and after he delivers the uppercut of the film's title to Bubi's chin, he and Carolin become a happy couple.

Read allegorically, the message of the story to the East German consumer might be summarized as follows: "The closed border is there to protect you from yourself, to stop you from prostituting yourself for Western goods. Though you may have sold your love in the past, we'll afford you a second chance at respectability. And if you wait patiently, we'll soon have the very products here for which you were selling yourself there." In this way *Der Kinnhaken* participates in the effort to create a consumer culture in the GDR to rival that of the West. Though the film does admit shortfalls in the East German production of consumer goods, it predominantly showcases the quality and variety of East German commodities: in the store where Carolin and her friend are cashiers, in Georg's gadget-filled apartment, in the factory where Georg works (the VEB Electro-Apparate Werke), and on the streets of East Berlin, *Der Kinnhaken* reminds East Germans that they are surrounded by a wealth of socialist commodities, a wealth that is only increasing. To avert the danger of undifferentiated commodity fetishism, the film makes it clear that what is responsible consumption in one state is base prostitution in the other. Essentially *Der Kinnhaken* is about marking boundaries: just as the "Antifascist Wall of Protection" (Antifascistische Schutzwall), had to be built to protect East Germans from Western exploitation and aggression, the film seems to say, a clear distinction has to be drawn between socialist consumption and capitalist prostitution.

And so we are back where we started, searching for the thin line between "wahre Liebe" (true love) and "Liebesware" (wares of love). It seems that the only thing keeping the former from becoming the latter is the state's intervention: the Wall of Protection, the commissioner and Dieter's brother, Georg's uppercut, the man in the trench coat. As we will see in chapter 2, this intervention, a facet of the control strategy known broadly as Stalinism, in fact implies the failure of Stalinist ideology—in large part a failure to offset the pleasures of capitalism. This discrepancy is particularly apparent in the East's attempts to find a romantic mode that could compete with the glamorous allure of Western love stories. In this light the increasing commodity orientation of East German romance seems to be a strategic retreat, buying time until the GDR could produce adequate commodities to romanticize. Chapter 2 will track the effort in the early 1960s to develop a "neue Romantik" (new romance) that would lend romantic valence not to the gratifications of consumption but to the rigors of production.

2

Love, Labor, Loss

Modes of Romance in the East German Novel of Arrival

Und wenn kein Unterschied ist zwischen der Liebe zueinander und der Liebe zu
einer Tätigkeit? Auch die Liebe ist eine Produktion.

And what if there's no difference between love for one another and love for an
activity? Love is also a production.

—Volker Braun, *Das ungezwungene Leben Kasts*

As we saw in chapter 1, the GDR of the 1950s came to look rather like a
consumer culture. This had practical consequences, but also, and perhaps more
importantly, philosophical and ideological ones. After all, consumer culture is essentially a response to the questions "Why do we work?" and "What do we get,
both as individuals and as a society, for our labor?" Consumer culture answers
these questions with commodities: the worker exchanges his or her labor for buying power; society works together to produce more and more consumer goods.

Officially, the GDR would never have endorsed this view of work's motivation.
In Marxist understanding, work represents a more fundamental, more essential
activity. The entry on "labor" in the East German *Kleines politisches Wörterbuch*
(Compact Political Dictionary) suggests this primacy with a quote from Friedrich
Engels's essay "The Part Played by Labour in the Transition from Ape to Man":
"[Labor] is the prime basic condition for all human existence, and this to such an
extent that, in a sense, we have to say that labour created man himself" ("Arbeit,"
47). Even the meaning of the word "labor" (*Arbeit*) changed under socialist rule
in East Germany. An article by Joachim Höppner in the September 1963 issue
of the East German literary journal *Weimarer Beiträge* maps the development of
the word's meaning from the "toil" of the bondservant—and thus also "drudgery,

hardship, necessity"—in Middle-High German to "productive activity" in the age of commodity production, culminating in its elevation under socialism to the "creative, productive employment of energy toward the complete fulfillment of the social and personal needs [of human beings]" (584).[1] Yet, as the SED discovered to its dismay, this etymological evolution was not enough to inspire the East German workforce to norm-breaking productivity.

The problem of incentive was one of the most pressing challenges of the East German planned economy—and remains an important topic in GDR studies today. Jana Scholze's contribution to the volume *Fortschritt, Norm und Eigensinn* (Progress, Norm, and Self-Will), a collection of essays on the history and historiography of everyday life in the GDR, begins with an extended meditation on this question:

> Why, in the face of…growing mismanagement and scarcity, did people in the GDR work? No pressure to perform, no fear of being fired or of unemployment "forced" them. Was it an understanding of social necessity? Was it the obligations of the tradition of "good German workmanship" and the pride of being a miner, doctor, or saleswoman? Was it the binding cohesion and the social control of the collective, the brigade, or the household? Was it a "fighting spirit" that, spurred by socialist competition, stimulated increased performance in production as though in a chess game? Or was it in fact just financial incentives, wages, bonuses? (85)[2]

This chapter will approach the question of incentive in its cultural articulation, tracking some of the hopes and anxieties regarding work in the East German public imagination.

Every socialist-realist industrial novel offers tracts on the subject of incentive, as do such films as Konrad Wolf's 1957 *Sonnensucher* (Sun Seekers), in which Jupp König (Erwin Geschonneck) takes the time to explain to his coworkers why it is in their best interest—indeed, in their class interest—to mine uranium for the Soviets. In these texts and films, the motivation to work is usually cast as a matter of the *collective;* it is not individual gratification or reward but rather group benefit that should incite the worker to greater productivity. A paradigmatic example of the rhetoric of collective incentive is found in Eduard Claudius's 1951 production novel, *Menschen an unserer Seite* (People on Our Side). To give a sense of the urgency with which Claudius takes up this theme, I will quote the passage at some length. In this scene, Wende, the new party secretary at the Berlin factory where

---

1. I was pointed toward this article by a passage in Bernhard Greiner's *Von der Allegorie zur Idylle: Die Literatur der Arbeitswelt in der DDR* (19).

2. In the end, Scholze suggests that a combination of these factors motivated East German workers. The strongest of these influences, however, seems to have been material gain. Prestige and recognition were gratifying, but it was the cash bonus attached to the "activist" title that made it worth struggling for.

the novel is set, interrogates the workers about the possibility of rebuilding the blast furnace while it is still in operation:

> Now Reichelt rumbled: "It depends what we stand to earn. I set no store by 'peoples' own' and such nonsense, and not by 'two-year plan,' not me!"
>
> "Oho," said Wende, amused, and smiled. He liked this fellow. Rare that someone had the courage to speak so openly.... Wende sat down on the edge of the kiln chamber, looked into the dirty faces, at the dusty, rough hands, became serious. He asked Reichelt: "Should we talk for real or do you want to just have a go at it?"
>
> "Leave me alone! I only talk to workers."
>
> "I'm a metalworker," Wende said thoughtfully, and his eyes sparkled impudently. "But that's not what's at issue now. I was listening earlier. Look here, you said the factory doesn't belong to you. You personally, certainly not, and you can't sell it or raffle it off because it belongs to us, understand? All of us! And we own other factories too, and you ask: What good does that do me? Well then, you're all doing work here that's saving some hundred thousand marks, and you're asking: What good does it do me? I don't feel it in my wallet. Aside from the fact that that's wrong, since you do feel it in your wallet and on your buttered bread, I want to clear something else up. You make export goods, but not just for export, and with your products it's not quite as obvious. Let's take another branch of production. Here in the Republic, in a factory that belongs to us, the people, we make thermometers. We've got the world monopoly, right? OK, the factory belongs to all of us, but let's assume for now that it only belongs to the workers who work in that factory. They have a kind of cooperative, and all the money that comes in from other countries gets divided up between them. Nice deal, no? Really a good deal, and boy can they buy things...the workers in the factory, I mean ...import goods, I mean, for the foreign currency they earn. Butter and bacon, my God, unbelievable what all they have! And you here...nada! You, you just lay bricks, your bricks don't bring in any foreign currency, and now you're standing here and watching how those guys are living large, how they've got bacon coming out their ears, how they're just busting at the seams. Nice, isn't it? Real nice, excellent!"
>
> Reichelt made a face as though someone had poured a bucket of cold water on his head. Without saying a word Wende stood up and walked away. (209–10)

Here, responding to Reichelt's reluctance to begin a job without a clear idea of what it might pay, the aptly named Wende ("reversal" or "turning point")—whose hands-on approach will eventually turn things around at the troubled factory—gives a spontaneous lesson in socialist economics. In the *Aufbau*-era production novel, a glance at the big picture is assumed to be motivation enough to get the job done.

In the early 1960s, however, a new kind of production narrative came into being: the *Ankunftsroman,* or "novel of arrival."[3] The *Ankunftsroman,* which takes its name

---

3. In this genre I would include such works as *Ankunft im Alltag* (Brigitte Reimann), *Beschreibung eines Sommers* (Karl Heinz Jakobs), *Der geteilte Himmel* (Christa Wolf), *Egon und das achte Weltwunder*

from Brigitte Reimann's 1961 novel, *Ankunft im Alltag* (Arrival in the Everyday), is a socialist *Bildungsroman,* a coming-of-age story in which the ultimate goal is integration into socialist society. The *Ankunft* genre was a direct product of the Bitterfeld Way, an initiative intended to bring together cultural producers and production workers under the dual slogans of "Schriftsteller an die Basis" (Writers to the Base!) and "Greif zur Feder, Kumpel!" (Grab that Quill, Buddy!). Bitterfeld's proponents hoped that if writers and artists spent time on farms and construction sites, in mines and factories, they would better understand the perspective of the average worker. Workers, meanwhile, would make their voices heard in anthologies, literary journals, newspapers, and *Wandzeitungen* (public information boards that functioned as a cross between a group diary and a bulletin board).[4] Echoing the ambitions of the Bitterfeld program, the *Ankunftsroman* insists on the transformative potential of production work: through the experience of industrial production, the novel's young protagonists eventually find their place in the socialist community.

In this sense, the *Ankunft* genre may be seen as an examination of the subjective experience of socialist society—and especially of socialist work—in which questions of individual motivation and satisfaction gain equal footing with socialist realism's established themes of solidarity and sacrifice. Thus the *Ankunft* narratives represent a break from the collective coming-of-age stories of the 1950s production novels, in which an emphasis on group development generally precludes a nuanced view of the incentives and compensations in the individual experience of socialism.

In the *Ankunftsroman,* a central love story tends to structure the plot and contribute to the "arrival" of the protagonist(s). The curious thing about these love stories, however, is that they usually fail. In Christa Wolf's *Der geteilte Himmel* (Divided Heaven), for instance, the lovers are parted when one of them emigrates to the West. In Karl Heinz Jakobs's *Beschreibung eines Sommers* (Description of a Summer), the main characters' extramarital love affair is subjected to a severe party correction, and they are forced to separate. The second volume of Dieter Noll's *Die Abenteuer des Werner Holt* (The Adventures of Werner Holt) ends with the protagonist leaving for university; we are led to believe his relationship will not survive the distance.

As a rule, the *Ankunftroman*'s love affair fails because it has in some way come into conflict with the integrative project of the whole—often because the intensity and exclusivity of the protagonists' relationship have alienated them from the

---

(Joachim Wohlgemuth), *Die Abenteuer des Werner Holt* (Dieter Noll), *Mein namenloses Land* (Joachim Knappe), *Wir sind nicht Staub im Wind* (Max Walter Schulz), and *Der Hohlweg* (Günter de Bruyn). As Dieter Schlenstedt suggests in his article "Ankunft und Anspruch," the genre can be subdivided into two groups: works that narrate the socialist conversion process of young ex-soldiers after the war (Noll, Schulz, de Bruyn) and works that describe the experience of young men and women "going into production" in the late 1950s and early 1960s (Reimann, Jakobs, Wolf, Wohlgemuth, Knappe). I will concentrate primarily on the latter group, in order to draw attention to the economic and cultural developments of the 1960s, developments that are central to my argument as a whole. For an excellent analysis of the mechanisms and implications of postfascist conversion narratives, see Hell, *Post-Fascist Fantasies,* esp. 115–23.

4. For more on the Bitterfeld Way, see Ingeborg Gerlach, *Bitterfeld: Arbeiterliteratur und Literatur der Arbeitswelt in der DDR.*

group. In a study of love motifs in East and West German literature, Ilse Braatz succinctly describes this dynamic in the *Ankunftsroman:* "When social and individual bonds no longer agree, the 'private' relationship has to give way" (56–57). Here Braatz identifies the unwritten (and sometimes written) rule of East German love stories from this period: the pair relationship is to remain subordinate to the claims of the socialist collective.[5] This hierarchy accounts for a great deal of the internal tension in these narratives—indeed, it often forms their fundamental structuring principle. For this reason, it may be tempting to read the abortive love stories of the *Ankunftsromane* as didactic exercises in the tradition of the Brechtian *Lehrstück* (didactic play)—that is, as lessons in social priorities and personal accountability. I would argue, however, that if these love stories fail to hold up—or, persisting, fail to convince—this owes less to the polemical intent of their authors than to the peculiarity of their erotic economy. In the *Ankunftsroman,* the romantic framework becomes uncoupled from the love story proper and is deployed instead in the service of the genre's overarching ideological project: to reconfigure the East German desiring imagination in line with what I will call the "neue Romantik" (New Romance/Romanticism). This reconfiguration does not entail simply abandoning one way of desiring for another, but rather abandoning desire altogether. Indeed, according to this model, the demands of desire *can* be met, the clamor of desire stilled, as long as the desiring subject chooses the right object. The "right object," however, is not an object at all, but rather a process: that of production itself.

To explore the distinctive interplay of love and production underlying the "neue Romantik" I will look at two representative *Ankunft* novels: Brigitte Reimann's *Ankunft im Alltag* (the novel that lent the genre its name), and Karl Heinz Jakobs's *Beschreibung eines Sommers.* These close readings will illustrate how the *Ankunft* genre functioned—and why it ran afoul of the cultural politics of 1960s East Germany. Like the Bitterfeld Way, the "neue Romantik" foundered on its own radicality: its uncompromisingly progressive vision threatened to release social forces that the party, as it turned out, preferred to contain.

Halbstarker or *Fußlatscher:* The Stakes of Romantic Choice in *Ankunft im Alltag*

Ankunft im Alltag describes the experiences of Recha, Nikolaus, and Curt, three students spending a year at the Schwarze Pumpe brown-coal refinery in Hoyerswerda before going to college. From the start, Curt, Recha, and Nikolaus find themselves

---

5. The written rule is found, for instance, in the entry on "Liebe" in the *Kulturpolitisches Wörterbuch:* "Because of its social conditionality and importance to the community, a sexual-erotic relationship between a man and a woman does not transcend the responsibility to the community nor stand outside society's moral assessment" ("Liebe," 343).

in a love triangle as both men compete for Recha while her attraction oscillates between them.[6] Nikolaus is kind, diligent, strong, and politically conscious—in other words, the quintessential worker-hero of the socialist-realist mode. Curt, on the other hand, is the textbook image of a *Halbstarker,* a Westernized rebel à la Marlon Brando or James Dean.[7]

In essence, the love story in *Ankunft im Alltag* is the story of competing modes of romance. At first, Recha is drawn to Curt's version: the romance of dates and driving tours, the allure of conspicuous consumption.[8] Focused more on pleasure than on principles, in affect more sentimental than idealistic, this is the glittery romance of Hollywood, and Curt's the appeal of the leading man. At one point Recha compares him to the "glossy photos of movie stars" that she and her roommate used to collect (174). Curt's affluence is not without its attractions for Recha. When they go for a drive in his father's Wartburg, she admits: "It really is quite pleasant, seeing the world from a car" (144). Curt is pleased with this revelation: "It's about time you figured that out. Unfortunately you have a tendency toward idealism—but idealism, my dear, is not pleasant and certainly not comfortable. Pedestrians [*Fußlatscher*] are not *up to date*.[9]... A few fools still haven't figured that out. Consider our Parsifal" (144).

Nikolaus, the "Parsifal" of Curt's ridicule, has a very different idea of romance. Seeing the industrial panorama of the Schwarze Pumpe for the first time he thinks: "This is the new Romantic [*die neue Romantik*]. What seemed dry and doubtful in books is beautiful reality here" (35; see fig. 6). Nikolaus dreams of heroic deeds in the name of socialism: "He surreptitiously squeezed his powerful muscles and dreamed, full of hazy longing [*verschwommener Sehnsucht*], that he was in a still-wild landscape, in a romantic, sweaty life among bold men who would fight against the forest with heavy axes—and he forgot that there were chain saws and bulldozers" (43). Content not only to be a *Fußlatscher* (pedestrian), Nikolaus's heroic longing here draws him out of the machine age altogether: he forgets about chain saws and bulldozers.

As this anachronism suggests, the "neue Romantik" seems to be romance in the older sense of the term, a kind of socialist chivalry. In *Ankunft im Alltag,* the chivalrous code of the "neue Romantik" would include not only such virtues as diligence, honesty, and loyalty, but also a chastity appropriate to courtly love. Walking with Recha one night, Nikolaus has an urge to kiss her: "In that moment he wished—and his head spun at the thought—he could find the courage to take the girl in his arms and kiss her. But he stood motionless...and then he said

---

6. As Julia Hell points out in *Post-Fascist Fantasies,* Recha's romantic choice is the real test of her "arrival"; when she ends up with Nikolaus in the end, her integration seems complete (126).

7. See above, p. 23.

8. This romantic mode is also investigated in chapter 1 above, under the rubric of what Eva Illouz calls "commodified romance."

9. In English in the original.

Figure 6. "Neue Romantik"? The sublime vista of the Schwarze Pumpe brown-coal refinery in 1958, seen from above. Source: SLUB Dresden / Deutsche Fotothek / DZL, 1958.

to himself: What a primitive notion, my friend! You can't solve problems that way" (110). In this moment of temptation and self-denial, Nikolaus exposes the incapacity of his romantic mode—the idealistic and chaste "neue Romantik"—to accommodate the "problem" presented by desire. Thus, when Nikolaus and

Recha finally do kiss, he appeals to a different mode of romance to process the experience:

> She threw her arms around his neck, and he kissed her, fervidly, clumsily, and anx-
> iously, his head was spinning, and he believed he could feel how the thoughts fell out
> of his head, all the good and beautiful words, and there was nothing left but a silly,
> vulgar line of song, all the heavens open, a song that he had heard somewhere some-
> time and had long since forgotten and that now circled insistently in his head, all the
> heavens open, my God, what nonsense, and he was ashamed that he could think this
> nonsense in the same moment as he covered the closed eyes and the mouth of the
> Mahogany-girl with his chapped, clumsy, boyish kisses. (158)

Something about this experience, then, breaks the frame of the "neue Romantik." The language Nikolaus used to take in the sublime landscape of the Schwarze Pumpe "falls out of his head," and he turns to an idiom more appropriate to his rival: the "silly, vulgar" lyrics of a pop song. The failure of the "neue Romantik" to frame this "romantic" moment is telling. Especially given his designation as "Parsifal," we might be tempted to push the correlation of Nikolaus's socialist chivalry with medieval courtly love to claim, with Denis de Rougement, that this kind of love is actually a love of its own obstacles.[10] In fact, such an appeal to anachronism would be the *fantasy of the fantasy* at work here. In other words, the portrayal of Nikolaus as a medieval knight, thwarted in the consummation of his love by a rigid code of honor, loyalty, and decorum, represents a wishful overlay upon a more fundamental (but still imaginary) hindrance to interpersonal libidinal ties within the symbolic matrix of *Ankunft im Alltag*.

This deeper fantasy, the second layer of the "neue Romantik," would posit a subject without desire—one who has no *need* for romantic love in the first place. Indeed, on closer inspection, the "neue Romantik" is revealed to have little to do with interpersonal relationships at all. This romantic mode is more about labor than about love; what is being romanticized is not a relationship between individuals, but instead an attitude of the worker toward his or her work. The "romance" of work, according to the model of the "neue Romantik," lies in the experience of labor as a wholesale sublimation.[11] Production work, in this conception, would be wholly

---

10. Rougemont locates the appeal of chivalrous romance in the figuration of its own obstruction: "Unless the course of love is being hindered there is no 'romance'; and it is romance that we revel in— that is to say, the self-consciousness, intensity, variations, and delays of passion, together with its climax rising to disaster—not its sudden flaring" (52).

11. On a related note, Hell points out in passing that *Ankunft im Alltag* "explicitly thematizes the Communist discourse on the nexus between sexuality and the work ethic, the 'revolutionary sublimation' of the Soviet Freudian Zalkind" (*Post-Fascist Fantasies,* 127–78). It would be a fascinating and no doubt rewarding project to trace the lines of influence from the "revolutionary sublimation" of the early Soviet period through East German *Aufbau* culture and into the *Ankunftsroman*. One possible approach

satisfying—it would leave nothing to be desired. In discussing their foreman Hamann's extraordinary dedication to the brigade, Nikolaus and his roommate, Rolf, articulate succinctly the economic logic at work here, according to which relations of production are exchanged for other social relations—in this case, familial ones:

> "He doesn't have a family," Rolf said. "At least he never talks about one."
>
> "Who's he beating himself up for then?"
>
> Half with astonishment, half with reluctance, Rolf said: "For the factory. For us." (96)[12]

The hermetic libidinal economy of the "neue Romantik" represents a significant quandary for Nikolaus and Recha's love story. The problem, as Recha perceives it, is that Nikolaus "is indifferent to her. He only thinks about his work" (110). Even when narrative interventions indicate that Nikolaus cares more than he lets on, such interest can only be a deviation from his romantic ideal. As one might imagine, these are not very encouraging conditions for a romantic relationship. In a moment of frustration, Recha attempts to provoke the phlegmatic Nikolaus: "'We're always so terribly virtuous,' Recha said unhappily. 'We never go dancing—work all day, and after work drawing-lessons...It's worse than jail!' Nikolaus said nothing, and she added spitefully: 'Curt was more fun'" (169). Nikolaus simply agrees. Though Recha insists she was just trying to annoy him, she later thinks: "He's a block of ice, he's just a block of ice..." (170). And that night, she goes to the Schwarze Pumpe bar with Curt.

Indeed, Curt *is* more interesting—not just for his money and social skills, but, more importantly, because he seems to *need* her. His wealth, his social grace, his physical attractiveness, are all fairly manageable variables within the novel's libidinal equation; Nikolaus's "neue Romantik" has an equivalent for each. It is Curt's need—the negative value of his desire—that leaves a stubborn remainder. The nature of this need is revealed by Curt's preoccupation with Recha's "Egyptian eyes" throughout the novel. Curt's desiring gaze is the one that is returned: his attraction to Recha is a product of her acknowledgment of him. As Recha seems to sense, Curt relies on others to guarantee his wholeness as a subject. At one point she wonders "why he needed an audience even for his feelings" (167). Without the "fixed point" of a love object, Curt is left only with a "disquiet" or "uneasiness" (*Unruhe*) (149). "I simply can't be alone," he says (166).

Just as Curt requires Recha's gaze to lend consistency to his inchoate, *unruhige* subjectivity, Recha finds herself captivated by his need. This need brings her back

---

would track the way these ideological configurations played out as fantasies of the body, as Keith Livers has for revolutionary- and Stalin-era Soviet literature in *Constructing the Stalinist Body*.

12. As we later discover, Hamann does in fact have a son, though he is away, at a clinic. Hamann's visits to his developmentally disabled son inevitably result in a twenty-four-hour drinking binge.

to him again and again, apparently against her will. Recha's stubborn attraction to Curt may be read in line with what Mary Ann Doane, in her study of the woman's film of the 1940s, calls a "desire to desire." Vis-à-vis the question of female desire, Doane claims: "The representations of the cinema and the representations provided by psychoanalysis of female subjectivity coincide. For each system specifies that the woman's relation to desire is difficult if not impossible. Paradoxically, her only access is to the desire to desire" (9). According to Doane, the female spectator is "stranded between incommensurable entities," stranded with a desire she is said to embody but never to possess (7). As Doane points out, the paradoxical role of the female spectator is particularly apparent in her relation to consumption and the commodity form: "The feminine position has come to exemplify the roles of consumer and spectator in their embodiment of a curiously passive desiring subjectivity" (32). In the parallel logic of film and advertising, the female spectator/consumer is both active and passive, consumer and commodity: she buys, but only insofar as she has been "seduced" to do so.

This interplay of spectatorship, consumption, and seduction can be observed in a scene near the middle of *Ankunft im Alltag* when Curt visits Recha in her room to persuade her to take him back after a breakup. Before Curt's arrival, the novel's free indirect discourse dips temporarily into the perspective of Recha's roommate, Lisa, as she reads one of the sentimental West German potboilers (*Groschenhefte*) that circulate among the young women at the Schwarze Pumpe. Lisa is moved by the potboiler's melodramatic suspense, though she knows that "after seventy pages of love, sorrow, and renunciation, everything will come out all right, and wedding bells will ring for the poor but pretty nurse" (131). Lisa is interrupted in her reading when Curt rings the doorbell (an echo, perhaps, of the potboiler's wedding bells). That Curt's visit coincides with this gratuitous rendition of the romance novel's formulaic plot underscores his association with Westernized romantic clichés: he would be the well-heeled surgeon to Recha's poor but pretty nurse. Like a suitor in a romance novel, Curt brings chocolates and roses. "I thought one gave roses only in pop songs," Recha says (134).

We see the other side of romance-novel melodrama, however, when Curt forces his advances on Recha, foreshadowing a more perilous attack later in the novel:

> Silently and wildly he fell over her and held down her hands and covered her eyes and her mouth and her throat with kisses. She bit his lips, but he felt no pain. He whispered as though out of his mind: "…you damned cat…, I'll get you…, go on, scratch, it won't do you any good…, I kill myself for you and you…" She suddenly stopped defending herself and kissed him, benumbed and trembling. (136)

Only a few pages after satirizing the kitschy language of the romance novel, Reimann falls into equally ludicrous prose here. Though perhaps inadvertent, this juxtaposition serves as a warning to the consumer of the potboiler's fantasy; its sensuous pleasure, we learn, has a violent core. As we discover when he attacks Recha, Curt's magnetic charisma is backed by force. Yet even this coercive violence seems to have a certain appeal as Recha, "benumbed and trembling," succumbs (temporarily) to his desire.

Having pushed Curt away, Recha rearranges her hair in the mirror. "I'm not as thin as a starving cat anymore," she says. "With time…I'm getting more curves, don't you think?" (137). It is telling that, in this appeal for affirmation of her desirability, Recha refers to herself as a "cat," falling into the language Curt used during his attack ("you damned cat"). Naming herself here with Curt's epithet, Recha reveals an important aspect of what she later calls Curt's irresistibility (139). Even, or perhaps especially, at his most menacing, Curt does something that Nikolaus cannot do: through his fervent—indeed violent—passion for her, he draws Recha into the economy of desire.

By reading Recha's relationship with Curt as a "desire to desire"—a longing, that is, to participate in desiring exchange—we can better understand Curt's powerful hold on Recha's romantic imagination. In this "seduction" scene, framed by the description of a melodramatic "woman's novel," Recha becomes both the subject and the object of romantic fantasy, the consumer and the commodity. By allowing herself to play into Curt's commodified romance, she becomes an object for his consumption: "I'll get you yet," he says.

In the East German cultural context, the concept of a "desire to desire" takes on an added significance, for in the psychological discourse of the GDR it was not just the woman who had a problematic relation to desire. The dominant psychological model in the GDR, adopted from Soviet psychologists such as S. L. Rubinstein, did not recognize desire at all—desire, that is, as defined by psychoanalytic theory as a lack, a space of unconscious agency that incessantly demands satisfaction yet cannot be appeased by specific objects. Instead, the Soviet model understood human activity as rational and goal oriented. Desire, according to this model, is always determinate and can be satisfied. For Rubinstein, the psyche exists as a unity of experience—the product of activity—and self-consciousness, or introspection (24). There is no "unconscious" in the Freudian sense, but rather that of which the subject is conscious (*das Bewußtgewordene*), and not yet conscious (*das Nichtbewußtgewordene*). The psyche is knowable through an observation of the subject's activity and an understanding of the motives for this behavior (40–41).[13]

According to this model, lack is not constitutive, but pathological. The "cure" for desire is conscious activity toward a known goal. As Curt seems to suspect, a "fixed

---

13. According to Rubinstein, one's motives, though sometimes hidden, are likewise knowable: "Every human activity proceeds from certain *motives* and is directed to a certain *goal;* it accomplishes a certain *task* and expresses a certain relationship of the person to his environment.…A person who is moved by a drive [*Trieb*] will act differently when he becomes aware of the drive, that is, when he chooses an object toward which to orient himself, than he will before he becomes aware of the drive" (29).

point" would alleviate his "unrest." Nikolaus, who has a "fixed point" in his work and his art, seems immune to the kind of inner turmoil that plagues Curt, who considers endless discontent "his personal tragedy: he worked hard to put something together, but he had no pleasure in what had been done; once reached, the goal did not interest him, and (this is how he formulated it for himself, wallowing in his own pain) every fulfillment left him sad" (81).[14] Curt's "personal tragedy," described here with no small sarcasm by a less-than-sympathetic narrative voice, is actually that of consumption in general: the commodities thought to offer satisfaction inevitably disappoint at the moment of acquisition, and the consumer must look ahead to his or her next purchase. Through an endless series of material acquisitions, the consumer attempts to alleviate his or her ever-increasing sense of lack.[15] An overabundance of goods and services ensures that consumers will never run out of things to want.

In contrast to the consumerist economy of the West, the productionist economy of the GDR functioned according to a dynamic in which the overabundance was on the side of the producer, rather than the consumer. As though embodying this principle, Nikolaus is often bested by his own physical strength. In one scene he splits the shaft of a hammer in his enthusiasm, nearly injuring Hamann with the shrapnel (64). This individual-psychological model of the "overflowing" worker paralleled the condition of the GDR labor force as a whole. One clear illustration of this is the case of material shortfall, a phenomenon depicted in nearly every East German film or novel of production. Shortfalls occurred when a given workforce exceeded the materials needed to complete their work. In the GDR's economy, the labor force was overabundant, but material was lacking. Even more than the inadequate supply of work material, however, the East German consumer market suffered from a critical scarcity.[16] The East German consumer was left "desiring to desire," hoping for something to want.

---

14. When Curt suggests that Nikolaus will sell himself out to make a living as an artist, Recha replies: "Nikolaus? Never!... You're just saying that because you're jealous that he has a fixed point he's marching toward while you just stagger around" (144).

15. In *Jazz, Rock, and Rebels,* Poiger also draws a connection between psychology and consumer culture. She points out that the refusal of GDR policy-makers to acknowledge the individual psychological mechanisms at work in the "youth problem" led to an inability to find an adequate solution to—or even model of—this problem. The East German "youth problem," in both Poiger's account and my own, occurs at the intersection of desire and consumption:

> The contradictory behavior of the East German regime that engaged with the West in the battle over consumption and at the same time attacked Western culture was not simply the result of a failure of socialist production to fulfill a population's consumer desires. Rather it had deep ideological roots. The study of psychology, which played such an important role in making consumer culture both understandable and acceptable in West Germany in the 1950s, was long repressed in East Germany. In West Germany, psychological models of adolescent development assigned consumption an increasingly important function, although this embrace coexisted with uneasiness about consumer culture. In East Germany, the focus on the individual in psychology—and on individual satisfaction in consumer culture—remained suspect for a long time. (217)

16. In fact, one of the greatest dangers for the GDR economy was that of calcification; too much money was in savings and too little in circulation, because there was simply not enough to spend it on. In his book *The Politics of Economic Decline in East Germany, 1945–1989,* Jeffrey Kopstein points out

"Der Blacksmith Blues": Forging the "neue Romantik"

Though she is reminded again and again of Curt's ignoble intentions and dangerous tendencies, Recha does not learn her lesson: she returns to him three times in
the course of the novel. Eventually the plot itself is forced to intervene. Literalizing
all of the party's warnings against the dangers of Westernized culture, Curt lures
Recha into the woods and attempts to rape her. As Julia Hell points out in her insightful reading of Reimann's novel in *Post-Fascist Fantasies,* this scene contains
"an intricate, complex entanglement of desires and prohibitions" (126). In Hell's
reading, Recha's desire renders Curt's assault a transgression of both political and
psychic taboos: "Recha's relationship to Curt is highly ambivalent. He represents
what is most forbidden—both the fascist father/past *and* the proto-fascist West/
present—and Recha's physical attraction is as strong as her moral revulsion" (126).
When Nikolaus comes to her aid, then, he rescues her as much from herself—from
her own forbidden desire—as from Curt. Following the pair into the woods, Nikolaus pulls Curt away from Recha and pummels him—a "throwback to the Stone
Age," Nikolaus remarks later (212). By the end of the book it would seem that,
with Nikolaus's help, Recha has rejected her participation in Curt's consumerist romance and embraced the "neue Romantik."[17]

The decisive moment in this breakthrough takes place when, abandoning a
date with Curt, Recha returns to the factory to help with an all-night overtime
shift. As she works with Nikolaus on this shift—or, more precisely, watches him
work—Recha discovers the "neue Romantik" for herself. By a process of triangulation, the experience of communal labor, both on this long night and over the
whole year at the Schwarze Pumpe, has become the shared "fixed point" of Recha
and Nikolaus's relationship. Theirs would be a relationship, in other words, in the
mode of the "neue Romantik," upheld not by mutual consumption, but by collective production.

Recha's arrival (*Ankunft*) into the libidinal economy of the "neue Romantik" can
be observed in the language of her inner monologue as she watches Nikolaus chisel
cracks in a massive slab of concrete:

> Now that he had enough practice, his hands struck swiftly, in a measured rhythm,
> and the sound of metal on metal echoed off the walls and the high ceiling. Recha,
> who was still so close to the age of fairy tales and romantic stories, thought haz-
> ily [*verschwommen*] about a mythical smithy in a forest clearing: Landgrave, become

---

how the yearly increases in personal savings throughout the 1980s indicate "pent-up demand" in the
East German economy. Thus, he argues, one can view the events of autumn 1989 "largely [as the] political actions of dissatisfied consumers, not . . . of dissatisfied producers" (192–93).

17. The structural logic of this scene is similar to that identified in chapter 1 as operative in *The Uppercut.* Just as Georg's intervention stops Carolin from prostituting herself to Bubi and Onkel Franz,
Nikolaus's violent "throwback" saves Recha from being raped by her own desire. Timely constraint, in
other words, once again saves the GDR consumer from herself.

hard! [*Landgraf, werde hart!*] In England there was a legendary blacksmith who, in his apron…and at the anvil, married lovers who had eloped. (185)

Recha's hazy (*verschwommen*) thoughts here echo Nikolaus's hazy longing (*verschwommener Sehnsucht*) for a "romantic, sweaty life" fighting back the forest with a heavy ax. It is significant that, in each case, the "romantic" aspect of the fantasy lies in its anachronistic mode of production: Recha compares Nikolaus to a blacksmith in a fairy tale, while Nikolaus imagines life as a woodcutter, before the advent of chain saws and bulldozers.

These anachronisms suggest one way to read the ideological function of the "neue Romantik": to reinvest atavistic modes of production with a new libidinal charge. As I have suggested in chapter 1, one of the fundamental contradictions in East German ideology during the *Aufbau* years was that between the party's utopian claims to have transcended capitalist modes of production and the starkly nontranscendent experience of the East German worker. Seen from the production floor, the East German factory actually appears to contain the worst of both presocialist worlds: Taylorist repetitiveness and isolation combined with the inefficiency and labor-intensiveness of preindustrial production. Like the industrial work taking place throughout the GDR at the time, the labor depicted in *Ankunft im Alltag* is physically taxing, repetitive, and dangerous, and carried out with outdated tools and inefficient methods. More importantly, it is hardly collective production at all: the GDR's radically Taylorized industrial workplace tended more toward atomization than collectivity. If not *alienated,* the starkly divided labor was at least *alienating.*

The "neue Romantik," however, attempts to recode the backwardness of East German working conditions as a romantic ideal. The absurdity of having to cut concrete by hand with a chisel, for instance, becomes the fairy-tale scene of a blacksmith working in a forest clearing. What fuels this romance is the fantasy of a kind of prelapsarian labor, an image of "satisfying" work before alienation and Taylorization took away what might be called the *jouissance* of production.

There is another mechanism at work in the "neue Romantik." Watching Nikolaus, Recha does not just compare him to a blacksmith, she compares him to several particular blacksmiths. The first, in a "mythical smithy in a forest clearing," is the Blacksmith of Ruhla, a figure of Thuringian legend and the eponymous hero of an 1894 play by Martin Pfeifer. In Pfeifer's play, the young landgrave Ludwig is more interested in hunting than in ruling and allows his vassals, in particular the reeve Kurt von Tenneberg, egregious abuses of power. While hunting one day, Ludwig loses his way and seeks shelter in the smithy at Ruhla, claiming to be the landgrave's huntsman. The blacksmith lets the "huntsman" stay, but he has no good words for the weak landgrave: "We need a just and stern [leader], with a hard head and an iron fist—in short, a man! And not—…With your permission, sir, not a weakling" (Pfeifer, 49). Deep into the night, the blacksmith hammers away on his anvil, repeating with each stroke: "Landgrave become hard [*Landgraf, werde hart!*], landgrave become hard like this iron!" (57). After his night in the smithy, Ludwig resolves to take a more active role in the governance of his lands and begins by arresting Tenneberg. The blacksmith approves, saying: "If you are the landgrave, and remain the landgrave, that I saw today…then far-off centuries will pronounce your name with pride, and in Thuringia you will be called the just, the iron landgrave!" (81).

In the second transformation effected by Recha's "hazy" thoughts, the Thuringian blacksmith becomes a "legendary blacksmith" from England who joins eloped couples at his anvil (Reimann, 185). Though the exact referent is unclear, this passage seems to allude to Scotland's "anvil priests," blacksmiths and other tradesmen who, according to a loophole in England's marriage laws, were able to marry young couples without parental consent.[18] The important aspect here is the legendary smith's unifying authority, the fact that he marries runaway couples at the locus of production, the anvil.

Recha's "hazy" free associations in this scene help us to map the layers of fantasy at work in the romantic mode that *Ankunft im Alltag* puts forward to its readers. On one level, the evocation of prealienated labor compensates for the failure of the GDR's claim to have transcended alienation. Insofar as the depiction of exhausting and repetitive industrial labor can hardly be sold as "romantic," a glorification of outdated modes of production lends the image a certain anachronistic charm. Beyond alienation (though retrograde rather than progressive), such work is portrayed as "satisfying," that is, as addressing—and fulfilling—the full potential of the worker. This notion is supported by the understanding of psychic economy prevalent in the GDR at this time: rather than insatiable desires, the East German subject has material (hence satiable) needs and acts on achievable goals. If he or she is unsatisfied—*unruhig* like Curt—then it is due to a failure to integrate him- or herself adequately into the process of production. The libidinal economy implicit in this ideal of labor, however, presents a significant problem for the novel's love story, and for the question of socialist Eros in general: if work is indeed "satisfying," then what happens to the romantic relationship? Without the bonds of reciprocal need, of mutual desire, what would bring and hold a couple together?[19]

Within the consumerist romantic framework occupied by Curt, the commodity represents a unifying third term in the relationship: the act of mutual consumption—namely the "date"—provides the "romance" that constitutes the couple as such. Despite the party's propagandistic efforts, however, the "romance" of

18. To this end Lydia, the youngest Bennet sister in *Pride and Prejudice,* runs off with Wickham to Gretna Green, Scotland (Austen, 257). In *The Mill on the Floss,* Maggie and Stephen set out for Scotland with the same intent (Eliot, 477).

19. As I suggested in the introduction (and in note 11 above), such questions were discussed with some urgency during the years after the Russian Revolution.

production was never commensurate with that of consumption. This was due both to historical circumstances—the decidedly unromantic conditions of production in the GDR—and to a fundamental *economic* difference in these modes of romance. While consumerism follows and fosters an economy of desire, of constitutive lack on the part of the subject, the libidinal economy of the ideal socialist subject is one of abundance: he works not for the purchasing power to assuage his own sense of lack, but rather to meet the needs of the socialist community. Yet, as mentioned above, the disavowal of desire necessary to the ideal of "satisfying" work, of wholesale sublimation, renders extraproductive ties dispensable or problematic.

For the "neue Romantik" of socialist production to be romantic—for it to become a discursive space of courtship and coupling—a third term is required. This third term is found in Recha's vision of the "anvil priest," an outside authority who will bring people together "at the anvil," that is, within the space of production. Following the interpretive schema suggested by Hell's reading of *Ankunft im Alltag,* I would locate this "anvil priest" in the symbolic space once occupied by Stalin.[20] In chapter 1, I characterized the "Stalinist" symbolic order as one that anchors its legitimacy not in the horizontal relations of collective production and social equality, but in the vertical relations of power. In the logic of the Stalinist personality-cult, socialist subjects are united not through shared (class) interest, but rather through their collective relation to a centralized authority. As ideological fantasy, Recha's "blacksmiths" attest to an illicit nostalgia, a secret longing for the rigid certainties of the Stalinist social order. In this reading, Stalin becomes both the authoritarian kingmaker of the Thuringian tale, galvanizing the East German leadership to root out injustice and incompetence, and the "anvil priest," forging abiding bonds in a fractured and alienating socialist society.[21]

---

20. In her analysis of *Ankunft im Alltag,* Hell uncovers "a problematic that while never openly thematized, ultimately structures the entire narrative, namely Stalinism and the dilemma produced by the revelations of the Twentieth Congress" (*Post-Fascist Fantasies,* 124).

21. Franz Liszt's song "Biterolf und der Schmied von Ruhla" (Biterolf and the Blacksmith of Ruhla), from the 1873 *Wartburg Lieder,* combines both the unifying and the vulcanizing aspects in one figure:

> Thuringia this day sends the huntsman and the smith
> To pay the bride obeisance with music and with gifts.
> The sight of this fine maiden, of virtue in its splendor,
> Has Ruhla's blacksmith saying:
> Young Landgrave be tender! Young Landgrave be tender!
> But if the foe should clench his fist, as westward breaks the dawn,
> *Herr Major,* then we'll hammer this, we'll hammer this:
> Young Landgrave be strong! Young Landgrave be strong, be strong!
> (Liszt, 142–45)

> [Thüringens Wälder senden den Waidmann und den Schmied
> Brauthuldigung zu spenden mit Gaben und mit Lied.
> Vor hohem Frauenbilder, so tugendlicher Art,
> Singt Ruhlas Grobschmied milde:

As Hell points out, Reimann's novel stabilizes its turbulent symbolic order through the deployment of another cult of personality, that surrounding the students' brigadier Hamann: "If the loss of Stalin is the novel's unspoken problem, then the figure of Hamann is the solution to this silence. This model father figure with a 'minor' flaw fills the absence thematized by Curt's story, but Hamann also acts as a stabilizing force for the whole narrative, for each protagonist's 'novel of education'" (*Post-Fascist Fantasies*, 130). Hamann's personality cult can best be seen in his micromanagement of the brigade. No workplace incident, no after-hours occurrence, escapes his attention: "As foreman he felt obligated to see and hear everything that went on in his brigade" (Reimann, 77).[22]

Indeed, the love triangle between the brigade's newest members does not escape his notice:

> In the first weeks he had observed the three new members of his brigade. He had studied them with the passionate involvement of a man who has to get to the bottom of everything—whether a technical problem or the most fitting translation of a foreign word....
>
> He liked Nikolaus entirely.... But he didn't like the friendship between Curt and Recha at all....
>
> The boy's not right for her, thought Hamann now, watching her defiant yet sheepish bearing. She's still totally unformed. Someone had better give her something to do. (78)

In the end, Hamann's interventions help bring Recha and Nikolaus together. His influence alone, however, is not enough to guarantee the stability of their relationship. Instead, their conclusive union occurs only after Curt shows his true colors and Nikolaus, in a "throwback to the Stone Age," beats him up.

If Nikolaus and Recha participate in what might be called a "Stalinist" mode of loving, then the precariousness of their relationship alerts us to a deficiency in this mode, a gap in its libidinal network. This gap is not just that left by the loss of Stalin, but a structural deficiency inherent in the Stalinist mode of legitimization. The ties of projection and identification that should bind Stalinist subjects to each other and to the state proved inadequate to their task—a deficiency, I argued in chapter 1, that necessitated the Stalinist state's notorious apparatus of repression. In *Ankunft*

Jung Landgraf, werdet zart! Jung Landgraf, werdet zart!
Doch wills im Westen dämmern, und streicht ein Feind den Bart,
Herr Major, dann wollen wir hämmern, dann wollen wir hämmern:
Jung Landgraf, werdet hart! Jung Landgraf, werdet hart, werdet hart!]

22. Hamann does not snoop, however. Instead, the workers come to him with the details of their private lives: "Not a day went by in which someone did not come to him, to lay his sorrows and annoyances on the broad, patient shoulders of the foreman. And thus he was in fact better informed than any other foreman" (Reimann, 77).

im Alltag's climactic scene, Nikolaus's violent intervention recapitulates—and, to the same degree, legitimates—the direct coercion that compensated for the failure of the Stalinist symbolic machinery. When Nikolaus has to rescue Recha, it is because she has allowed Curt to lure her away from a meeting of the brigade's youth group. Appropriately, the group's focal point in this scene is Hamann. While Curt leads Recha into the woods, Hamann holds his young audience spellbound with accounts of his heroic antifascist activities. Given the reading that I have been suggesting, Recha's decision to turn her back on the collective formed around Hamann's storytelling and follow Curt would demonstrate the limitations of the affective ties of Stalinism. It is this failure that is being "covered up" by the multiple layers of fantasy in *Ankunft im Alltag*. Ultimately, the novel's melancholic longing concerns not so much the loss of the specular bonds of Stalinism as their always-already having failed.

Indeed, for the majority of East German workers, the impetus to work had never been the glowing ideals of the "neue Romantik" or Stalin's personality cult or even the naked coercion of the Stalinist state. Instead, they were motivated by a decidedly unsocialist concern with wages and bonuses. In this respect, the attitude of the East German worker would have resembled Curt's far more than Hamann's. Describing the brigade's efforts to produce electrodes otherwise available only from West German sources, Hamann says: "You can imagine what we'll save the GDR if the experiments succeed."

> "Big premium to be had, right?" Curt said and laughed, rubbing thumb and fore-finger together.
>
> "A couple of drinks might come out of it. But it's not about that," Hamann said coolly, turning away. Behind his back Curt grinned. He thought: Look at that, Napoleon's acting like an idealist, and the role suits him pretty well. He can tell it to his party secretary, but not to me. As if he doesn't care about making as much money as possible, saving up the premiums, buying a car once it's enough.
>
> He stared at the broad back of the foreman and thought with a surge of hatred: How they get on my nerves, these damned hypocritical idealists! Work for its own sake [*Arbeit als Selbstzweck*]—what a life. (49)

As the June 17 uprising made clear, East German workers were not interested in "Arbeit als Selbstzweck." As Curt explains to Recha, the brigade's agreement to an all-night extra shift had more to do with the expected *Prämie,* or "overproduction bonus," than with the opportunity to participate in the romance of production: "You think the others hollered from excitement? If there weren't a big premium, no one would have gone along with it" (176). Like most brigades in the GDR, Hamann's is more interested in the premium than in the inherent value of work. Consumer culture, in other words, is alive and well, even under Hamann's watchful eyes.

Recha denies that Hamann's brigade is motivated by materialistic considerations. Yet in her relationship with Curt, we see that she, too, is not immune to the allure of consumer culture. And returning to her thoughts while watching Nikolaus chisel concrete, we can observe the depth and subtlety of Western culture's insinuation into her imagination—and into the fantasy production of the GDR in general. There is a third blacksmith in Recha's vision, one that departs from the fairy-tale pattern: "And now, not like a fairy tale at all, a dance melody in her ear: the 'Blacksmith Blues,' which had been *Top Hit* for a number of weeks back then, when we had dance class" (185). Though it seems odd that the "Blacksmith Blues," an American radio hit from 1952, would be played in an East German dance class, Recha's reference to the song here is telling.[23] Just as Nikolaus, forgetting all his "good and beautiful words," resorted to a pop song to frame his first kiss, Recha's "romantic stories" here drift from work through fairy tales and into (Western) popular music.

Likewise, the "neue Romantik" of production slid toward the romance of consumption. Given the conditions of production in the GDR, the romance of work had to remain a cover story for that of consumption: one worked, as Curt tells us, for the premium and for the car it might one day afford, not for the fanciful ideals of the "neue Romantik." And, as the adoption of the consumer-friendlier New Economic System (NÖS) made clear, the party saw the writing on the wall.[24] Meanwhile, in the gap between *Aufbau* Stalinism and the arrival of the still-scarce socialist commodity, the GDR consumer was suspended between libidinal economies—poised, as it were, between the stick of Stalin and the carrot of the NÖS. The following section will explore this precarious liminal condition, the temporary stasis upheld by an "anticipatory consciousness" that was the GDR's greatest hope—and its most critical liability.

Love and the Perils of Affect: *Beschreibung eines Sommers*

From the first pages of Karl Heinz Jakobs's 1963 novel, *Beschreibung eines Sommers* (Description of a Summer), it is clear that the narrator, Tom Breitsprecher, has a

---

23. If Recha is thinking about the Ella Mae Morse version of the "Blacksmith Blues," the lyrics (written by Jack Holmes) are undeniably "American":

> Down in old Kentucky
> Where horseshoes are lucky
> There's a village smithy
> Standin' under the chestnut tree
> ....
> He sings the boogie blues
> While he's hammerin' on the shoes
> ....
> You'll get a lot o' kicks
> Out of the Blacksmith Blues

(Holmes, "Blacksmith Blues," http://www.oldielyrics.com/lyrics/ella_mae_morse/the_blacksmith_blues.html)

24. See chapter 1, esp. pp. 58–60.

problem. He first describes the weather "that summer," then, with the same dispassionate tone, recounts a series of vacation love-affairs:

> That summer I took my vacation early and stayed as long as I saw fit. First I went to Warnemünde, then to Zempin, and then to Kloster. In Warnemünde I had a second-rate affair with quite a few tears at the end. In Zempin, where I went with Lotte, there was a lot of anger, since she cheated on me with a stylish lifeguard.... Just before I went home I met a swell blond, but we broke up when she found out that I didn't have a car. (5–6)

Reading further in Jakobs's novel, we learn that Tom's emotional detachment extends beyond the romantic sphere. When Tom returns from vacation to his job as an engineer in Berlin, party cadre-leader Trude Neutz pays a visit to convince him to join a youth construction project at Wartha. She has some reservations about sending him there, however: "I'll tell you exactly what's wrong," she tells him. "You're our best engineer, but morally, you're awful [Moralisch aber bist du ein Dreck]" (14). In the ensuing dialogue, Tom's political position (or, more to the point, his lack thereof) becomes clear:

> "What do you want from me?"
> "We know that you'll work. We know that you'll work day and night. But we don't just want your work there, like here in Berlin. There we want all of you. Head and heart."
> "And what do I have to do for that?"
> She looked me in the eyes.
> "Stop drinking and whoring."
> "That's possible," I said, "but I don't know what my heart should have to do with it. I get paid, well paid, and I do my work for it. It has nothing to do with emotions."
> She said quietly: "Every undertaking demands the whole person. I mean, if one's heart isn't in it..."
> ...And I said: "To build, one doesn't need heart, but understanding [Verstand]."
> "But the understanding to see that our way is right and not Adenauer's—that you don't have." (14–15)

Despite its air of self-evidence, Neutz's argumentation here warrants a closer look. What *does* emotion have to do with construction? If socialism is built on scientific principles, then why is Tom's "understanding" (*Verstand*) not enough to see that "our way is right and not [West German Chancellor] Adenauer's?" Why must Tom—and the reader—"put his heart into it [mit dem Herzen dabei (sein)]?" Like many East German cultural products of its time, *Beschreibung eines Sommers* sets out to answer these questions with no small urgency. Indeed, all of the novel's narrative machinery is brought to bear on Tom's slumbering affect. By the end of the novel, Tom will find himself invested personally, politically, and romantically in the collective project of the GDR—even if, as we will see, this investment yields a surprising return.

To illuminate the narrative strategy by which Tom's change is effected, I propose to start at the point of solution—the moment, as it were, when Tom finds his heart—and work backward. The scene I have in mind is that in which Tom admits to himself that he loves Grit, a young machinist at Wartha. Tom had met Grit at a bar with his friend Schibulla, who was the leader of Grit's FDJ group.[25] Tom, the callous connoisseur, found in Grit a new object of consumption, literally: "She looked good enough to eat" (55). The only thing standing in his way was her marriage to Georg, a miner and party functionary in Oeslnitz. Tom tackled the problem head-on and, in a flagrant abuse of his power as brigadier, demanded that she remove her wedding band (technically a safety hazard) while on the job.

Tom's cynical stratagem worked: Grit took off the ring (with Tom's help, when it got stuck), and a short while later, they began their love affair. This inaugural subterfuge makes for an unpropitious start to Tom and Grit's relationship; from the first, it seems that the roué will corrupt the ingénue. To a certain degree, this turns out to be the case. With this extramarital affair, the party-loyal Grit puts herself at odds with her own ethical "compass" (44) and the moral codes of the party. At heart, however, Grit does not undergo the radical transformation that Tom does. She begins and remains a passionate, politically engaged idealist. Tom, on the other hand, will abandon his apathy and cynicism under Grit's influence: "I might as well admit it," he says, "I had fallen for her" (204). Here we find ourselves at the end of what seems to be a fairly standard love-plot, a narrative conforming to the template that Mark Rubinfeld, in a book on the Hollywood romantic comedy, calls "the coldhearted redemption plot." Rubinfeld explains: "Simply put…the coldhearted redemption plot…features a bitter hero who is incapable of love. He is heartsick.…What the hero most needs, it turns out, is a redemptive heroine" (13–14). Yet when Tom reveals his love for Grit, it becomes apparent that the redemption plot in *Beschreibung eines Sommers* reverses this model. Tom comes to the conclusion that it was not his love for Grit that revived his emotion, but rather it was his emotional revitalization that made him capable of love:

> And suddenly I knew how it was that I had fallen for Grit.… The experience of the last months had brought me to it, the experience: Wartha; the experience: youth construction project; the experience: forest and in the middle of it the future chemical

---

25. For more on the Freie Deutsche Jugend, see chapter 1, p. 55 n. 30, and chapter 3, p. 97.

factory;…I had lived every second at Wartha to the full. Everything had penetrated into me and prepared the ground for Grit. (Jakobs, 204)

It is the whole Wartha experience, then, that enables Tom to overcome his apathy and listlessness, and to achieve, by the end of the story, a strong emotional commitment and a tentative political consciousness. In this redemption plot, the love story is not so much the engine of change as the proof and product of Tom's transformation.

That *Beschreibung eines Sommers* modifies the traditional redemption plot in this way is due to the novel's distinctive affective economy. In Jakobs's novel the romantic plot becomes a site less of the quickening of emotions than of their containment, providing a supple framework to accommodate the novel's contradictory agenda. As I argued at the beginning of the chapter, this contradiction can be seen to revolve around the problems of motivation and sublimation. Even more than in *Ankunft im Alltag,* the underlying ideological dilemma of Jakobs's novel is this: how can the productive power of the East German workforce be unlocked without unleashing the destructive potential of its collective desire?

Mit glühenden Herzen: Enthusiasm and Sublimation

In Jakobs's novel, the interplay of motivation and sublimation is inscribed in the opposing poles of *Herz* and *Verstand* ("heart" and "understanding or intellect"). These signifiers do not simply refer to emotion and reason but rather represent broader ideological positions. Tom's abundance of *Verstand* is the characteristic that makes him an effective construction manager, and is the grounds for his employment at Wartha. His is the calculating *Verstand* of the mathematician, the practical insight of the engineer. Yet his calculations also have a politically problematic side, as we see in the conversation with Trude Neutz that brings Tom to Wartha. Neutz asks: "And you're not for the SED either…but what *are* you for?" Tom replies: "I'm for mathematics" (16). By Tom's figuring, work is a rational exchange, rather than an expression of ideological commitment: "I get paid, well paid," he says, "and for that I do my work" (19). Tom's calculations extend even to the romantic sphere: "Love," he insists, "is really nothing other than technology. The scientist will triumph over the poet, the head over the heart. Emotion is just fine and can be charming, but the refined and well-executed approach is irresistible" (203).

Having mocked Neutz's suggestion that the socialist worker needs *Herz,* Tom admits to himself that his logical arguments do not address the real source of his dispassionateness. Instead, we learn the psychohistorical origins of Tom's lack of affect in a long inner monologue recounting his childhood experiences in the Third Reich. With remarkable candor and detail, Tom describes the thrill of the fascist mass spectacle and outlines his emotional and practical complicity with the crimes of the Nazi regime, both at home and on the Eastern Front. As Tom explains to his imaginary interlocutor, all of these experiences render excitement impossible, and any kind of engagement questionable:

> And after you had lived through all that, that all and POW camp and flight and the years '46, '47, '48, then there was nothing in the world that could get you excited. Besides mathematics. And music. But they were worth getting excited about, since they were the only things that seemed to touch on objective laws, therefore the only things with any constancy. (23)

Too young to have experienced fascism and the war, Wartha's young volunteers—including Grit—operate with a very different emotional palette. The youth brigades are brimming with *Herz,* even if *Verstand* is somewhat lacking. As Tom remarks sarcastically to Martin Kamernus, a foreman at Wartha:

> I know it all: they came here voluntarily, and they're young fighters for socialism, and they've come here with hearts aflame [*mit glühendem Herzen*]…I'll tell you what, my good man, if their glowing hearts help to put together a top-quality tank foundation and pronto, then they might as well glow. But if they don't understand anything…

In response, Kamernus reminds Tom that it is their job to guide this enthusiasm into productive channels: "If they don't understand," Kamernus says, "then we have to teach them" (50).

From the earliest days of the GDR, the productive enthusiasm of youth was considered an essential component of the party's economic strategy. As one of the earliest formulations of East German youth policy puts it,

> We need real enthusiasm for the plan.…I believe the youth can contribute the most to this effort.…It shouldn't just be a matter of inspiring the young people, but rather of the youth with their enthusiasm infecting the rest of the population and sweeping them along.…In the mobilization of ideological energy for this plan the youth, with their ability to be inspired [*Begeisterungsfähigkeit*], can really be the avant-garde. (F. Selbmann at the Zentralratsplenum, 1948; qtd. in Skyba, 51)

Here it is hoped that, inspired by the heroic *Aufbau* project, the youth will "infect" the rest of the population with their enthusiasm. Soon, however, the idea of a young avant-garde gave way to a more cautious policy. Youth enthusiasm was still considered a powerful productive force, but one that had to be steered and contained. In the words of the Politburo resolution "Enthusiasm and Activity of the Youth for the Realization of the Great Ideas of Socialism" (September 3, 1957),

We have to take into account much more strongly than before the adventurousness and revolutionary romanticism of the youth, above all in the work of the FDJ and GST.[26] Both adventurousness and revolutionary romanticism reveal the active spirit of youth, which must be guided into the right channels and made useful for the construction of socialism. (Jahnke et al., 436)

Here, the "revolutionary romanticism" and "adventurousness" of East German youth is not to be denied, but neither should it be allowed to divert into unproductive channels. East German youth institutions such as the FDJ and the GST were expected to find a middle ground between enthusiasm and discipline. The emphasis here on "guid[ance] into the right channels" attests to a growing concern, as we saw as well in chapter 1, that the party's leadership function could be hijacked by the propaganda of the Western media.

By the mid-1960s, youthful energy had come to be seen as a liability, and enthusiasm as an extremely dangerous and unstable force. A resolution of the SED's Leipzig district leadership, entitled "On Several Questions of Youth Work and the Appearance of Groups of Rowdies" (October 13, 1965), asserted:

The goal of the enemy is to instigate ideological maceration and to provoke licentiousness and anarchy, especially among the youth, in order to turn segments of the young population against their own Workers' and Peasants' State and to foment violations of the public peace. The enemy cleverly carries out this agitation through radio and television stations…by means of the decadent culture [*Unkultur*] of Westernized music and dancing, Beatles ideology, loafing, and slacking. (Qtd. in Rauhut, "Beat in der DDR," 377)

In this passage, the Western "enemy" attempts to provoke young East Germans to a twofold betrayal: on the one hand, Western *Unkultur*—music and dance—is used to drive GDR youth into a frenzy of riotous, anarchic licentiousness. At the same time, however, the enemy uses these methods to encourage loafing (*Gammlertum*) and slacking off from work (*Arbeitsbummelei*).

Underlying this only apparently contradictory set of effects is a simple economic logic: if young workers squander their energy on rock and roll and boogie-woogie, their performance at work is sure to suffer. Behind this logic, however, is a more complex ideological fantasy concerning the body and its susceptibility to outside influence. In an essay on the rhetoric of the GDR "youth problem," Dorothee Wierling calls attention to the trope of "undisciplined bodies" in the party's descriptions of youthful rebellion: "The 'standing on corners, loitering, and loafing' [*Eckenstehen, Herumlungern und Gammeln*] imputed to youth, like the wild, destructive dancing [*Auseinandertanzen*] and frenzied guitar-playing described with horror [by party

---

26. The Gesellschaft für Sport und Technik (Society for Sports and Technology), or GST, was an East German youth club.

reports], were part of an undisciplined, unmanly, and out-of-control corporeality" (410–11). The SED's rhetoric vis-à-vis youth culture betrays a profound anxiety concerning the corporeal dimension of the West's influence on East German youth. In the party's descriptions of Beat fans in orgiastic, Dionysian ecstasy, for instance, we can observe an explicit sexualization of Westernized popular culture. The 1965 Leipzig resolution quoted above insists:

> We are fully in favor of a modern and refined dance music. We are also not against fiery rhythms, but we strongly reject those groups who violate every principle of morality and ethics, who take the stage barefoot and half-naked, who contort their bodies and use inflammatory rhythms to drive young people into a frenzy and tempt them to excesses. (Qtd. in Rauhut, "Beat in der DDR," 377)

One can identify in such rhetoric a constellation of related concerns: What is the proper affect of enthusiasm, the correct embodiment of youthful energy? What are the appropriate expressions of individual, interpersonal, or collective passion? The consistency of these concerns attests to a particular logic—a particular economy, to use the language of this book—of control and release, discipline and desublimation.

As they were perceived at the time, the stakes of these questions were nothing less than the security and stability of the socialist order, for the series of quotes above narrates the transformation of youth "from great hope to security risk" (*von Hoffnungsträger zur Sicherheitsrisiko*), to borrow the title of Peter Skyba's history of East German youth policy. This group, which in the *Aufbau* period had been a cornerstone of the GDR's ideological optimism, came eventually to be considered a significant threat to the East German state. Though the quotes here span a period of nearly twenty years, Skyba designates the decisive moment of disillusionment as occurring quite early: "The youth of the GDR, who in 1950 were still considered the great hopes of the party, had by 1953 become particularly unreliable politically...in the eyes of the SED" (277). The reason for this initial break, in Skyba's account, was the disproportionately high numbers of youth who participated in the June 17 uprising in 1953.[27]

In the wake of the 1953 uprising, the increasing involvement of GDR youth in Western popular culture was a cause for great alarm, especially because it seemed to open the doors to a second June 17. The bourgeois imperialist powers, according to this line of argument, were bombarding the GDR's youth with Western popular culture "to make them into willing tools of the warmongers"—in other

---

27. See Skyba, 253: "In general the FDJ had to conclude that in those places where strikes and demonstrations had broken out, a 'large proportion' of young people took part in them. This statement has all the more weight insofar as it could not have been in the youth organization's interests to call attention to the strong participation of its clientele in the riots. In the larger striking factories it was even the 'majority'...of adolescents, in some factories the entire youthful workforce, who took part in the walkout. A reliable quantification is not possible on the basis of the reports."

words, to incite them to revolt against the East German state. And this revolt did in fact occur, in the famous "Leipzig Beat riots" in the fall of 1965. These illegal demonstrations—which, with more than 2,500 participants, were the largest since the June 17 uprising—broke out after the Leipzig district leadership revoked the licenses of fifty amateur rock-and-roll bands.[28] Enraged by this seemingly arbitrary attack on their lifestyle, Leipzig's Beat fans took to the streets, chanting: "All we want is Beatles." The youthful protesters were dispersed by policemen and water cannons, but the riots cast a long shadow: the shock of the Leipzig demonstrations can be felt in the tone and content of the notorious Eleventh Plenary Session of the SED in December 1965, which censured and censored East German cultural producers for their "corrupting" influence on the young.[29]

Beschreibung eines Sommers was written well before the Leipzig riots, but the conditions that led to the uprising are emphatically present in Jakobs's novel. *Beschreibung eines Sommers* can be said to occupy the field of force stretching between June 17, 1953, and the Leipzig Beat riots. It articulates, on the level of its underlying fantasy-structure, the continuity of ideological anxiety that would link these two traumatic events. The fear is that the powerful, unstable, libidinal energies of young workers, released in part by their not-so-harmless leisure-time interests, would erupt into a mass expression of frustration and resentment. Reflecting this concern, the novel's *Ankunft* plot turns on the question of infectious youthful enthusiasm and its proper containment. Working, talking, and falling in love with the young idealists at Wartha, Tom will overcome his apathy and listlessness and achieve a tentative political consciousness by the end of the story. His budding enthusiasm, however, must be channeled and controlled. The novel's love story, integral to Tom's revival of affect, will be essential to this second process as well.

In a pivotal scene in the novel, Tom surreptitiously watches the Wartha FDJ group read passages from a Soviet novel around a campfire. The book, which is never named (but fits the description of *The Second Day,* aka *Out of Chaos,* by Ilya Ehrenburg), narrates the construction of a steelworks in the Russian town of Kuznetsk. "Why did I come here? thought Kolya [the protagonist of *The Second Day*]. Sverdlovsk was cleaner and quieter.... Can I live in a dump like this? Kolya read further on the bulletin board. 'We're building a giant.' He smiled incredulously: all around him he saw only tired and unhappy people" (73). Tom looks around the circle of listeners and tries to imagine their reaction to this story: "I knew that somewhere in [their heads] lurked the thought, why did I come here? And day after day they looked tired and unhappy as they struggled not to collapse under the merciless sun.... Some of what was written in the book they had experienced themselves" (73–74).

---

28. See Wierling, 408.
29. Rauhut, "DDR Beatmusik zwischen Engagement und Repression," esp. 130; and Agde, *Kahlschlag.*

His young coworkers, however, take a wider historical perspective: "In every face you could see the work going on in their heads: 1917 the revolution [to] 1931 this in Kusnezk [where *The Second Day* is set], that's fourteen years. 1945 the liberation plus fourteen years equals 1959. NINETEENFIFTYNINE." By this logic, the GDR in 1959—the year *Beschreibung eines Sommers* takes place—is at the same level of revolutionary development as the Soviet Union in 1931, the year in which *The Second Day* is set. Though the living conditions described in *The Second Day* are primitive and harsh, the Soviet Union has come a long way since then: as one of the FDJlers points out, they had Sputniks by 1957. According to this calculus, the GDR has a great future in store. By 1985, the FDJlers decide, they will have full-fledged communism and fly to Venus and Mars. Finally, Morlock, the youth-group brigadier, spells out the moral of the equation:

> How else could they have started in the Soviet Union after the intervention, since they had nothing but their hands? Of course, they could have said: We'll only build steel-works when we have decent barracks, reasonable tools, and if there's plenty to eat. If they had said that, though, then their state wouldn't have lasted the next ten years. I think the new can only grow when there are enough bold people. And who can be bold if not us, the youth? It doesn't do us any harm to work.... The Comsomols of 1931 are now enjoying the fruits of their labor. We'll certainly have something tomorrow out of our work today. (76–77)

The FDJlers have come to the conclusion that, as the party slogan puts it, "wie wir heute arbeiten, werden wir morgen leben" (as we work today, so shall we live tomorrow).[30] They are willing to overlook the privations of the present for the sake of future prosperity.

Thinking back on the campfire scene, Tom is struck by the volunteers' forward-looking optimism:

> What they were saying owed a lot to popular science from books and magazines. There was a lot of fantasy in the way they embellished and misinterpreted scientific fact.... But most of all there was romanticism, what you could call socialist romanticism. In the newspaper I had once read the formulation "forward-dreamers" [*Träumer nach vorn*]. It had amused me at the time. This was exactly the kind of dreaming being done that evening around the campfire. (82)

One of the most eloquent "forward-dreamers" of the GDR's early years was the philosopher and theologian Ernst Bloch. Bloch's magnum opus *The Principle of Hope,* a sprawling study of the question of socialism and utopia, was written

---

30. See also chapter 1, p. 44.

in American exile in the 1940s and first published in three volumes by East Berlin's Aufbau Publishers in 1954, 1955, and 1959. Echoing Lenin's *What Is to Be Done?* Bloch's *Principle of Hope* calls for precisely the kind of forward-dreaming being practiced around the campfire at Wartha.[31] The "anticipatory consciousness" necessary to socialist revolutionary thinking, Bloch writes, is the proper affect of youth. When the utopian enthusiasm of youth comes together with historical circumstances fostering change, revolutionary results are possible (121–22).

What is realizable in spirit, however, is trickier in practice. Throughout *The Principle of Hope,* Bloch makes an effort to distinguish between "abstract" and "concrete" utopias. The "abstract utopia," a wistful dream of a better world, is the product and propagator of false consciousness, whereas the "concrete utopia" would represent the anticipatory consciousness of a partially realized and fully realizable revolutionary program (157–58). The "concrete utopia," in other words, must eventually come into being. To paraphrase Engels, it is a pudding proved only by the eating.

For Bloch, as for a number of other prominent East German intellectuals of the time, the tentative political "thaw" after the Twentieth Congress provided an opportunity to begin realizing the "concrete utopia" of the GDR.[32] Bloch joined with other leading academics and scientists such as Robert Havemann, Rudolf Bahro, Wolfgang Harich, Walter Janka, Friedrich Behrens, and Hans Mayer in calling for a comprehensive course of democratic and economic reform, codified by Harich and Janka in the "Platform for a Special German Path to Socialism."[33] As Wolfgang Engler points out, the "Platform" recapitulated many of the demands made by the striking workers on June 17, 1953: an immediate change in party leadership, full democratization of party and society, the dissolution of state security (the Stasi), guaranteed freedom of expression and assembly, the right of workers to organize and strike, and a limited licensing of small businesses. The "Platform" also contained a provision for German reunification, as long as certain socialist characteristics were retained (Engler, 94). While distinct in certain ways from the platform of the striking workers in 1953, the "concrete utopia" outlined in the 1956 "Platform" grew out of the same basic demand: it was time to see some of the changes promised by the sloganeering of the SED.

As the workers had been in 1953, the 1956 reform movement was suppressed with fierce efficiency. The Soviet intervention in Hungary afforded party leaders in Berlin an opportunity to clean out the GDR's "Petőfi sympathizers," and the resulting purge sent Harich and Janka, among others, to prison.[34] Bloch was

---

31. In *What Is to Be Done?* Lenin defends the right of a Marxist to dream, as long as that dream is anchored to a realizable goal (167).

32. At the Twentieth Congress of the Soviet Communist Party, Nikita Khrushchev revealed and denounced the crimes perpetrated under Stalin.

33. For more on this group of reformers, see Engler, 88–107; Bathrick, 57–83.

34. The Petőfi Club was a group of reform-minded intellectuals in Hungary in 1956. The "club" included Georg Lukács, Tibor Déry, and Julius Hay (Engler, 95).

forced to resign from his teaching position at the Humboldt University and to re-linquish his editorship of the *Deutsche Zeitschrift für Philosophie* (German Journal for Philosophy).

"Day X": Conspiracy and Containment

As the party's reaction to the 1956 reform movement makes clear, it was not yet ready to cash the check its slogans had written. In the late 1950s the party contin-ued to rely on the kind of optimistic futurism embodied by Wartha's young vol-unteers, who were content to work and wait for the payoff—Wartha, after all, is a homophone for *warte,* the imperative of *warten,* "to wait." Tom considers himself incapable of summoning up this kind of forward-looking enthusiasm. His trau-matic encounter with fascism has rendered him emotionally disengaged and polit-ically cynical. Near the end of the novel, however, a new narrative emerges. At the party hearing called to discuss Tom and Grit's affair, Tom's friend Schibulla speaks up to defend Tom's character. To do so, he brings a new element into the mix: the events of June 17, 1953.

As Schibulla tells it, he and Tom were working together on a construction site in Berlin when the strike began. Apparently worried that Tom might join the dem-onstration, Schibulla suggests that they walk home together. They see the hordes of West German invaders held at bay by East German police at Potsdamer Platz and streaming through the Brandenburg Gate. Schibulla describes a solitary Soviet tank under attack by hordes of West German invaders—a historical inaccuracy of obscene boldness. Though exact numbers of the killed and wounded strikers are not available, historians agree that the suppression of the uprising by Soviet troops was quick, brutal, and bloody. In its factual distortion, Schibulla's story mir-rors exactly the party's official account of the uprising, which blamed the events of "Day X" on instigators and provocateurs sent across the border by "the Enemy," the United States, and the BRD (Zentralkomitee, *Dokumente* 1954, 438).

Schibulla goes on to recount how he and Tom were beaten by a mob, then arrested by the West German police and held for interrogation. Schibulla ex-plains that Tom refused to cooperate with the police, declaring: "I am a citi-zen of the German Democratic Republic, and I demand to be set free" (206). "On the seventeenth of June," Schibulla concludes, "Tom saw fascism in action again. There's nothing that he hates more than fascism. Fascism made him into a cynic" (206).

Though Schibulla insists that it was fascism that made Tom a cynic, his evoca-tion of the June 17 uprising allows us to reevaluate our understanding of the origins of Tom's cynicism, and to reinflect the story of his transformation. If we tell Tom's story as that of the East German worker after June 17, the underlying ideological tension in *Beschreibung eines Summers* begins to come into focus. In this reading, June 17 would indeed be, as Schibulla suggests, a traumatic revisitation of fascism.

However, the "fascism" of June 17 would be found in the naked display of coercive, totalitarian violence on the part of the workers' state rather than in the tactics of West German agitators. The revolt was successfully neutralized, but at a high cost: the ideological credibility of the party was weakened, and the motivational efficacy of its slogans and promises destroyed. To borrow language from Tom's other trauma, "After that, there was nothing in the world that could get you excited." Thus Tom and his generation are motivated not by socialist conviction, but by what, from the party's perspective, would be alarmingly unsocialist considerations: "I get paid…and for that I do my work."

If the party's promises were bankrupt for workers of Tom's age, there was still hope for ideological credibility with the succeeding generation. They could still be convinced to mortgage the present against the future, to work under the assumption that "as we work today, so shall we live tomorrow." Viewed programmatically, then, Tom's story is that of a disgruntled East German worker being "cured" by the optimism of the post–June 17 generation.

Yet, as the East German reform movement in 1956 showed, the repressed will always return. And, albeit on slightly different terms than the June 17 demonstrations, the repressed did return in 1965 when Leipzig's youth took to the streets for the Beatles and rock and roll. In *Beschreibung eines Sommers,* the anxiety about a "return of the repressed"—a repetition of the events of June 17—does not materialize as an explicit thematic concern: here we do not have, for instance, the fear of workplace anarchy that is openly discussed throughout Erik Neutsch's 1964 novel *Spur der Steine* (Trace of Stones). Instead, the uneasiness and tension that permeate *Beschreibung eines Sommers* manifest themselves in more indirect ways. By one such circuitous route, the landscape itself becomes the principal antagonist in the novel, as constant forest fires hinder and undo the work of the youth brigades. In a now-familiar logic, these fires are attributed to the efforts of Western saboteurs. Tom is skeptical of this explanation, but when the chimney of the boiler house collapses, even he is forced to conclude that "sabotage was the only possible cause of the mishap" (137). This time, however, the cause turns out to be accidental: the boiler house had been constructed over an underground tunnel. This tunnel, according to Wartha legend, was dug by a local count as a secret escape route for his wife.

In a conversation with Tom shortly after this accident, Grit draws a connection between the chimney's collapse and the acts of sabotage that continue to plague the Wartha site, thereby suggesting a second repository of ideological tension in *Beschreibung eines Sommers:*

> "See who all is conspiring against us," said Grit.
>
> "Against us?" I said.
>
> "Yes, against us, against the chemical factory," Grit said. "Even the margrave is playing along. Adenauer's East Ministry and Heinrich Emanuel—same brothers, same caps." Then after a short pause: "But aren't we two actually on their side?"

"We?" I said. "Why?"

"Oh, Tom, don't ask," said Grit. "You know very well that in loving you, I'm hiding from my party." (139)

In Grit's mind, the margrave and the arsonists from the West are in league against the construction of the chemical factory—as are, she suggests, she and Tom. How can it be that this love, the proof and product of Tom's emotional and political reawakening, has become as dangerous as arson and entangled Grit and Tom in a conspiracy with Adenauer and a centuries-dead margrave?

From Grit's perspective—and the perspective of the party—the question is quite readily answered. In betraying her husband and her marriage vows, Grit has also betrayed the party. As Schibulla puts it, "Grit's husband is in the party, and Grit is in the party. So it *is* our business" (175). For this reason, she is summoned to a party hearing, given a stern rebuke, and sent off to Oeslnitz to straighten things out with her husband.

In Tom's case, however, the moral significance of the love story is more ambivalent. This love affair, though illicit, is the token of his emotional and political reawakening. Within the novel's narrative logic—that is, within the redemption plot that forms its core—Tom's newfound capacity to love must be regarded as a positive development. Why, then, is the catalyst and object of his desire forbidden to him in the end when the party steps in to end the affair? Which is also to ask, why must Grit be married in the first place?

Tom's always-already foreclosed relationship with Grit reflects a fundamental contradiction at the heart of Jakobs's novel, a disturbance in the economic logic that informs the narrative. The problem ultimately comes back to the question of incentive: why should Tom do what Trude Neutz demands and "put his heart" into his work? To put a finer point on it, why should he, or any of his coworkers, work on faith alone? How long can production be maintained by promises and payment deferred? On this question, *Beschreibung eines Sommers* mirrors the ambivalence of a wavering party line. On the one hand, if the SED had learned anything from June 17, it was that slogans alone would not increase production or keep the producers satisfied. In chapter 1 we saw how, by the logic of the New Course of the 1950s and the "New Economic System" of the early 1960s, consumer goods were to provide the impetus for individual and collective labor. An overriding concern with buying power, however, was a far cry from the socialist consciousness that policy makers were trying to foster. Through Tom's conversion narrative—the story of his *Ankunft*—*Beschreibung eines Sommers* attempts to supplant the materialistic calculations of an apathetic *Verstand* with the "forward-dreaming"—the *Herz*—of Wartha's volunteers, who are willing to endure hardship and hard work for their part in "building a giant."

Such revolutionary enthusiasm, however, carries with it a significant danger: what if the "giant" never materializes? What if the boundless energies of youth—and of East German workers in general—become truly unbound, no longer held in check by an investment in the *Aufbau* project or in its prospective returns? If Tom's newfound capacity for romantic passion corresponds to the enthusiasm he acquires from his young coworkers, then the party hearing that ends the affair would represent the steering and containment that must accompany the risky project of inspiration. The ideological fantasy at work here, in other words, is that the party could have it both ways: releasing the energies of revolutionary romanticism while retaining control over its objects and effects.

The perceived stakes of this undertaking become clear in the sudden violence of the novel's penultimate scene. Having convinced Grit to visit him once more before she leaves for Oeslnitz, Tom waits for her in his Berlin apartment, drinking cognac and fretting. When Grit arrives, a drunken Tom begs her not to leave him and says he can't live without her. Grit replies that she loves him, but that they have to be apart for a time while she sorts out her life. Suddenly, the scene turns violent and degenerates into a near rape. Here, Tom seems to have lost his *Verstand* completely: "I was out of my senses....I had lost all trace of control" (215–16). Fortunately for Grit, he eventually loses consciousness entirely and collapses to the floor.

Like the similar scenario of near rape in *Ankunft im Alltag,* Tom's attack here would prove the wisdom of separating the two lovers in the first place. The party's intervention, it seems, is intended only to save them from themselves—that is, from the violence of Tom's uncontrolled desire. In light of the reading I have suggested here, this scene would rehearse an anxiety about the potentially explosive effects of productive energy bound neither by the satisfactions of nonalienated labor nor by the pleasures of consumption. Tom's ferocious loss of control would represent the fear on the part of the East German state that the citizens' desire—desire the state itself had helped create—would, when thwarted, turn to violence. If the Leipzig Beat riots in 1965 represent such an outbreak of frustrated collective desire, then the state's reaction to this event demonstrates that the ideological apparatus of the GDR was unable to metabolize this mass dissatisfaction: the SED had to resort consistently to direct coercion.

In this light it is significant that when Tom comes to, he raves feverishly about escaping with Grit "to freedom": Toronto, he thinks, or Madrid (217). Once again, the party will have to protect Tom from his own madness. And in August of 1961, just after the first installments of *Beschreibung eines Sommers* began appearing in the FDJ newspaper *Junge Welt,* the Berlin Wall was built to do just that.

In the introduction to this book, I suggested that stories of romantic love share a potent narrative capacity: acting as an unmotivated motivator, love can instigate, sustain, convolute, or resolve a plot. As we have seen, the *Ankunftsroman* avails itself of this potential, employing a romantic framework to structure and stabilize its account of social assimilation. Both *Ankunft im Alltag* and *Beschreibung eines Sommers* insist, however, that it is not love that facilitates the "arrival" of the protagonists, but rather it is their "arrival," their harmonious integration into socialist production, that makes love possible. This reversal is the basic machinery of the pattern of libidinal investment I have been calling the "neue Romantik." In essence, the "neue Romantik" represents an effort to romanticize the process of production, wresting the passionate attachments of the East German citizenry—and especially of the youth—away from the desiring economy of commodity culture. Subordinated to production, romantic love becomes both a source of inspiration and motivation and a force of containment, directing and channeling the unstable energies of productive drive.

In a way, we can characterize the "neue Romantik" as an experimental narrative technology, part of the broader cultural experiment known as the Bitterfeld Way. As we will see in chapter 3, the radical productionism of the Bitterfeld Way was not destined for longevity. Ultimately, East German cultural and social policy followed the path marked by the NÖS, placing its faith once and for all in the sphere of personal fulfillment—including the satisfactions of consumer choice—rather than in the realm of collective production.[35] The short-lived genre of the *Ankunftsroman,* the culmination of a decade of *Aufbau* culture, stands as a signpost of a road not taken: the development and cultivation of a distinctly socialist libidinal economy in the GDR.

---

35. In the cultural sphere, this shift has been characterized variously as a "subjective" turn (Emmerich, 174 ff.) or a "retreat into interiority" (Zimmermann, 4).

3

Corrective Affinities

Love, Class, and the Propagation of Socialism

Zwischen Wand- und Widersprüchen
machen sie es sich bequem
Links ein Sofa, rechts ein Sofa,
in der Mitte ein Emblem

Between convictions and contradictions
They live like kings and queens
A sofa left, a sofa right
A party emblem in between

—Kurt Bartsch, from the poem "Sozialistischer Biedermeier"

In *Pursuits of Happiness,* Stanley Cavell explores a genre of American film he calls the "comedy of remarriage." In the films that comprise this genre, all of which were made between 1934 and 1949, "the drive of [the] plot is not to get the central pair together, but to get them *back* together, together *again*" (1–2). Cavell identifies a consistent utopian thread in the remarriage plot, a vision of social transformation that explores the terms and conditions of human happiness. These film comedies, Cavell suggests, are involved in what he calls a "conversation" with American culture, testing it against its own utopian aspirations (152). For Cavell, the trope of marriage relates both to the reality and to the potential of society. It is microcosm as well as utopia. If marriage is an emblem of a better way of living, then *re*marriage represents a necessary reaffirmation of this vision: "Our genre emphasizes the mystery of marriage by finding that neither law nor sexuality (nor, by implication, progeny) is sufficient to ensure true marriage and suggesting that what provides legitimacy is the mutual willingness for remarriage, for a sort of continuous reaffirmation" (142).

This chapter will consider a number of East German novels and films made between 1968 and 1978 that share with Cavell's remarriage comedies a concern with the conditions under which estranged married couples achieve (or fail to achieve) reconciliation. While none of the East German examples are, strictly speaking, comedies, they share the Hollywood comedies' utopian stakes. Through the lens of the marital relationship, the fulfilled and unfulfilled promises of culture and society come into focus; the utopia that is the implicit referent of the Hollywood comedies becomes an explicit theme in the remarriage narratives analyzed here. These are, in effect, studies in the conditions of utopian possibility, meditations on the interplay of idealism and resignation, expectation and disillusion. The terms according to which each couple chooses, abandons, then reconfirms—or fails to reconfirm— their romantic union trace the borders of real and imagined socialist community in the GDR of the 1970s.

From Production to Reproduction: The Crisis of Post-*Aufbau* Cultural Pedagogy

As suggested in the previous two chapters, the most urgent project in postwar East Germany was the rebuilding of a devastated industrial base and the remobilization of a decimated workforce. For this reason the ideological drive in cultural products from this period—known generally as the *Aufbau* (reconstruction) era—is directed primarily toward fostering the extraordinary levels of productivity necessary to the reconstruction effort, as well as toward counteracting various impediments to this productivity.[1] Bluntly put, in the productionist ethos of the *Aufbau* period, everything comes back to work. Even in texts steeped in New Course consumer culture, consumption is never an end unto itself, but rather an attempt—sometimes a last-ditch effort—to motivate production.[2]

In *Aufbau*-era cultural products, however, work is not simply a means to an end: the process of production serves a key pedagogical function. As Marc Silberman notes in his study of the East German industrial novel, for the literature of this period "the working world represents not a peripheral social activity but the *formative* sphere of social relationships and material productivity" (2). While East German workers rebuild their homeland, in other words, the experience of socialist labor would rebuild the workers. In particular, *Aufbau* public culture depicts the workplace as the primary site of denazification. Collective labor was to be a panacea for the damages caused by National Socialism, gathering together the pieces of

---

1. Wolfgang Emmerich observes: "Literature and other cultural activities were not only supposed to promote human productivity in general while expanding consciousness, but also very concretely to stimulate a readiness for physical work in order to help socialism toward victory in the clash of the economic systems" (115).

2. For more about the New Course, see chapter 1, pp. 42–49. For a discussion of the problem of motivation in the GDR workplace, see chapter 2, pp. 61–64.

a shattered nation and absolving its politically compromised citizens. Through the production process, workers would learn to be socialists. As the motto would later have it, "Sozialistisch arbeiten, leben und lernen" (Work, live, and learn socialistically) (Deutsches Historisches Museum). Perhaps nowhere is the pedagogical function of labor more accentuated than in the *Ankunftsroman,* which relies on the transformative experience of work to bring about the social integration, the "arrival," of the novel's troubled young protagonists.[3]

By the mid-1960s, however, the extreme productionism of *Aufbau-* and *Ankunftsliteratur* was destined for a crisis. As National Socialism and the war fell one and even two generations back in the collective experience, both the focus and the site of pedagogical and didactic efforts had to shift. The *Nachgeborenen*—those born after 1945—could hardly be expected to relate to narratives of socialist reeducation, in which soldiers and refugees, perpetrators and victims, skeptics, diehards, and neophytes all learn to live—and especially to work—together. In this sense, the *Ankunftsroman* represents the outermost limit of this paradigm: the young heroes of the *Ankunftsroman* belong to the last generation that should require reeducation. Subsequent generations would experience only the socialist order.

Given these conditions, a cultural template that emphasized reeducation through collective labor had to give way to one that could address socialist education prior to entry into the workforce. Officially nearing the end of its transition from capitalism to socialism, the GDR needed urgently to attend to the social institutions that would transmit socialist values to subsequent generations.[4] A preoccupation with production, in other words, had to be replaced with a focus on reproduction. In using the term *reproduction,* I have in mind both Marx's definition, as adopted by the SED, of the "constant process of renewing and widening social production" ("Reproduktion," 554) and a more current sociological understanding of cultural or social reproduction, in Anthony Giddens's gloss the "remaking [of] what is already made in the continuity of praxis" (171). *Reproduction,* according to these definitions, refers to the way a society replicates and renews itself over time. For Marx, reproduction encompasses a wide range of activities that, although external to the sphere of production, are nonetheless indispensable to the labor process, from the replenishment of an individual worker's labor power (sleeping, eating, doing laundry, and so on) to the maintenance and expansion of social and state institutions (*Capital,* 711–17, 732).

At the same time, it is important not to lose track of the vernacular meaning of the term. In a sense, biological reproduction is the crux of the matter: without successive generations, the question of social reproduction is moot. For Mary

---

3. See chapter 2, p. 64.

4. The Sixth Party Congress, in January 1963, announced the triumph of socialist production in the GDR and promised that the "transitional period" would be over by the end of the current phase of socialist development, the "comprehensive construction of socialism [umfassende Aufbau des Sozialismus]" (Zentralkomitee, *Dokumente* 1965, 209).

O'Brien, Marx's systematic devaluation of biological reproduction represents "one of the great defects" of his work, leading to an only "partial" conception of history: "Mode of production follows mode of production in providing subsistence for the reproducing of man on a daily basis. The daily reproduction of the *species* in the birth of *individuals* is not perceived as an essential dialectical moment of historical process, which of course it is" (10). The dialectical interrelation of individual, species, and social reproduction is at stake in the following analysis, as well as in chapter 4, which investigates the asymmetrical demands of reproduction on men and women.

In their influential study *Reproduction in Education, Society, and Culture,* Pierre Bourdieu and Jean-Claude Passeron focus on cultural reproduction through education, understood as all the institutions that inculcate successive generations with the ideology of the ruling class. "Education," they write, "is the equivalent, in the cultural order, of the transmission of genetic capital in the biological order" (32). From the beginning, the party recognized the crucial importance of pedagogical institutions to the health and longevity of East Germany's socialist experiment. Immediately following the fall of National Socialism, officials in the Soviet Occupied Zone aggressively restaffed primary and secondary schools with party-affiliated teachers to ensure a thorough and consistent restructuring of East German society, starting with its youngest members.[5] Beginning with the handpicked *Neulehrer,* the East German educational system was carefully monitored and guided by the party, from the preschool education of crèche and *Kindergarten* to the *Arbeiter- und Bauern-Fakultät* (ABF—a kind of precollege for workers and their children) and the universities. Children's extracurricular life was also structured extensively by the institutions of the state. Participation in the recreational and pedagogical activities of the Young Pioneers (ages six–eight) and the Thälmann Pioneers (ages nine–thirteen) was nearly mandatory.[6] For youth between the ages of thirteen and twenty-five, the FDJ offered organized leisure-time activities, special-interest clubs, athletic facilities, vocational training, and political education.

In February of 1965, the Central Committee of the SED announced the inauguration of the Standardized Socialist Educational System, the culmination of a reform process begun officially in 1963.[7] According to its architects, the new educational system would better prepare students for the demands of the Scientific-Technical Revolution (WTR), as well as helping them to develop into "all-around and harmoniously developed socialist personalities" (Uhlig, Günther, and Lost, 572). As its name suggests, the primary objective of the school reform was to unify the various elements of the GDR pedagogical system, ultimately bringing all the

---

5. See Brigitte Hohlfeld, *Die Neulehrer in der SBZ/DDR 1945–1953.*

6. By 1985, 99 percent of East German children between the ages of six and thirteen belonged to the Pioneer movement (Edwards, 36).

7. For analysis of the genesis and genealogy of East German school reform in the 1960s, see Baske, 15–43.

institutions of intergenerational social reproduction under one roof: "The Standardized Socialist Educational System will unite the educational effects of all state and social institutions and organs involved in the education and formation of the youth, uniting as well the efforts of school, home, factory, children's and youth organizations" (567).

As this grandiose promise of social orchestration indicates, another important institution of social reproduction was also undergoing judicial and legislative scrutiny in the mid-1960s. In 1965, the Central Committee adopted a sweeping set of reforms in family law. The family law reform, as outlined in the *Familiengesetzbuch* (Family Law Code), had a unifying function similar to that of the Standardized Socialist Educational System: one of its primary goals was to ensure the political integration of the family by bringing the domestic sphere under the protection—and influence—of the state. As the preamble to the *Familiengesetzbuch* explains,

> The task of the *Familiengesetzbuch* is to advance the development of familial relations in socialist society. The *Familiengesetzbuch* should help all citizens, and particularly the youth, to shape their family life consciously. It serves to protect marriage and the family and the rights of each individual member of the family unit. It should help to prevent family conflict and recurrent problems....
>
> The *Familiengesetzbuch* directs the attention of the citizens, the socialist collective and the social organizations toward the great personal and social importance of marriage and the family and toward the duty of each individual and the whole society to contribute to the protection and development of every family. (Kanzlei des Staatsrates, 118)

Although the family's "great personal and social importance" was clear to the authors of the *Familiengesetzbuch,* the ideal character and composition of the socialist family were somewhat more murky. On the one hand, the familial model presented by the *Familiengesetzbuch* is quite traditional and conservative, emphasizing the desirability of two-parent households and identifying the telos of marriage as procreation.[8] On the other hand, the *Familiengesetzbuch* claims that "with the development of socialism in the German Democratic Republic, new kinds of family relations emerge" (Kanzlei des Staatsrates, 117). These "new" family ties by no means constituted a radical challenge to the traditional nuclear family—East German family planners did not, for instance, revisit the domestic experiments of the early Soviet period. Though it stops far short of restructuring the East German family in the eyes of the law, the Family Code does acknowledge the changing structure of modern socialist families: it calls for special measures to ensure

---

8. E.g., § 5.2: "The family should grow out of marriage, which finds its fulfillment in shared life together, in the raising of children, and in the mutual development of the parents and children into principled, all-around developed personalities" (Kanzlei des Staatsrates, 120).

adequate support for single parents (§ 3.2) and insists that the harmony of the family should not be placed above the career aspirations of either partner (§ 2) (Kanzlei des Staatsrates, 119).

The most decisive innovation of the fairly traditionalist Family Code can be found in what might be called its strategy of legitimation. The new family law takes pains to locate the legitimacy of the family not in its congruence with pre-established norms or modalities (the two-parent household, for instance, or pre-defined spousal roles), but rather in its imbrication with the institutions of society and the state. The *Familiengesetzbuch* is adamant in its rejection of bourgeois notions of the domestic "private sphere" as an autonomous area distinct from society at large. Responding to West German criticisms of the new family law as a "regimentation" of the private sphere, East German Staatsrat representative Heinrich Homann argues that there has never been a "private sphere." "Bourgeois society has always exercised objective influence on marriage and the family," Homann observes, "and bourgeois law and the bourgeois state sanction this influence." Yet where the influence of capitalist society on working families must be antagonistic, in the GDR "an objectively present harmonious consonance exists between socialist social relations and family relations. Socialist relations exert a positive influence on family and marriage" (Kanzlei des Staatsrates, 42).

Homann's argument seems somewhat self-defeating: if there were in fact a "harmonious consonance" of socialist social relations with familial relations in the GDR, then why was the *Familiengesetzbuch*'s intervention necessary in the first place? The portrayals of domesticity analyzed in this chapter will help begin to construct an answer to this question. The novels and films we will examine all focus on an apparent asymmetry between the social order being reproduced within the "private" domestic sphere and the one intended by public policy and nurtured by the institutions of the state. The problematic insularity of these families directly reverses the poles delineated by Homann: where he imagines a working-class family in the West besieged by a hostile bourgeois order, these works describe islands of bourgeois domesticity within the Workers' and Peasants' State.

The cultural phenomenon—one might say, the presenting symptom—that motivates this chapter is a recurring plotline in East German cultural products from the 1970s: a young, married, career-driven urbanite suddenly finds his or her home life intolerable and leaves it behind to pursue another way of living, an alternative embodied in a new love interest.[9] What lends this narrative a particularly East German flavor is the class dynamic that informs it: the new lifestyle and lover are

---

9. In addition to the four works analyzed here, one could include Günter de Bruyn's novel *Preisverleihung* (1972), Karl Heinz Jakobs's *Die Interviewer* (1973), Dieter Noll's *Kippenberg* (1979), Frank Vogel's film *Das siebente Jahr* (1968), Egon Günther's *Der Dritte* (1972), and Frank Beyer's *Das Versteck* (1977). An interesting precursor to these narratives of romantic rearrangement is Slatan Dudow's 1959 film, *Verwirrung der Liebe,* which, as Joshua Feinstein convincingly argues, uses the genre of romantic comedy to examine the utopian ambitions of East German socialism (78–109).

distinctly proletarian, the home and spouse left behind unmistakably bourgeois. Given the tendencies of East German public culture from the *Aufbau* period on, such an impulse toward proletarization seems fairly unsurprising. In fact, I would argue, the magnetic pull of these working-class characters attests to the lingering influence of the "neue Romantik," the trend in East German public culture of romanticizing the sphere of production.[10] Even after cultural policy had left *Aufbau* productionism behind, the industrial narrative's characteristic pattern of libidinal investment continued to shape the public imagination.

A thornier problem, from the perspective of official ideology, was the presence of these class distinctions in the first place. According to the SED's understanding of social class, the nationalization of the means of production should have eliminated the basis for meaningful class distinctions in the GDR.[11] Though by the 1970s the SED was willing to concede that the GDR was still a "class society," it insisted that the East German class system was "nonantagonistic"—in other words, that its conflicts could be solved gradually and peacefully.[12] A 1977 treatise entitled "Development of the Classes and Social Strata in the GDR" reports

> [an] incremental growth of the similarity between the classes and strata in accordance with the worldview and ideals of the working class, as well as a gradual overcoming of remaining social distinctions, particularly the fundamental divisions between city and country and between manual and intellectual labor. (Parteihochschule "Karl Marx," 6)

The claim that the class system in the GDR unfolded "in accordance with the worldview and ideals of the working class" seems dubious; as we saw in chapter 2, East Germany's fraught labor relations bore witness to a far more antagonistic contradiction between labor and management than the official account would have it. Nor does the promise of a "gradual overcoming of remaining social distinctions" hold up well to historical scrutiny. In fact, the opposite appeared to be the case. In the course of the 1960s, under the aegis of the New Economic System (NÖS) and the Scientific-Technical Revolution, a new class of managerial, technical, and political elites began to assert itself—not only in the workplace, but also in the cultural life of the GDR.

Speaking at the Second Bitterfeld Conference in 1964, SED General Secretary Walter Ulbricht announced a new cultural line corresponding to the advances of

---

10. In chapter 2, I argue that the romantic aura attached to production, which was widespread in socialist-realist production narratives, reached its zenith in the short-lived genre of *Ankunftsromane,* "novels of arrival."

11. The *Kleines politisches Wörterbuch* spells out clearly the party's understanding of the origins of class distinctions: "In every case, the ownership-relation to the means of production is constitutive of class difference" ("Klasse," 402).

12. On the theme of "antagonistic" and "nonantagonistic" contradiction in GDR literature, see Jochen Staadt's comprehensive study *Konfliktbewusstsein und sozialistischer Anspruch in der DDR-Literatur.*

the NÖS and the WTR: "An artist who wants to achieve the Truth and the Whole cannot [do so] by assuming the perspective of an empirical observer, nor by taking on the point of view of a simple worker. He absolutely needs the perspective of a planner and leader. That is what we ask of him" (81). With these words the Second Bitterfeld Conference essentially reversed the mandate of the First Bitterfeld Conference five years earlier. Where participants at the 1959 conference were urged to immerse themselves in production, to assume the "point of view of a simple worker," they were now being told to shift their focus to the "planners and leaders." In his remarkable historical survey of East German industry literature, Peter Zimmermann characterizes this shift as a definitive indicator of the GDR's growing class divide:

> Surveying the history of *Industrieliteratur,* one sees that the most radical change in perspective occurred in the middle of the 1960s: this marks the transition from workers' literature to the literature of the planners and leaders. After the working class had done its part [in the *Aufbau*],...the "new socialist intelligence"...declared itself the most important force for economic and social progress. (39)

As we will see, however, this bid for power on the part of the "planners and leaders" was not the end of the story. Throughout the 1970s the "planners and leaders" and the working class vied for the attention of East German public culture. Ultimately, this was a struggle less for the GDR's head than for its heart, less for political power than for dominance in social reproduction. Would GDR society take a fancy to the new technocracy, realigning its ideals and ambitions to those of the intellectual and scientific elite? Or would it recommit to the principles of the Workers' and Peasants' State? The works examined in this chapter literalize this metaphor, weighing the attractions of both suitors in a scenario of romantic choice.

"Do dialectics excuse adultery?": *Buridans Esel*

Günter de Bruyn's 1968 novel, *Buridans Esel* (Buridan's Ass), follows the romantic adventures of Karl Erp, a librarian in Berlin. Erp lives with his wife, Elisabeth, and their two children in a posh suburb on the Spree. The Erps enjoy all the comforts of their middle-class status: a large house, a garden, a car. Legally (and importantly) these luxuries all belong to Elisabeth, who inherited them from her wealthy parents when they retired to the West (16). Erp allows himself another bourgeois luxury as well: an extramarital affair with a young, idealistic new colleague at the library, Fräulein Broder.[13] Elisabeth knows about her husband's affair, though she assumes it to be a short-lived and shallow fling. She rationalizes the situation to

---

13. Broder's first name is never revealed in the novel.

herself as a necessary consequence of the growing gulf in their marital relationship: "Karl had changed, that was true, but everything changes. Standstill doesn't exist. Do dialectics excuse adultery?" (41). This formulation captures the implicit question governing de Bruyn's novel: does the infidelity at the core of this narrative represent a positive development—a dialectical advance—for Erp, or does this explanation simply cloak more ignoble motives?

If the former is the case, it would be because Erp's affair reawakens his revolutionary consciousness, dormant since his FDJ years. Near the beginning of the novel, the free, indirect narrative dips into Erp's memories to depict the earliest days of his romance with Elisabeth:

> Country road, deserted lakeshore, pine forest, bare roadside trees reminded him of that Sunday thirteen or fourteen years ago when he first came here, on the back of a truck, freezing, in a blue shirt [the FDJ uniform] (he still had it, wore it sometimes gardening), a flapping flag above him, one arm draped over Elisabeth's shoulder. The best students at the librarian school went into the village as harvest helpers and culture bringers, sang something about the vanguard of the proletariat, and were so convinced to be just that that Elisabeth was ashamed to call a villa in this eastern Dahlem her home. (13)[14]

Here, in a description touched with the novel's characteristic wry irony, we see Erp and Elisabeth as FDJlers, full of *Aufbau* enthusiasm and caught up in a courtship under the sign of the "neue Romantik." Later, recounting these years to Broder, Erp invokes a classic text of *Aufbau* youth-movement nostalgia, Hermann Kant's 1965 novel, *Die Aula* (The Auditorium): "Surely she knew Kant's *Aula,* that's how it was, just like that, tough and splendid, splendid and tough" (45). In its periodic revisitations of the "tough and splendid" *Aufbauzeit, Buridans Esel* provides an insightful commentary on the ideological standpoint represented by *Die Aula* and prompts a reevaluation of the lasting significance of the GDR's heady early years.

In Kant's novel, Robert Iswall, a journalist, has been commissioned to give a speech for the closing of the *Arbeiter- und Bauern-Fakultät* (the Workers' and Peasants' College, or ABF), where he was once a student. Iswall's efforts to frame his experience occasion a great deal of anecdotal reminiscing, as well as a where-are-they-now of his former classmates. Kant's narrative voice, like de Bruyn's, treats the exuberance and pretensions of the young students with a good deal of irony, even if *Die Aula* tends to be more cheerful and forgiving than *Buridans Esel.* Though it touches on some of the excesses of the Stalin era and raises a few questions about the motives and methods of participants in the *Aufbau* effort, *Die Aula* finds in general that the experiment of the ABF was a success, as measured by the career trajectories

---

14. Dahlem was a well-to-do suburb of West Berlin.

of its graduates: "If it were up to me, distinguished guests," Iswall imagines saying in his speech,

> I'd forget about the speech. I'd do something totally different. I'd raise my finger and point at you, fellow class of '49, at each one of you and I'd say: Stand up, say your name and say your occupation, the one from then and the one now, and then sit down, and that's all. All we need are facts. Now stand up, you facts, and let's see you!
>
> Irmgard Strauch, shopgirl—lecturer; Joachim Trimborn, fisherman—chemist; Rose Paul, farmhand—sinologist; Vera Bilfert, seamstress—ophthalmologist. And now the next row, please: watchmaker—physicist; hairdresser—high-frequency-radio technician...(363)

Overall, *Die Aula* casts the *Aufbauzeit,* the time of the ABF, as a period of radical and salutary change that saw the construction of socialism and the dismantling of class barriers.[15] Such a rehabilitation of the *Aufbauzeit*—which, after all, was also the time of East German Stalinism—has significant consequences for *Die Aula*'s evaluation of the present.[16] Indeed, the epigraph from Heinrich Heine reminds us: "Today is a consequence of yesterday. We have to discover what the latter intended, if we would know what the former holds" (Der heutige Tag ist ein Resultat des gestrigen. Was dieser gewollt hat, müssen wir erforschen, wenn wir zu wissen wünschen, was jener will).[17] Ultimately, *Die Aula* presents a continuity between the class-leveling efforts of the ABF and the social structure of the narrative's present time. That the ABF is being dismantled would attest then not to the abandonment of the goals it represents, but rather to their achievement; the *Arbeiter- und Bauern-Fakultät* would no longer be necessary in the classless society of the "comprehensive expansion of socialism."[18]

Buridans Esel, on the other hand, posits no such correlation between the social restructurings of the *Aufbauzeit* and the present class structure. In Erp's case, material success represents a betrayal of his former ideals—or perhaps reveals the

---

15. Zimmermann writes: "Kant means nothing other than that socialism has brought the fulfillment of the dream of the poor—that their children might become something better than they—within reach....[In *Die Aula,*] the achievements of the GDR at the level of education-politics are indisputable. Equal opportunity for workers' children, thus far an unmet goal in West Germany, had been secured in the course of the *Aufbau*" (206).

16. That Kant's intervention constitutes a rehabilitation can also be seen in his account of the genesis of *Die Aula:* he recalls being inspired to write his novel after reading a "dry and lifeless" report about the ABF in a *Festschrift* for the Fifth Centennial of Greifswald University. "I told myself," he explains, "that it would be a shame if this was all that remains of the subject [of the ABF]...I was motivated by a very palpable anger at a nearly heartless treatment of a very important time in the lives of many people in our Republic. I think that when we talk about our socialism, we downplay too much one of its great achievements, namely, as I see it, the educational revolution" ("Ein verregneter Urlaub!"; qtd. in Krenzlin, 59).

17. From the *Französische Zustände,* Artikel VI, Paris, 19 April 1832.

18. See note 4 above.

insubstantiality of those ideals in the first place. In his youth, Erp participated in *Aufbau* efforts to revolutionize the GDR's rural populace and aspired to do cultural work in those backwaters "where the cultural revolution was still revolutionary" (127). Since then, however, his revolutionary ideals have given way to a thoroughly bourgeoisified lifestyle, a "retreat into the comforts of prosperity: home, garden, car" (58).

In light of this apparent political regression, Erp is able to justify his extramarital affair with Broder as a social gain: "That's what made it so hard to judge this affair," he thinks. "It was a boon—for her, for him, for everyone (the kids maybe—maybe!—excepted). *He had awakened from a years-long lethargy*" (80, italics mine). After storming out of his house following an ideological showdown with his antisocialist West German father-in-law, Erp moves into Broder's rather squalid *Hinterhaus* apartment, and his youthful idealism burgeons once again (see fig. 7).[19] Broder, though usually quite critical of Erp's posturings, concedes that he has "shattered" his former bourgeois complacency (134). When Erp and Broder go public with their relationship, even the party seems to agree that this affair has had a positive influence on Erp's political consciousness. Party Secretary Theo Haßler recommends that Erp be reassigned but points out that his leaving will be a great loss for the Berlin library: "I know what we'll lose in him: a comrade who has found a new start through the productive power of love!" (116). Erp's friend Fred Mantek goes even further, arranging a promotion for Erp based precisely on his affair, arguing that his commitment to the relationship shows a "staunchness of character, resolve, and sincerity" that has allowed him to overcome his "inactivity and resignation" (178).

Eventually, however, Erp's true colors begin to show. Annoyed by the privations of Broder's apartment, Erp finds himself longing for the comforts of home and garden on the Spree (176). And when Broder, taking Erp up on his revolutionary rhetoric, tells him that she has requested to be transferred to the country, she does not get the reaction she was expecting. Instead of waxing ecstatic about youthful dreams long deferred, he asks bluntly: "Why did you do that?" (187). This moment reveals to Broder the insufficiency of Erp's transformation:

> Because of course two souls resided, alas, in his breast, which had warred but had not yet defeated each other, and the second, the love-and-activity soul, was still alive and produced pain and genuine objections when the beloved...spoke the awful truth, that his love was not big enough to jump the hedge and fence around the paradisial goal. (188)

Erp's two souls, the bourgeois and the revolutionary, give rise to the guiding allegory of *Buridans Esel* (Buridan's Ass): Erp would be the ass in the sophism (mis)

---

19. The back-courtyard apartment (*Hinterhauswohnung*) was the traditional and quintessential proletarian dwelling in Berlin.

Glück im Hinterhaus
Von einem, der Brücken abbrechen, aber einen Fußsteg stehenlassen will

Figure 7. "Happiness in the *Hinterhaus*." In Herrmann Zschoche's 1980 film adaptation of Günter de Bruyn's novel *Buridans Esel* (Buridan's Ass), Karl Erp (Dieter Mann) looks with disgust on the trappings of his bourgeois life. The caption reads: "About a man who wants to burn his bridges while leaving a gangplank behind." Source: Bundesarchiv [FilmSG1/BArch/25251 *Glück im Hinterhaus*].

attributed to the fourteenth-century philosopher John Buridan. Confronted with two indistinguishable piles of hay, the donkey starves to death because he cannot decide between the two.[20]

Of course, Erp does not starve, even metaphorically, but rather goes back to Elisabeth toward the end of the novel. Here, the novel's far-from-impartial narrative voice reveals the full extent of its preference: "The proper ending for the story would be this: when Buridan's ass finally decided for one of the two piles of hay, both were gone!" (196). After receiving a well-earned rebuke from Haßler, Erp would return to Elisabeth but find no welcome in her home. Eventually, he would spend a gloomy, rainy night in his prized Trabant. "That," we read, "would be the proper ending" (196).

---

20. G. E. Hughes comments: "[It] seems safe to say that to many generations of students of philosophy [Buridan's] name has brought no more to mind than 'Buridan's ass'—the donkey that starved because it was equidistant between two equally succulent bundles of hay; and yet no one has found this example in any of his writings" (Buridan and Hughes, 1).

But the novel is not finished yet. The narrator picks up the story again: "Since reality seldom has novel endings at the ready and since this report strives for clarification [*Klärung*], not transformation [*Verklärung*], the actual ending is less pretty, less clear-cut, less just" (197). The real ending, according to de Bruyn, could be summed up as follows: "A man returns to his family. The neighbors, friends, colleagues, comrades say: Thank God, finally, what luck! And they call it a moral victory. But the writer asks himself and his reader: Was it really?" (198). In this satirical reversal, the "less pretty, less clear-cut, less just" ending becomes a "moral victory" in the eyes of friends, neighbors, and party—in everyone's eyes, that is, except those of the narrator, and perhaps, by proxy, the reader. On the surface, the criticism implied in this discrepancy is directed at a petit-bourgeois morality that deems the preservation of the nuclear family good a priori, regardless of circumstances or consequences—unless the irony here goes deeper, suggesting a reversal of a reversal. How might this work?

It is tempting, as I have done thus far, to posit Elisabeth and Broder as opposing poles, bourgeois and revolutionary, between which Erp chooses—wrongly. Wolfgang Emmerich, for instance, remarks in his summary of de Bruyn's novel:

> The successful, conformist library director Karl Erp...and his masculine self-confidence are not equal to the revolution that would be necessary to realize his love for his emancipated, clever colleague "Fräulein Broder" in the long term. Spinelessly, he returns to his ostensibly idyllic family life—a "decision" that de Bruyn hardly presents as a triumph of socialist morality, but rather the opposite. (211)

Or as Karin Hirdina summarizes it, "The question—a moral victory?—is developed with great irony. But the irony is not aimed at the fact that love develops, pulls one out of the secure, definite world of habit, activates the best in those affected, makes them ready for a new, a better, life. The irony applies to the characters. Especially Erp" (36). Under closer examination, however, we will find that Erp's personal culpability is less binding than it might at first appear. Here we must remember that the story of Buridan's ass presents not simply a choice to be made, but rather a choice that *cannot* be made: there are no logical criteria by which to distinguish between the two options. This is *not* the choice template of the *Aufbau-* or *Ankunftsroman*—for instance, the *Entscheidung* (decision) between East and West in Anna Seghers's novel of the same name, or Recha's fraught decision between Curt and Nikolaus in Brigitte Reimann's *Ankunft im Alltag*. In fact, Erp's "choice" of the bourgeois lifestyle, the life of the *Spießer* (bourgeois) or *Wohlstandskommunist* (prosperity communist, 103), is already made for him: he is bourgeois not by virtue of a character flaw or a decision wrongly made, but rather by his position of privilege within the existing class structure of the GDR. Seen from this systemic perspective, both Erp's bourgeoisified home life with Elisabeth and his only apparently radical *Hinterhaus* life with Broder are in fact two sides of the same coin.

This complementarity is brought out by a perhaps inadvertent intertextual resonance between Erp's love story and that of the petit-bourgeois "revolutionary" Gottfried Kinkel, as retold in Marx and Engels's satirical pamphlet *Heroes of the Exile*. Kinkel, like Erp, must make a difficult decision: between the clever Johanna Mockel, a romantic revolutionary of his own stamp, and the "gentle,...dear, innocent" Sophie Bögehold, a match suggested by his sister (149).[21] Marx and Engels observe:

> Naturally, Gottfried soon began to make "comparisons"...between Mockel and his fiancée, but he had "had no time hitherto"—much against his usual habit—"to reflect at all about weddings and marriage."...In a word, *he stood like Buridan's ass between the two bundles of hay, unable to decide between them.* (153, italics mine)

In the end, Kinkel makes the opposite choice from Erp: he breaks off his engagement with Bögehold and opts for the radical-intellectual Mockel. Here, though, the joke is on Kinkel for thinking that his amorous posturing constitutes a real revolutionary breakthrough. Marx and Engels's blistering satire makes it clear that whether Kinkel marries Bögehold or Mockel, he is still as laughably bourgeois as before.[22] Given these circumstances, whichever bundle of hay one chooses, the result is the same.

If Erp deserves reprobation, I am suggesting, it is not for abandoning the "revolutionary" path of the *Hinterhaus,* but rather for arrogating it in the first place. This guilt, then, would fall equally on Fräulein Broder—as much a member of the bourgeois intelligentsia as Erp. Through narrative "digressions" depicting the habits and attitudes of Broder's working-class or petit-bourgeois neighbors, the text alerts us to the gap between library and *Hinterhaus.* This dynamic comes into focus when Broder's neighbor, Frau Wöllfin, makes a cameo. "Why all these digressions?" de Bruyn asks. "Certainly not because after all these figures of planner- and leader-literature it would perhaps be an accomplishment to rediscover the old washerwoman" (124). With this sardonic reference to "Planer- und Leiterliteraturgestalten," the narrative voice calls attention to its own participation in shifting the focus of East German culture from the working class to the bourgeoisie.

Against the backdrop of a self-reflexively exclusive planner-and-leader narrative, Erp's attempt to relive his radical youth through an only superficially cross-class love affair seems even less meritorious—and even more ludicrous—than it first appears. Erp's personal revolution, like Kinkel's, is more appearance than essence, more guilty conscience than transformed consciousness. In the end, the

---

21. Marx and Engels describe Mockel as "a female Kinkel, his romantic alter ego. Only she was harder, smarter, less confused, and thanks to her greater age she had left her youthful illusions behind her" (*Heroes of the Exile,* 150).

22. Ultimately, the polemic of *Heroes of the Exile* locates Kinkel's primary fault not in his romantic choice, nor even in his class of origin, but rather in his conception of history: like his fellow would-be revolutionaries in exile, he fails to see that the reactionary times are wrong for radical social transformation (Marx and Engels, *MEGA,* 794–95).

adjudicating reader is put in the place of Buridan's ass, confronting the forced choice of pseudo-revolution or *embourgeoisement.* The two warring souls of East German public culture—the soul of the *Hinterhaus* and the soul of the "planners and leaders"—are set adrift in the bottomless irony of *Buridans Esel.* Yet where Faust's dual souls cling to the earth and the heavens respectively, the GDR's two souls seem caught in a feedback loop: the latter dreams of becoming the former, the former turns out to be a fantasy of the latter.

"Who else could do it, if not lovers?": *Karen W.*

In many ways, Gerdi Tetzner's 1974 novel, *Karen W.,* constitutes an attempt to circumvent this feedback loop. By traversing the divisions of labor that separate the two spheres, Karen Waldau searches for a stable foundation on which to build her own life and the life of her daughter. Tetzner's novel begins in medias res: "Now, tonight, I have to do it!" the narrator declares (5). She composes a note: *"We've degenerated nicely. Apparently you feel fine. I'm leaving to start over another way"* (6). Taking her young daughter Bettina with her, Karen leaves her life in the city and husband of eight years and moves into her childhood home in the rural village of Osthausen. The grounds for Karen's decision are not immediately clear and throughout the novel remain irreducible to one distinct motive.

A number of critics have interpreted Karen's move as an inaugural act of feminist emancipation and have identified the motivating contradiction in the novel as that between Karen's "roles"—housewife, mother, professional—and her quest for self-knowledge and personal fulfillment. Sonja Hilzinger, for instance, sees Karen's development as a model of "female self-realization" (90), a condition of which is the rejection of preestablished roles. Pairing Karen W. with the eponymous hero of Brigitte Reimann's 1974 novel, *Franziska Linkerhand,* Hilzinger explains that "both women fight in their own way for freedom from the confining roles they have learned and internalized through the socialization of family and community." Hilzinger goes on to describe "Karen's rebellion against the alienating, deforming everyday of the workplace, against the masculine standard that leaves no room for self-fulfillment and happiness" (125).[23]

Although it cannot be denied that *Karen W.* engages in a strong critique of calcified social roles—particularly gender roles—I would suggest that such a reading

---

23. Further proponents of a subjectivist, role-based interpretation of *Karen W.* include Sara Lennox: "*Karen W.* depicts problems in the professional and personal fulfillment of women from a female perspective" (236); Dorothee Schmitz: "In Tetzner's novel, bourgeoise women's roles are lived out again, but in the end such a life proves no longer possible, at least not for the protagonist....So she rejects the fundamental orientation of her female role-models and searches for living possibilities that are adequate to her individuality" (170); and Jochen Staadt: "[Tetzner] emphasizes...the search for subjective self-realization. The heroine of the novel does not just break with her husband, but also with her career and her social position, in order to keep her life hopes from suffocating under the bondage of social roles" (237).

contributes less to our understanding of the novel than might first appear. Indeed, Tetzner's novel nestles all too comfortably into this interpretive framework. Considering her friend Linda's career-driven life, for instance, Karen thinks: "I don't want a life like Linda's. Where is my own model?" (207). In the course of the novel, Karen considers a number of *Muster*—"models, roles"—but ultimately rejects them all, having decided that self-fulfillment must be sought outside any predefined spheres of activity. The straightforward critique of roles, in other words, recapitulates the viewpoint of the novel but sheds little light on the underlying tensions that drive the plot and determine its narrative arc.

Without diminishing the importance of the personal, the following analysis will focus on the social, exploring the implications of Karen's actions for the vision of society—actual and potential—put forth in Tetzner's novel. In fact, Karen herself casts her decision to move to Osthausen in precisely this light. Considering her conflicted relationship with her own father, Karen imagines how Bettina, her daughter, might judge her parenting:

> But Bettina now, in six years she'll be as old as I was when I left home.... What could she charge me with? The betrayal of our breakthrough through careers and the dictatorship of consumption…wait! You can't lump me in with that part of my generation; I took off when you were eight so as not to belong to that group, to set an example. (168)

Here, anticipating Bettina's future accusations, Karen gives a clear account of her intentions in moving to Osthausen; in her family, at least, the sins of the parents will not be visited on the daughter: Bettina will not inherit her parents' "betrayal" of their revolutionary "breakthrough."

A closer look at the terms of this "betrayal" reveal why the circumstances of Karen's life in the city demand such a radical break. After studying law at the university, Karen embarks on an upwardly mobile career in the legal profession. Like Karl Erp, she begins her career with revolutionary ideals, agitating among the GDR's rural farmers for collectivization: "To change a centuries-old mode of production in a few weeks! Unheard-of things were happening in this country, and I was there!" (48). After a while, however, she finds that law lacks the interpersonal connection, the "human warmth," she had expected. "Life happens outside of the courtroom," she says (213). She eventually abandons her career path to become a stay-at-home mother. Yet the life of a housewife also becomes meaningless for Karen: "My daily activities lost their meaning, you know? I became a stranger to myself" (34).

Karen explains this development partly in terms of her changing relationship with her husband, Peters. Earlier in their relationship, she says, their partnership had been based on an exchange of ideas and opinions. Over the years, though, he has become more and more dogmatic and supercilious. As a professor he reveals himself to be a rank opportunist, the kind of teacher who would (and did) change his whole pedagogy overnight to conform to the worldview of a new boss (33). The new Peters has a new circle of friends, successful academics whose elitist attitudes repel Karen: "They live in their calculated circle, these people, and pronounce judgments about this and that...I lose myself in the shuffle and become a stranger to myself, I can't do anything about it, you know?" (157). Karen is appalled not only at the bourgeois worldview of Peters's friends, but also at her own bourgeoisified, consumerist lifestyle:

> I walk across the parquet floor between all the chair legs and plant pots as big as buckets. I lived here...where? Between the *Schrankwand* and the *Kastensesseln* from some furniture showroom we ate dinners and entertained guests.[24] Any young woman could have lived here. Where am I? At least in the bedroom.... No, these carefully made beds with the senseless runner around the bottom belong to some solid married couple, but not to me and him. For whom and for what eternity did I collect all this junk around us? For guests? For Bettina? (93)

The common thread in these characterizations of life in the city (designated as "L." in the novel) is a profound sense of alienation—vocational, social, and personal. Working as a law clerk, Karen feels distanced from the lives of others and sapped of her own vitality; in her life with Peters and her interactions with his circle, she feels distanced from herself; having assembled a house full of comforts and luxuries, Karen finds she no longer has a place there.

What are we to make of all this alienation? Is it a subjective condition—an incidental "feeling"—or does it derive from the material circumstances of Karen's life? Dorothee Schmitz suggests the latter, applying a Marxist conception of alienated labor both to Karen's domestic disaffection ("The life of a housewife confines her, alienates her from herself and her environment" [70]) and to her vocational estrangement ("Karen W. suffers the most from a loss of the emotional-sensual connection to work. The lack of connections to other people creates feelings of objectification and dehumanization" [61]).[25]

At a theoretical level, the claim that exclusively domestic labor could be alienated—in the Marxist sense—should not cause much surprise. Feminist criticism has consistently emphasized the disparity created by a division of labor between wage earners and homemakers—an unequal partnership analogous to the dependence of the worker on his or her employer. Michèle Barrett, for instance, points out that

> capitalism not only took over and entrenched the differentiation of tasks, but divided the workforce itself into wage earners and those dependent upon the wage of others. Capitalism did not create domestic labour, or the "feminine" areas of wage labour, but

---

24. The *Schrankwand* (built-in shelving unit) and *Kastensessel* (armchair) were fashionable and ubiquitous in GDR homes of the 1970s.

25. Marxist alienation, in Schmitz's gloss, is "a reduction of the human being in the labor process" (60).

it did create a set of social relations in which pre-existing divisions were not only re-produced but solidified in different relations in the wage labour system. (182)

Even within noncapitalist countries like the GDR, Barrett notes, fundamental in-equalities remain.[26] Though the exact relationship between domestic work and wage labor is a matter of great debate, it seems legitimate to claim that exploited labor-power within the home is no less alienated than comparable work outside the home.[27]

And yet, though we are not obligated to take her word for it, we should not overlook the fact that Karen directly addresses and denies the supposition that do-mestic work is tantamount to alienated labor. In a letter to Peters, she writes:

The formulas that say that a woman shrivels up as a person between wash-bucket and stove and doesn't really work when she's only a wife and mother because her life—seen from outside—doesn't have any economic or otherwise quantifiable purpose—I'm honestly past such formulas, please believe me, it's not that at all, not even in a hidden corner of my heart. (29)

We can infer from this denial that Karen would not characterize her alienation as intrinsic to domestic labor as such, but rather as arising from the specific circum-stances of her home life. This impression is compounded by the fact that Karen is equally discontented when, in the early days of their marriage, she and Peters oc-cupy the opposite domestic roles. While she works as a notary public, he stays home to cook, clean, and take care of Bettina. Yet where housework had merely left her unsatisfied, this arrangement begins to produce physical symptoms of repulsion: "My revulsion toward judicial categories was no longer to be channeled into ratio-nal objections and began to take embarrassing forms: in meetings I would suddenly fall out of my chair, or I would throw up on irreplaceable documents" (205). Is this repugnant work, as Schmitz suggests, alienated?

In his *Economic and Philosophical Manuscripts,* Marx characterizes alienation as a product of the objectification of the worker, the exploitation of his labor power, and the appropriation of the product of his labor by the property owner: "The realization of labour is its objectification. In the sphere of political economy this realization of labour appears as a *loss of reality* for the worker, objectification as *loss of and bondage to the object,* and appropriation as *estrangement,* as *alienation*" (Marx, *Early Writings,* 324). It would be absurd to claim that Karen's high-level career exploits her labor power in the sense described by Marx. Far more, her profession

---

26. "The tenacity and intractability of gender ideology, and the failure of socialist societies to social-ize domestic labour and childcare to any significant degree, must lead to the conclusion that these pro-cesses are not restricted to capitalist systems of production" (186).

27. For an account of one such debate, see Maxine Molyneux, "Beyond the Domestic Labour De-bate." Barret draws attention to Molyneux's useful summary (173).

would make her one of the "planners and leaders," the East German elite. In fact, her elevated social position is precisely the problem both in her home life and in her career trajectory. From the "daily ordering, assessing, judging" (204–5) required by her leadership position to the accumulated "junk" of her middle-class home, Karen's very privilege—her *embourgeoisement*—seems to be at the root of her alienation.

This intriguing reversal of the Marxist paradigm, an inversion by which class privilege appears to cause social and self-estrangement, can be found in a number of texts from this period. The logic at work here is similar to the redoubled *ressentiment* described by Fredric Jameson in *The Political Unconscious*. In a chapter on the novels of George Gissing, Jameson turns Nietzsche's theory of *ressentiment*, the slavish resentment of one's masters, on its head:

> What is most striking about the theory of *ressentiment* is its unavoidably autoreferential structure. In *Demos*, certainly, the conclusion is inescapable: Gissing resents Richard [the novel's militant working-class hero], and what he resents most is the latter's *ressentiment*. We are perhaps now far enough distant from this particular ideologeme to draw a corollary: namely, that this ostensible "theory" [i.e., Nietzsche's theory of *ressentiment*] is itself little more than an expression of annoyance at seemingly gratuitous lower-class agitation, at the apparently quite unnecessary rocking of the social boat. It may therefore be concluded that the theory of *ressentiment*, wherever it appears, will always itself be the expression and the production of *ressentiment*. (202)

This autoreferential *ressentiment*, the resentment of resentment, can be seen in nearly every "planner-and-leader" narrative. For instance, it is behind the recurring trope identified by cultural historian Jochen Staadt as "the loneliness of the planner-leader": "They worry about their workers, while the latter only in exceptional cases show any concern for their harried leaders, upon whose shoulders rests the weight of broad economic, scientific-technical, and moral responsibilities" (81–82). The roots of worker-party estrangement, in other words, appear to reside in the workers' failure to appreciate the selfless efforts of the party leadership on their behalf. For Staadt, this estrangement would constitute an inversion of the actual conditions— a transposition, like the one described above, from privilege to alienation:

> Taken together, these factors account for the loneliness and solitary struggle of the heroes: as representatives of social progress, they still remain separated from the class to whom this progress is guaranteed because the leap over the shadow of their real prototypes (privileged state functionaries…) comes only at the price of a blatant distortion of real conditions. (84)

In *Karen W.*, the mutual *ressentiment* between "planners and leaders" and workers in the GDR can best be seen in Karen's relationship with her neighbor, Paul

Werlich. Karen's split with Werlich, the father of her first boyfriend, occurred just before she began studying law at the university. Home from boarding school, Karen visits Werlich to confront him about his continued obstinacy in resisting agricultural collectivization. In the ensuing argument, she accuses him of being a selfish petit bourgeois, and he calls her a "stuck-up and pigheaded girl" who, despite her education, has forgotten where her bread comes from (Tetzner, 69). This altercation is the essence of mutual *ressentiment:* Werlich resents Karen's presumption of knowing what is best for him, while Karen resents Werlich's resentment, made manifest in his stubborn refusal to recognize the benefits of communal farming.

Karen's biography illustrates the double-edged nature of the GDR's emphasis on the upward mobility of its working class. On the one hand, Karen's opportunity to attend a college-preparatory high school—as the first in her village to do so—typifies one of the real achievements of East German socialism. The party's efforts to make higher education readily available to workers and their children represented a concerted attempt to address the problem of class at the level of reproduction. As we have seen in the previous section, however, such initial mobility does not spell the end of class stratification. In fact, as Peter Zimmermann points out, to a certain degree it actually highlights the inequalities of the social system: "The socialist version of 'rags to riches' refutes exactly what it wants to prove, for this kind of ascent is only possible in a society in which social hierarchies have been largely maintained" (210).

This contradiction activates the utopian impulse behind Karen W.'s remotion. In leaving her bourgeoisified life in L. and moving to Osthausen, Karen redresses her drift away from her agrarian, working-class origins, traversing each of the divisions of labor represented by her personal trajectory: physical versus mental labor, agricultural versus urban production, domestic work versus work outside the home.[28] In Osthausen, Karen learns again "where her bread comes from," and even takes part in the process of agricultural production: to make ends meet, she gets a job picking potatoes on the local LPG (*Landwirtschaftliche Produktionsgenossenschaft,* a communal farm). She literalizes this learning process when she visits an egg factory near Osthausen. Noticing the distinctive packaging of these eggs, she thinks:

> I remembered when I first saw this silvery packaging on the shelf. I asked the cashier about this new kind of egg The women standing around jumped in: those are the eggs of chickens that never see the light of day, that never go outside, those aren't real eggs! At home I carefully tasted the yolk; tasted like real egg yolk. A few months later one took the silver packet off the shelf and put it in the shopping bag with butter and cheese. One didn't ask oneself: Why are there fresh eggs in February? One has forgotten that seven years before…there were only cold-storage eggs in the winter. (224–25)

---

28. For a more thorough examination of divisions of labor in *Karen W.,* see Staadt, 237–49.

In circumstances updated for the age of the factory farm, Karen discovers where eggs come from. This visit to the egg factory represents a twofold reconciliation. On the one hand, it symbolically reclaims her agrarian roots. By overcoming the urbanite's indifference to the origin of his or her food, Karen would shift her allegiance from the side of the consumer to the side of the producer.[29] At the same time, her tour of the factory represents a literal bid for rapprochement with Werlich: she has come to the factory to find him a job.

If Tetzner's novel ended here, it would be a fairly straightforward back-to-production narrative. Having decisively rejected her *embourgeoisement,* Karen would settle in Osthausen and work on the LPG. She would continue to live with Dieter Steinert, the veterinarian who had rented a room in her house and with whom she has gradually become more intimate. Her daughter would have the childhood she herself had left behind. Yet just when it seems that this provisional household might become permanent, might even increase, Karen balks. "I could live here with Dieter," she thinks (235), then continues:

Why not have a child with Dieter? A child is a child and a new beginning! We would live well together. We would give each other warmth and security. And one day I would not love him less than he loved me…what good would it do to ask for more? I lost what I had before. I'm turning thirty. I shouldn't want everything anymore.

And yet I blushed in the face of Dieter's fervent caresses like a liar. (236)

Karen suddenly decides to return to L., where she intends to renew her connection with Peters. "How long can one talk oneself out of a longing?" she asks by way of explanation (237).

Why does Karen return to Peters? Which is also to ask, why were they together in the first place? Their first real encounter is occasioned by a student hearing at the university in 1957. Peters stands accused of counterrevolution on account of his radical writings: "If we believe the magic formulas of the politicians and social scientists," he had written, "we have already overcome war and existential scarcity. I mean, the revolutions of many centuries cannot be finished with social changes. The most important step begins there: the freeing of the human being as a personality!" (111). Karen is intrigued by Peters's attitude and ideas, which are so out of keeping with the dogmatism of the times. "What kind of time and place was that?" Karen thinks later. "I was always getting tangled up for or against something, and every choice included the unchosen flip-side. Was there never a perfect, round yes? Not even in love?" (113).

Theirs is a relationship, then, based on the utopian ambitions of post-Stalinist reform. Peters is looking for "the freedom of the human being as a personality,"

---

29. At a more literal level, this process begins with her work on the LPG and culminates with her job at a similar egg factory near L.

Karen "a perfect, round yes." When she returns to Peters at the end of the book, Karen hopes to renew her earlier ideals and aspirations. "Consistent, wholehearted openness and trust!" Karen thinks on another occasion. "Who else could do it, if not lovers?" (120).

In this respect, the novel's two utopian impulses seem to be mutually contradictory: Karen's optimistic appraisal of love's potential contrasts with the disappointing results of her experiment in Osthausen. Thus, Staadt argues, *Karen W.* seems suspended between disillusionment and hope:

> Disillusionment with a society that can offer no general perspective on the possibility of overcoming fundamental social contradictions (the divisions of manual and intellectual labor, city and country). Hope in the readiness of the individual for personal revolt and noncompliance. This hope expresses itself in the encouragement to break out of preestablished roles, to refuse to adapt and subordinate oneself. But since this hope does not find itself born up by social progress, this literary anticipation of concrete utopia must find its expression in individual emotional depth and sensibility, the social unfolding of which remains unrepresentable. (253)

As much as Karen seems to be able to slough off and take on new roles more or less at will, one might ask whether her fellow potato-pickers in Osthausen have the same palette of choices available to them.[30] They are well aware of the class divide that separates them from Karen, as we learn when Karen defends the much-maligned potato-harvesting machines:

> "The first machines are always imperfect," I said. "The first cars were too, but in ten years…" I don't get any further. "Whaaat? Maybe the cows will believe that! Or are you going to eat bread this winter that'll be baked in ten years? You're one of them!" shouts Erna Meink. Everyone gangs up on me. They can finally unload their fury on a city slicker. (52–53)

Karen, it seems, has not made the transition from city to country, from intellectual to manual labor, as smoothly as she had hoped. Her planner-and-leader optimism and citified impracticality expose her to Erna Meink's *ressentiment,* which is every bit as virulent as Werlich's. Here, however, the foreman jumps to her defense: "She's standing here in the same muck as you!" (53). The logic of this retort mirrors the reasoning behind the Bitterfeld Way, which hoped to overcome social

---

30. To follow this line of thought, one could look to the debates within Western (Anglo-American) feminism in the late 1970s and 1980s over the role of class in the experience of gender, and vice versa. In this respect, East German feminist works were in a curious position: though necessarily materialist-Marxist in outlook, they could not adequately address the problem of class as a problem of women's emancipation. If the question could be raised at all, the available answers were limited.

stratification by enjoining writers, artists, and intellectuals to "stand in the same muck" as the workers.

Karen's decision to return to L., however, gives the lie to this "trading places" strategy of class convergence, for the experience of class is not entirely localizable to the production process but rather mediates all of one's attachments to the social environment. This view of class would be closer to Pierre Bourdieu's concept of a class habitus, "the internalized form of class condition and of the conditionings it entails" (101). According to Bourdieu, even the most apparently personal and arbitrary judgments of taste are in fact practices of class and as such are conditioned by one's familial, educational, and cultural background.

From this perspective, the driving conflict of *Karen W.* becomes the struggle between opposing modes of class habitus. In light of this internal tension, Karen's sojourn in Osthausen begins to take clearer form. The initial impulse to move to Osthausen arises from the friction generated between Karen's proletarian origins and the bourgeois class habitus demanded by her life in L. Once in Osthausen, however, the poles of this conflict reverse: now it is Karen's residual *embourgeoisement* that rankles, alienating her from her LPG coworkers and leaving her bored and frustrated with small-town life. While Karen is eventually able to adjust to most aspects of life in Osthausen, one barrier remains: she's left her heart in L.

Through this final twist of the novel's romantic plot, class habitus demands its due. The same social forces that raised Karen out of the working class—in particular, the privileges conferred by higher education—continue to draw her to Peters and her life in L. This is the "longing" she cannot talk herself out of. By this route, and in light of Karen's final decision in favor of Peters, we reach a conclusion quite different from the one the novel intends. In the end, Karen's rustication has contributed less to renewing her working-class ties than to breaking them. She has come to Osthausen, we might even conclude, precisely for the latter purpose. If the chief hindrance to Karen's well-being in L. is the residual class habitus of her upbringing, then it becomes possible to recast her return to Osthausen as a bid to remove this impediment. This process occurs through the resolution of her clash with Werlich.

That Werlich somehow impinges on Karen's happiness is suggested by a passage just before her visit to the egg factory. "Somewhere behind that dark hill," Karen thinks, looking out the window, "off to the east, Peters is walking through illuminated big-city streets, sits with friends, eats, sleeps, works—lives. And I can't get away from Werlich and can't live out my life" (212). Karen finally "gets away" from Werlich in the last pages of the novel. Having found him a job as a technician at the egg factory, she stops by his house to tell him about it. When she launches into a detailed description of his new opportunities and responsibilities, however, he cuts her off. In a drunken, paranoid rant, Werlich makes clear that he wants neither her job nor her sympathy.

In the context of the redoubled *ressentiment* theory outlined above, this conversation would absolve Karen of her culpability in the feedback loop of resentment.

She has tried to lead her stubborn neighbor into the Scientific-Technical Revolution. If he refuses her assistance, he has only himself to blame and no more right to resent her for her foresight than she has grounds to feel guilty for it. Or so she reasons, and returns to L. to start over with Peters. Ultimately, the reconciliation in question is as much with her own biography as with Werlich. In justifying her final rejection of Werlich, she also authorizes herself to enjoy the privileges of her well-earned—and socially necessary—middle-class status. If we generalize out of this logic, we discover a familiar ideological strategy, namely that of the "perspective of the planner and leader." In the forward march of progress, this is the class that sees the farthest; it therefore requires the highest cultural standing. When Karen W. decides finally to embrace her social role as a "planner and leader," she also validates the cultural dominance of the East German elite and secures the conditions of possibility for an established East German middle class.

Buridans Esel and *Karen W.* lead the reader to rather pessimistic conclusions about the possibility of overcoming class stratification within GDR society. *Karen W.'s* initial back-to-production enthusiasm and concluding subjectivist utopianism reveal themselves to be progressive facades over the novel's ideological raison d'être: to help clear the way for an expanding bourgeoisie of "planners and leaders." *Buridans Esel* takes a more explicitly skeptical position, presenting the allure of middle-class comfort and the temptation of pseudo-revolution as halves of the same whole. If *Buridans Esel* and *Karen W.* portray failed attempts at proletarization, the two texts discussed below are more optimistic about the durability of the protagonists' break with bourgeois complacency. Although *Die Legende von Paul und Paula* and *Es geht seinen Gang* share the basic romantic plot of the previous two novels, they achieve wholly different results.

"Paul is different from Paula": *Die Legende von Paul und Paula*

Heiner Carow's 1972 film, *Die Legende von Paul und Paula* (The Legend of Paul and Paula), may be the best-known East German love story of all. The most popular production in DEFA's history, Carow's film continues to enjoy cult status—so much so that Berlin's Börse cinema ran *Paul und Paula* several times weekly for eight years before closing in 2003 ("Wie soll das nur ohne 'Die Legende von Paul und Paula' weitergehen?" 23). Many reviewers have attributed the film's popularity to a universally and perennially engaging love story. In the words of a 2003 review from the *Neue Zürcher Zeitung,* "The film has retained its cult status. Young and old, from West and East, [even] people who did not experience the GDR are drawn into this story of a love that was stronger than communism" (Schwartz).

Like many classic love stories, *Die Legende von Paul und Paula* constructs a highly hermetic romantic scenario—a love story so fiercely independent that a viewer prone to Cold War cliché might call it "stronger than communism"—and challenges it with a similarly formidable social or economic impediment. Thanks to its relative autarky within the film's narrative economy, Paul and Paula's romance can navigate the perilous straits of class affiliation in "actually existing socialism."[31] These lovers accomplish the leap that was foreclosed in *Buridans Esel*: between the world of the "planners and leaders" and that of the *Hinterhaus*.[32] Yet the strain of doing so takes its toll; the problem of class ultimately shapes the tragic arc of the film's romantic plot.

After the film's title sequence, we see Paula, dressed in the brash height of 1970s fashion, exiting her apartment building, a crumbling Berlin *Altbau*. Paul, similarly stylish in Beatles-inspired hair and a leather jacket, steps out of a similar building down the street. As he walks past Paula, each mumbles hello and does a double take. This chance encounter is followed by another near miss at the Berlin fairgrounds, where Paula goes home with Colly, a carousel operator, and Paul with Ines, a shooting-gallery attendant. Paula lives with Colly until, returning from the hospital with his newborn child, she catches him in flagrante delicto with another woman. Paula kicks Colly out of her apartment and continues on as a single mother, struggling with the double burden of breadwinning and caregiving. Meanwhile, Paul marries Ines and begins a life trajectory more like Erp's or Karen W.'s: after finishing at the university, he becomes a high-ranking ministry official and moves into a posh new apartment building across the street from Paula's. In accordance with a logic by now familiar, Paul's bourgeois luxuries are bought at the price of an increasingly intolerable family life, and when he returns unexpectedly from his two years of army service, Paul finds Ines in bed with her lover. Though Paul and Ines patch things up, their marriage seems doomed. Ines remains as uncultured and materialistic as when they first met. The couple's spoiled son (who receives two identical new bicycles for Christmas) and Ines's parents, who are carnival barkers and inveterate capitalists, round out the picture.

Paul and Paula meet at a dance club, both seeking respite from their home lives. After a night together, they begin a tentative love-affair. The careerist in Paul equivocates about his commitment to the relationship, blaming the moral guidelines of his job. Paula, however, does not want to hear his excuses. As she covers and uncovers her ears, the film's sound cuts in and out. "My wife and I," Paul stammers, "that...she'll want a divorce right away. She's just waiting for a reason and I...can't afford a divorce in my position. There's no regulation against it, but that's

---

31. "Actually existing socialism" (*real existierender Sozialismus*) was the official term for the East German political system. It is used here (as it was in the GDR and still is in postcommunist scholarship, albeit sometimes ironically in the latter) to distinguish between the lived experience of the socialist order and socialist theory.

32. Joshua Feinstein also calls attention to the connection between Paul's class position and the preoccupations of East German public culture of the time: "Paul's position makes him precisely the *Leiter und Planer* (leader and planner) type celebrated in other DEFA films of the same era" (207).

how it is. They just tell me: Educate her!" (48). Paul's colleagues have a simple solution for the education gap in Paul's marriage: "Educate her!" This advice echoes
the party's broader strategy for ameliorating social friction in the GDR: with the
democratization of educational opportunity, the party reasoned, class difference
would simply wither away.

Instead of his wife, Paul tries to educate his mistress by taking Paula, against her
mild protestations, to a classical concert. By the end of the first movement, however,
the tables are turned. Moved to tears by the music, Paula stands up and applauds,
much to Paul's consternation. Eventually the entire audience joins in, inspired by
Paula's untaught, authentic enthusiasm. Surprised and pleased, the soloist takes a
bow. The next day, Paula takes Paul on an excursion of her own, an elaborate flight
of psychedelic fantasy. In this justifiably famous scene, Paul and Paula float down
a river on her bed—he wearing a ruffled tuxedo shirt, she a wedding dress—while
Paula's extended family looks on. In *The Triumph of the Ordinary: Depictions of
Daily Life in the East German Cinema,* Joshua Feinstein reads this moment as an
encounter between two modes of temporality:

> Inherent in this phantasmagorical image is nothing less than an alternative under-
> standing of time that contrasted markedly with the regime's transcendent vision of
> history. Here Paul, who as a family father and a loyal career man embodies conven-
> tional virtue, finds himself unable to resist the vital forces that Paula represents. If the
> premise of his lifestyle up to now has been the promise of steady material advance-
> ment in exchange for discipline, then she stands for an understanding of life empha-
> sizing cyclical renewal rather than endless horizons, tradition instead of progress.
> Thus Paul's vision is organized around a wedding, the rite of passage most closely as-
> sociated with genealogical replication. (209)

At her wedding, Paula literally introduces Paul into the continuity of proletarian
tradition: "This is Paul!" she says to her family. "I also have a son!" (Plenzdorf, 56).
That she mentions her son but not her daughter underscores the fact that this is a
question of symbolic lineage—apparently patrilineage. Paula comes from a long
line of bargemen, as she tells Paul in the previous scene:

> *[Paul] indicates the portrait of a stout old man in an oval frame that hangs in Paula's room.
> The man is wearing a sailor's uniform.*
>
> PAUL: Seadog, no?
> PAULA: Seadog?—We're rivermen! I was born on the "Paula." Six hundred tons—or
>   nearly. But the part about the six hundred tons is true. All women and all barges
>   are called Paula in our family . . .
> PAUL: So riverdog. And now?
> PAULA: Nothing. No men left in the family. Paul? Let's buy a barge! (52–53)

Now, with a raucous marriage ceremony aboard the barge "Paula," the family binds Paul to their line—actually draping heavy anchor chains over the couple.

Unsettled, perhaps, by the intensity of his connection to Paula—or perhaps by its implications for his career—Paul stays away for a few days, then makes it clear that for him the affair is over. "We can stay friends," he suggests. In the next scene Paula, visibly depressed, yells at her children for pestering her and sends them away with money to go to the movies. We see the children running toward the street, then hear squealing brakes. After the death of her son, Paula is inconsolable. She goes to work but otherwise withdraws from society completely. When Paul comes by her apartment, she turns him away: "You're right, Paul. What I want won't work. It had to happen this way" (68). Having given up on love, Paula begins to entertain the advances of Herr Saft, an elderly, well-to-do entrepreneur who has been wooing her unsuccessfully for years. A marriage to Saft would ensure a comfortable lifestyle and a secure future for her and her daughter. The trade-off for this security would be, if not happiness, certainly sexual desire: Paula tells her obstetrician she no longer needs birth control pills. "I'm getting married soon," she explains. "He's older, you see" (78).

Meanwhile, Paul has realized that he loves Paula after all. Although she refuses to speak to him, he camps out in front of her door and even follows her on an outing with Herr Saft. Finally, after he has missed a week of work, Paul's coworkers come to fetch him. Clean-shaven and wearing a new suit, Paul returns home to Ines with flowers, chocolates, and champagne, as well as a new bicycle for his son. It seems that this might become a remarriage narrative after all. Perhaps Paul, like Erp, will choose the path of comfort and career over life in the *Hinterhaus*. Back at home, Paul breaks out the champagne and sweet-talks Ines: "Let's drink to your beauty," he says. Suddenly he begins laughing, opens the closet door, and hauls out Ines's lover, who has been hiding there all along. "Let's do this another way," he says to them. "Another way entirely, colleagues!" (83). With that, the possibility of reconciliation with Ines collapses, and *Die Legende von Paul und Paula* diverges from the route taken by *Buridans Esel* and *Karen W.* Paul strides purposefully across the street and into Paula's building. When she does not answer his knock, he rings a neighbor's doorbell and requests an axe. The neighbor, who has hitherto glared with disapprobation at any goings-on in the stairwell, gladly hands over a massive woodsman's axe. As Paul batters down the door, Paula's elderly neighbors crowd around, shouting encouragement—an audience of well-wishers to match the throng of revelers at the barge wedding, most of whom were also of Paula's grandfather's generation.

Through a dramatic act of "mock chivalry" (Feinstein, 207), Paul turns his back on "planner-and-leader" *embourgeoisement* and interpolates himself into Paula's line. As we have seen in *Buridans Esel* and *Karen W.*, however, the initial *Aufbruch* (break, departure) alone does not constitute a revolutionary break with prevailing conditions. Significant change in this respect must be abiding, which is also to say, it must be reproducible. If Paul is to be inserted into the continuity of proletarian culture, the line must continue through and beyond him. Given this emphasis on lineage, it is not surprising that, to conclude the "legend," Paul and Paula would have a child together. Despite the near-fatal complications she experienced with the birth of her son, and against the grave warnings of her obstetrician, Paula insists that she wants a child with Paul. In the next scene, she descends into the darkness of a subway station. A sonorous voice-over declares: "Paula did not survive the birth of the child" (87).

The abrupt tragedy, even violence, of the film's ending can be read as symptomatic of unresolved anxiety in the film, of lingering doubts that disrupt the smooth resolution of the plot.[33] We might look for such anxiety in the film's underlying fantasy of the proletarization—or re-proletarization—of GDR culture in the 1970s. Like the other texts analyzed in this chapter, *Die Legende von Paul und Paula* responds to the GDR's increasingly pronounced class stratification and the growing hegemony of "planner-and-leader" culture by envisioning a scenario of class convergence through downward mobility. Where *Buridans Esel* and *Karen W.* cast doubt on the endurance of the protagonists' déclassé experiment, however, *Die Legende von Paul und Paula* sustains the new arrangement even into the next generation. The film's final shot is of Paul sleeping in Paula's bed with three children: Paula's daughter, Paul's son with Ines, and Paul's son with Paula.

Yet why does Paula have to be absent from this scene? How can we make sense of her death in light of the reading proposed here? In the film's internal logic, Paula's death is related to the leitmotif of destruction and renewal that runs through the film. This motif is most clearly captured in the demolition scenes that frame the narrative. At the beginning and end of the film we see footage of houses imploding, while the Puhdys (East Germany's Led Zeppelin) sing Ecclesiastes: "Jegliches hat seine Zeit / Steine sammeln, Steine zerstreuen" (For everything there is a season / A time to cast away stones, and a time to gather stones together") (9, 86). The script tells us that the final house to fall is Paula's, "the last old house on Paul and Paula's street" (87). According to Feinstein, the opening demolition sequence "efficiently establishes" one of the film's main themes, "the cyclical nature of human existence" (206). As he goes on to say, however, the endless replacement of old with new is not presented uncritically in Carow's film:

> [The] film's attitude towards progress as expressed in the ideological reinscription of urban space is at best ambivalent. Indeed, if anything, the lifestyle and the comfortable proletarian sociability that Paula represents appear threatened, an impression

---

33. h. sander and r. schlesier see this violence as a clear sign of the film's misogyny: "paula, the emotional, ambivalent woman-child finally has paul all to her self and can let her maternal instinct run wild again. she makes paul into the father of her third child, filled with the will-to-victimhood of the loving woman, since she knows she won't survive the birth.... paula's *liebestod* as self-sacrifice for a child from her beloved man is a fitting ending for this 'legend'" (22–23). Despite their overindulgent sarcasm and unsubtle argumentation, sander and schlesier make an important point: in Paula's maternal self-sacrifice, *Die Legende von Paul und Paula* falls all too easily into an age-old "patriarchal cult of the mother" (38).

heightened by premonitions of her premature death throughout the film. Arguably, the picture is ultimately about preserving what Paula embodies against the relentless pressures of supposed progress. (210–11)

Yet, while *Die Legende von Paul und Paula* is concerned with preserving the proletarian tradition embodied by Paula, the resolution of the film's narrative of class convergence also depends upon her disappearance; Paul's insertion into the lineage of the East German proletariat can endure only if the trace of difference that would exclude him from this lineage is removed. Just before the barge wedding scene, Paula and Paul discuss the question of difference as such:

> PAULA: Can you explain to me what an inequality [*Ungleichung*] is? My [daughter] asked a little while ago. Do you think I knew? Never learned that. One equals two?
> PAUL: Nonsense. One is smaller than two. That's an inequality.
> PAULA: Everyone knows that.
> PAUL: I'm bigger than you.
> PAULA: Everyone can see that.
> PAUL: You're different from me.
> PAULA: Of course! Where would we even start with each other otherwise?!
> PAUL: Be serious. Inequalities are...
> PAULA: I am. Very serious. Paul is different from Paula, particularly in certain...
> *Paul covers her mouth.* (Plenzdorf, 58)

Where Paula is interested here in the "little difference" of gender, Paul wants to focus on inequality: greater than, less than. In the latter sense, the governing inequality in this scene is (formal) knowledge: Paul, with his college education, sets out to teach Paula mathematics. Given this imbalance, we can imagine Paul and Paula's life together in terms of a familiar narrative, one in which a married couple from different educational and social backgrounds find these differences more difficult to negotiate than they had planned. In short, we would be right back where we started. The fantasy of proletarization at work in *Die Legende von Paul und Paula* can be maintained only by erasing the mark of difference that would give the lie to this vision of class convergence. The gap between the culture of the "planners and leaders" and that of the *Hinterhaus,* the film seems to suspect, is too wide to be bridged by love alone, however legendary. This symptomatic anxiety would help to account for the violence with which the plot casts Paula out, and the unequivocal finality with which Paul supplants her in the film's social universe.

"A typical GDR bourgeois": *Es geht seinen Gang*

Erich Loest's 1978 novel, *Es geht seinen Gang, oder Mühen in unserer Ebene* (It Runs Its Course, or Struggles at Our Level), presents one of the 1970s' most provocative

and involved literary explorations of the East German class system. The protagonist of Loest's novel is Wolfgang Wülff, a midlevel engineer at a washing-machine
factory. He and his wife, Jutta, live in a *Neubau* apartment building in the upscale
"Oktober" district of Leipzig. Wolfgang feels out of place in this posh neighborhood. As the son of a metal cutter he is, as he repeats throughout the novel, an *Arbeiterkind.* Like Karl Erp, Wolfgang married into his bourgeois lifestyle: Jutta, the
daughter of an industrialist, brought 43,576.56 marks into the marriage, as Wolfgang meticulously records (54). He feels much more comfortable, he tells us, in the
working-class neighborhood where his mother lives:

> I knew my way around in this neighborhood, I could talk to the people in any house,
> could sit at any table in a bar and say: I was a toolmaker, now I'm an engineer. Tool-
> maker is the king of all metalworking jobs, and engineer is so close to worker that
> every worker knows enough engineers to have a sense of it. If I were to say, I'm a his-
> torian or a doctor, it would be different. (28)

Significantly, there are no such bars near Wolfgang's new home. Instead of fre-
quenting bars, the residents of the "Oktober" district drink Bulgarian "Hemus"
wine in the comfort of their homes.

Though he misses the familiar sociability of his mother's neighborhood, Wolfgang is quite aware of the privileges that have been afforded him: "[I] found again
that I had it good, attractive wife and new apartment and a clever child…I lived
in a *Neubau,* was an engineer" (30). Though hardly at the top of his career ladder,
Wolfgang is far from the bottom. As his mother succinctly puts it, "Just be happy
you're not on the assembly line" (62). Like Karen W., Wolfgang feels uncomfort-
ably suspended between classes. Amid the bourgeois comforts of the "Oktober"
district he longs for the gritty familiarity of his mother's neighborhood, yet from
the perspective of the laborer, he is part of the managerial class, a "tie-wearer" and
"briefcase-carrier" (192).

Adding to this friction, Jutta is pressuring him to take courses to become a higher-
ranking *Diplomingenieur* (graduate engineer). She insists that the money and the
status are not at issue, but rather the principle. It is his duty, she says, to make the
most of the opportunities he has been given—he, like Karen W., was able to attend
a college-preparatory *Erweiterte Oberschule* (Extended High School) (55).

As Wolfgang explains it, his unwillingness to become a true "planner and
leader" goes deeper than laziness or complacency. He traces his reluctance to a
formative and traumatic encounter with state power: as a teenager, Wolfgang got
caught up in the Leipzig Beat riots of 1965.[34] When the police broke up the Leuschnerplatz demonstration, Wolfgang was attacked by a police officer and bitten by

---

34. For more on the Leipzig Beat riots, spontaneous demonstrations by young, frustrated rock-and-
roll fans, see chapter 2, p. 86.

a dog. This, Wolfgang explains to Jutta, his friends, his mother, and the reader, is the real reason that he eschews any position of power. In one formulation of this rationale, Wolfgang states: "I didn't want to work evenings and weekends, I didn't want to give myself digestion problems, but the main reason was this, that I didn't want to be a *boss,* that I dreaded the responsibility of power. I imagined the hot red face of the police officer in the Leuschnerplatz" (55).

In Wolfgang's view, his decision to remain a lowly engineer ought to be commended, rather than censured. Walking past the home of the district party secretary, one of his neighbors in the "Oktober" quarter, Wolfgang imagines receiving the public recognition his selflessness so richly deserves:

> I looked up at the windows of the high comrade and thought: Actually, you ought to be pleased with me. For whatever reason, I'm not increasing the oversupply of *Diplom*-engineers. On the contrary, I would be happy as a traveling washing-machine repairman. I imagined how the comrade would come out of the house and embrace me, in his hand a copy of *Die Aula,* one of the few books I've read, this book from the Stone Age, when every little bit of intelligence was scratched out of every corner. He'd say: Colleague Wülff, I congratulate your outstanding dialectical thinking! (80)

Here, as in *Buridans Esel, Die Aula* is used to signify the *Aufbau* period's sweeping changes in educational opportunity. Back in the "Stone Age," Wolfgang says, any and all educational advancement was necessary. Now, however, the Scientific-Technical Revolution's emphasis on qualification has led to an overabundance of planners and leaders.

Continuing with his fantasy, Wolfgang frames his story as a kind of anti-planner-and-leader narrative: "I imagined that a writer would interview me about my ideas and goals and write a book: a man forgoes a course of study and returns to his job as a toolmaker and works in three shifts" (80). This reversal levels criticism at the growing hegemony of planner-and-leader culture in the GDR. If this is a workers' state, why does its public culture foreground the managerial and intellectual elite? Shouldn't voluntary proletarization be a plausible—even an ideal—plot trajectory? Wolfgang's reverie then takes him into the party secretary's apartment:

> He had three children, I imagined. They sat peacefully at the table and ate potatoes with cheese and talked about their career goals. One was going to be a petty officer in the army, another was traveling to Orenberg for two years to work as a welder on the natural-gas pipeline, a daughter wanted to be a spinner in a three-shift factory; she had been offered a place in medical school but had turned it down. The second daughter wanted to become a *Zoo-Technikerin,* as we say—one used to say milkmaid. I thought: *Listen, comrade, on your honor, if you had four children, and they became a petty officer, a welder, a spinner, and a milkmaid, would you be happy about it? Would you be proud?* (80–81, italics mine)

Wolfgang's flight of fancy enables him to ask a naïve and incisive question, one that exposes the problem of class reproduction in the GDR. Why does it seem unlikely that this powerful official's children would forgo university to work in three shifts? Why is Wolfgang skeptical about whether the comrade would be happy, satisfied, and proud if his family did not reproduce as planners and leaders?

By the late 1970s the view that the GDR was a class society was not a heretical one. More problematic, however, was the increasingly undeniable actuality that the proletariat was not in fact East Germany's ruling class. One of the SED's strategies to overcome this dilemma was to expand the definition of working class to include party officials and technical intelligence. This expansion process seems to be underway in *Es geht seinen Gang:* Wolfgang's friend Wilfried Neuker, a historian, reveals at one point that he is part of a secret commission dealing with the definition of the working class, in particular the designation "of working-class origins" (186). Wolfgang sees immediately the personal implications of this inquiry: "I said: 'That's important for your son, if he wants to get into the EOS.'" As intelligentsia, the Neukers are having trouble getting their son Peter into the *Erweiterte Oberschule.* Wilfried's work with the commission might clear away such problems. Wilfried clarifies that the committee is in fact investigating "[what] the concept of class consciousness [means] today" (186).

This correction is significant. As indicators of working-class legitimacy, there is a considerable difference between class origin and class consciousness. In practical terms, the latter would include—even privilege—the political and intellectual elite (such as Wilfried). Meanwhile, Wolfgang, though an *Arbeiterkind,* has a highly questionable sense of class consciousness. "Everything has to fall into your lap," scolds his colleague Huppel, an old Communist Party veteran and ABF alumnus. He continues:

> "No interest in art, ideology, politics. Now tell me without thinking about it, off the top of your head: What do you think of when I ask, What's the difference between the GDR and the FRG?"
>
> "Spee und Dash, Trabbi und Volkswagen, Buschner und Schön."[35]
>
> "I thought so."
>
> "And what should I have answered?"
>
> "Who owns the means of production."
>
> "But I know that!"
>
> "Yes," said Huppel sadly. "You learned it, of course. But, believe me, back when I was an ABF student, you could have woken any one of us up in the middle of the night and asked that question, [and] he would have hit the nail on the head."
>
> "Yeah, back then."
>
> "Yes, Wolfgang.... You're a typical GDR bourgeois [Bist 'n typischer DDR-Spießer]." (212)

---

35. Wolfgang lists laundry detergents, cars, and soccer stars from East and West.

For Wolfgang, class ties are not predicated on consciousness ("art, ideology, politics") but rather on an unconscious set of shared interests and concerns—in short, on a shared habitus. Thus he asks Wilfried, only half facetiously, whether it was class consciousness "when as a 'Chemie' fan I carried my green-and-white banner to Leutzsch? We were all workers" (186). Though Wilfried dismisses this model of class affiliation as "clique mentality" (186), Wolfgang's point has been made. What really unites the East German working class, he suggests, is soccer.

In his descriptions of the working-class bar, Wolfgang advances a model of proletarian solidarity based not on politics or ideology but rather on entertainment, sports, and gossip:

> These people watched sports and variety-shows, they pontificated about Udo Lattek [a West German soccer star] and Rudi Carrell [a West German entertainer], and when an East German soccer team played a West German one, they rooted for the one from the GDR. They talked about politics only when something big was going on.... They rarely complained about the government, since complaining, they'd long since realized, doesn't help at all.... In these bars no one ever talked about a book or a play and certainly not about a concert. The debate about whether it was better in the East or in the West had run out of steam. There was always some Kurt Fritsche who was having an affair or a Helmut Paulik who had got in an accident or a Wolfgang Müller who was buying drinks. (28–29)

This is the class to which Wolfgang feels he belongs. It is less a bond of material circumstance than of shared mental and geographical disposition: "Others say: I'm from the country, from Silesia, from the working class, from a doctor's family. I can say: I come from this apartment, from the neighborhood behind Thälmannstraße, from East Leipzig; I talk like they talk here, I think like they think here" (89). Rather than focusing on the ownership of the means of production or the relative position of the worker within the relations of production, Wolfgang sees the operative differences between East and West as those of dialect, soccer allegiance, television personalities, and brand names. What seems to define the East German proletariat is precisely the refusal to engage with political distinctions of class consciousness. In this light, Wolfgang's rejection of power becomes more specifically a rejection of politics; to become a "planner and leader," he would have to discontinue his apolitical stance, and with it his working-class affiliation.

With this in mind, we can better understand the stakes of the marriage narrative that frames the plot of Loest's novel. As in the three texts discussed previously, the love plot in *Es geht seinen Gang* figures broader questions of social status and class mobility. Here, however, affective ties do not mediate class but rather constitute it, for if proletarian sensibility entails a refusal of class consciousness (in the Marxist sense), then class becomes an elective affinity, a product of one's attachments and desires, which in turn are conditioned by the circumstances of geography, family, and education. Thus, after agonizing throughout the novel about his relation to production—should he move up the ladder or down?—Wolfgang finally decides that his real problem is love. When the tension between his apathy and Jutta's ambition becomes too great, they decide to separate. He moves back in with his mother and reacquaints himself with her neighborhood. "I was working class again," he says (215). Now he is in the position to look for a partner who accepts him as he is, rather than as what he might become.

Eventually Wolfgang begins dating Margrid, a clerk at the post office. When he first sees Margrid, he mistakes her for Jutta: "After I few seconds I realized it wasn't Jutta, but a woman of her type; she had eyes like Jutta and a haircut like Jutta, and when she looked up, it was almost Jutta's gaze" (207). Unlike Jutta, however, Margrid is perfectly satisfied with Wolfgang's lack of ambition:

> I said: "And what if I worked as a metal cutter?"
>
>   "Do you want to?"
>
>   "I mean: Would you mind?"
>
>   "As long as I didn't have to cut." Margrid didn't seem to notice what I was driving at; Jutta's way of thinking was alien to her: "As long as you didn't have to work night shifts." (216)

In the final pages of *Es geht seinen Gang,* Wolfgang and Margrid settle into a life corresponding neither to Wolfgang's proletarian origins nor to Jutta's social-climbing aspirations, but rather to a comfortable, middle-class contentment. In an ongoing imaginary conversation with Huppel, the representative both of the revolutionary proletarian tradition and the party line, Wolfgang defends this contentment as a sign not of his own complacency but of socialism's success:

> Huppel, old Huppel, everything was different back in your day, you don't have to tell me. Of course you didn't arrange cold cuts and drink Hemus, but didn't you *long* for meat and wine? Didn't you *fight* for them? Or what were you fighting for? And why do you blame me for being content, isn't contentment the ideal? I do my work—ah, let's drop it, good old Huppel, if you don't get it by now, all the talk in the world won't help. (222)

In its very success, then, socialism seems to have driven a wedge between the party and the people. In this account, the politicization of everyday life demanded by party doctrine would only disturb the well-being of its citizens. Despite its internal tensions and contradictions, East German society seems to have achieved a certain equanimity. It has become postclass, but not in the way envisioned by the architects of East German socialism. Where politicized class-consciousness ought to have rallied the various social groups to the flag of the working class, the masses chose their own standard of differentiation. In the social world of *Es geht seinen Gang* there are two classes: the political and the apolitical. Within the latter, larger group, minor distinctions of income, status, or schooling do not disrupt the broader solidarity, a group cohesion based on the trials and satisfactions of East Germanness. In this way Wolfgang and Margrid's domestic pleasures—cold cuts and Hemus and a comfortable apartment—become signs of community and belonging, rather than of isolating privilege:

> Margrid brought a bottle from the kitchen: "Would you open this?" It was Hemus. I popped the cork and poured the wine, we made a toast and took a sip and gave each other a kiss, we ate salami and tatar and ham and cheese like thousands of people in Schönefeld and on Oktoberstraße and in Cranzahl and Gormorgsschdodd [Karl-Marx-Stadt] at the same time…
>
> …
>
> "You—it's nice being with you."
> "And with you." (222–24)

In this light, *Es geht seinen Gang* becomes a kind of remarriage narrative, one that recaptures the best aspects of Wolfgang's marriage with Jutta while bypassing the frictions—especially the lingering irritant of class difference—that led to its dissolution. For the founders of the East German socialist experiment, with their ideals of social leveling and permanent revolution, this solution would seem a contemptible and dangerous resignation. From the perspective of the GDR's apolitical class, however, it would represent a logical division between useful and futile, controllable and uncontrollable, participation in the social sphere. As Loest explains in an introductory note addressed to "spatially and temporally removed readers," that is, to his Western audience: "The phrase 'Es geht seinen Gang' [It runs its course], which was popular in the early '70s in the GDR, combines both a certainty of the forward march of society and a capitulation before the intensity of its pace" (5).

Returning to the guiding question of this book, we can ask, why does each of the texts examined here turn to a romantic plot to frame its treatment of class mobility? As in the texts and films already examined in chapters 1 and 2, the love stories considered here constitute a response to a vexing impasse within East German ideology: in this case, an aporia concerning the dynamics of socialist social reproduction. According to official theory, a transformed mode of production and greater educational opportunity ought to have elevated the whole working class. Indeed, the proletariat, as we read in the East German government study *Zur Entwicklung der Klassen und Schichten in der DDR* (On the Development of the Classes and Social Strata in the GDR), "is a class with a constantly increasing level of education" (Parteihochschule "Karl Marx," 96). In practice, however, the revolutionization of the educational system simply led to the creation of a new socialist elite, a bourgeoisie of "planners and leaders." Rather than raising their class with them, those workers who attended university, qualified for higher-status positions, or assumed management roles simply ceased to be working class. By this token, Karl Erp, Karen W., and Paul all find that their proletarian roots have been severed by their upward mobility.

Yet this continuous retrenchment of the working class had less to do with the failure of the party's efforts to elevate the proletariat than with the self-definition of East Germany's workers. As the above discussion of *Es geht seinen Gang* points out, East Germany's proletariat, though relatively disenfranchised for a ruling class, asserted control over the politics of inclusion and exclusion. The lines of in and out were not drawn according to the Marxist blueprint of politicized class-consciousness but rather traced the vague outlines of habit, taste, and tendency. As Wolfgang Engler puts it in the chapter "Eine arbeiterliche Gesellschaft" (A Workerly Society) in his study *Die Ostdeutschen,*

> The East Germans lived in a society in which the workers dominated socially and culturally and more or less "workerized" [*verarbeiterlichten*] the other social groups.
>
> It would be absurd to claim that East German workers wielded the political power. But they held the social scepter in their hand. Outlooks, opinions, social conventions, clothing, and consumption habits and everyday customs conformed to the norms and ideals of the working class. (200)

By ceding the political, Engler claims, the working class seized the reins of social reproduction in the GDR: "The 'vanguard role' of the working class seems to have gone a very different way than the one foretold by [Marxist] ideology—more social and familial than political and organized" (190). To the degree that the *Arbeiterklasse* became the arbiter of class, the legitimacy claims of party and state faltered. In the Workers' and Peasants' State, it seemed, political power was by no means in the hands of the workers and peasants, but rather in those of the scientific, intellectual, and political elite—who, despite their best efforts, remained categorically excluded from the putative ruling class, the workers. Against this backdrop of destabilized legitimacy, the cross-class love affairs examined in this chapter take on a distinct ideological valence. In each of these narratives, a "planner and leader" looks to a representative of the working class to relegitimate his or her proletarian credibility. This love affair then becomes a corrective affinity, a compensatory union that would undo the drift away from his or her class of origin. Karl Erp hopes that a sojourn in Broder's *Hinterhaus* apartment will validate his revolutionary self-image. Karen Waldau seeks rapprochement with Werlich and debates staying in the country with Dieter. After some wavering, Paul forces himself into Paula's life and lineage. Wolfgang Wülff, however, does not need outside legitimation. Although his job would locate him in the management class, he feels like a worker. And this, by the curious logic of class-as-habitus, seems proof enough that he is.

4

W(H)ITHER EROS?

*Gender Trouble
in the GDR, 1975–1989*

L'amour est à réinventer.

—ARTHUR RIMBAUD, "Une saison en enfer"

Die Liebe muß wieder erfunden werden.

—One of the mottos adopted by the "Nonsense Council" (*Unsinnskollegium*) of
witches and fools in Irmtraud Morgner's *Amanda: Ein Hexenroman*

Love must be reinvented.

In 1993, Nancy Lukens and Dorothy Rosenberg published an anthology of
translations called *Daughters of Eve: Women's Writing from the German Democratic
Republic*. In their preface, they explain that the title of the anthology is borrowed
from *Evastöchter,* Renate Apitz's volume of short fiction, "whose title is a tongue-
in-cheek reference to an uncomplimentary German term for a stereotypical female
and, in the GDR context, clearly ironic" (vii–viii).[1] In the starkly secular GDR, this
biblical reference calls attention to itself: when scientific evolutionism is doctrine,
what would it mean to claim (even metaphorical) descent from Eve? To judge
from the frequency of its appearance, the Eve myth retained a privileged position
in the allegorical imagination of the GDR—especially, as Lukens and Rosenberg's
anthology reminds us, for authors invested in the question of women's equality.
Indeed, the Genesis story consolidates the key themes of East German feminist (or
parafeminist) writing in the 1970s and 1980s.[2] On the one hand, the prelapsarian

1. In their *Deutsches Wörterbuch* (German Dictionary), Jakob and Wilhelm Grimm define "Even-
tochter" as a "vain, lightheaded girl."
2. The term "feminist" is a perennial problem in East German cultural studies. As Patricia Herminghouse notes, "When enthusiastic readers in the West furnished GDR women writers of the new

scene of Edenic harmony and companionship resonates with the utopian impulse in these works, which never cease trying to envision a more perfect union, whether interpersonal or political. The asymmetrical punishments meted out to Adam and Eve, on the other hand, encapsulate the imbalances of historically, culturally, or biologically conditioned gender roles:

> To the woman [God] said, "I will greatly multiply your pain in childbearing; in pain you shall bring forth children, yet your desire shall be for your husband, and he shall rule over you." And to Adam he said, "Because you have listened to the voice of your wife, and have eaten of the tree of which I commanded you, 'You shall not eat of it,' cursed is the ground because of you; in toil you shall eat of it all the days of your life." (Genesis 3:16–17)

Such explicit thematization of the division between "productive" and "reproductive" labor helps to account for the recurrence of this biblical leitmotif in East German gender discourse. As Julia Kristeva writes in her 1993 essay "Women's Time," this split represents a fundamental aporia in the Marxist understanding of human activity:

> Socialist ideology, which is founded on the idea that human beings are determined by their relation to *production,* has ignored the role of the human being in *reproduction* and the *symbolic order.* As a result, socialist ideology has been compelled, in its totalizing, if not totalitarian, spirit, to believe that the specific nature of women is unimportant, if not nonexistent. (209–10)[3]

Simone de Beauvoir makes a similar observation in *The Second Sex,* where she raises questions about the role of women—or lack thereof—within socialism:

> [The] fate of woman and that of socialism are intimately bound up together, as is shown also in Bebel's great work on woman. "Woman and the proletariat," he says, "are both downtrodden." Both are to be set free through the economic development consequent upon the social upheaval brought about by machinery. The problem of woman is reduced to the problem of her capacity for labour. Puissant at the time when techniques were suited to her capabilities, dethroned when she was no longer

---

generation with the label 'feminist,' this designation was usually rejected emphatically, since feminism was generally seen as a bourgeois attempt to reach women's liberation through the battle of the sexes rather than through an attack on the economic basis of oppression" ("Schreiben in gewendeten Verhältnissen," 478). Some cultural historians prefer a variant of the blanket term "women's writing," which has the dual disadvantage of implying a uniform agenda on the part of women writers and of excluding male authors concerned with the questions of gender equality.

3. Cheryl Dueck's study *Rifts in Time and in the Self: The Female Subject in Two Generations of East German Women Writers* alerted me to Kristeva's critique of the suppression of gender difference in socialist ideology; see esp. Dueck, 80–81.

in a position to exploit them, woman regains in the modern world her equality with man.... And when the socialist society is established throughout the world, there will no longer be men and women, but only workers on a footing of equality. (55)

The otherwise laudable analyses of Bebel and Engels, writes Beauvoir, are "disappointing" in their lack of depth and detail regarding the specificities of women's historical conditions. As she argues later,

> Woman cannot in good faith be regarded simply as a worker; for her reproductive function is as important as her productive capacity, no less in the social economy than in the individual life. In some periods, indeed, it is more useful to produce offspring than to plough the soil. Engels slighted the problem, simply remarking that the socialist community would abolish the family—certainly an abstract solution. (58)

According to Kristeva and Beauvoir, any advances for women brought about by socialism come at a price: an increased stake in the sphere of production is bought at the cost of a devaluation of reproduction. Though the political economy of industrial labor is laid bare by socialist social analysis, the value of both biological and social reproduction is effaced. In chapter 3 I suggested that the GDR's reluctance to confront the pressing question of reproduction returned symptomatically in the ubiquitous broken marriages of 1970s domestic narratives. Here, following Kristeva and Beauvoir, we see the wider consequences of the GDR's exclusive privileging of production. In disavowing reproduction, socialist ideology also elided gender difference: to paraphrase Beauvoir, where social activity is assumed to be coterminous with the sphere of work, "there will no longer be men and women."

Like these passages from Kristeva and de Beauvoir, many of the literary texts analyzed in this chapter make the case that biological reproduction constitutes the basis of an irreducible and ineluctable difference—a difference ignored at the peril of both the individual and society. In the wake of the deconstructionist strategies epitomized by the work of Judith Butler, such an emphasis on inherent gender difference may seem to veer toward an outdated and problematic essentialism. As Butler puts it in *Gender Trouble: Feminism and the Subversion of Identity*, "Recourse to an original or genuine femininity is a nostalgic and parochial ideal that refuses the contemporary demand to formulate an account of gender as a complex cultural construction" (36). More specifically, Butler takes issue with the prominent position of reproduction within Kristeva's theoretical system:

> Kristeva understands the desire to give birth as a species-desire, part of a collective and archaic female libidinal drive that constitutes an ever-recurring metaphysical reality....
>
> Insofar as Kristeva conceptualizes this maternal instinct as having an ontological status prior to the paternal law, she fails to consider the way in which that very law might well be the *cause* of the very desire it is said to *repress*. (*Gender Trouble*, 90)

In terms of the texts analyzed below, Butler's argument would suggest that it is not the case, as Kristeva claims, that socialism *represses* the archaic species-desire of women, but rather that paternalist socialism *causes* these texts to understand women's desire in terms of a repressed maternal "instinct." Do these texts, then, simply fall behind the curve set by contemporary feminist theory?

In her article "The American Feminist Reception of GDR Literature," Angelika Bammer juxtaposes developments in Western feminist theory and trends in East German literature. She suggests that 1980s East German women's writing was moving backward relative to Western feminist theory. In the 1970s, Anglo-American and West German feminists tended to focus on the problem of women's oppression as a transhistorical and transcultural phenomenon, a phenomenon rooted ultimately in the primary and essential difference between men and women. By the late 1980s, however, the emphasis had shifted: "The focus was now on the construction and role of gender in identity formation and its effect on the relations of power in both public and private spheres. From an insistence on the otherness of women, feminist attention had shifted to the otherness among and in women" (22). Following the signposts of deconstruction and Lacanian psychoanalysis, Western feminism was dismantling universalist notions of gender and identity. Meanwhile in the East, Bammer claims, a shift in the opposite direction was underway. Where GDR literature in the 1970s had subjected universalist categories of gender difference to radical materialist critique—in contradistinction to the more ahistoricist, cultural-feminist Western approach—it reversed this trend in the following decade:

> [In] the GDR [of the 1980s], precisely those writers most identified in the West with feminism, notably [Irmtraud] Morgner and [Christa] Wolf were producing texts like *Amanda* and *Kassandra* that to Western feminist ears had a distinctly cultural-feminist ring. This shift, not only in tone but, more importantly, in a view of history, is particularly striking in *Kassandra* where women are defined not only as separate from men, but in opposition to them. In *Kassandra* Wolf depicts the struggle for survival in gender terms. Moreover, as this text puts it, this struggle has the givenness of the mythic dimensions in which the narrative is cast. Gender, in other words, is not deconstructed, as had become critical practice in the West: rather, it is set in place with a vengeance. (22)

While the feminisms of West and East may indeed have been ships passing in the night, I will argue that the East German focus on "essential" difference, which seemed like a kind of theoretical atavism to Western feminists, was in fact a strategic response to the East German socialist context. In this sense, the East German example would approximate what Gayatri Chakravorty Spivak refers to as "strategic essentialism": "a *strategic* use of positivist essentialism in a scrupulously visible political interest" (205). In confronting the persistence of patriarchal domination within "actually existing socialism," East German feminist texts reached for the language of radical difference, a language foreclosed by socialist ideology's very definition of the human. Human existence, in East German Marxist understanding, was defined by the labor process: as we saw in chapter 2, the 1973 *Kleines politisches Wörterbuch* (Compact Political Dictionary), a standard reference for ideological correctness, endorses Engels's designation of work as "the prime basic condition for all human existence, and this to such an extent that, in a sense, we have to say that labour created man himself" ("Arbeit," 47).[4]

The productionist bias exemplified by this quotation and identified by Beauvoir and Kristeva also governs Siegfried Schnabl's description of the role of women under socialism in his canonical sex and marriage manual *Mann und Frau intim* (Husband and Wife Intimate), first published in 1971. After cataloging the ways in which women have been oppressed throughout history, Schnabl turns his attention to the new social order of the GDR:

> All of these considerations culminate in the understanding that the development of the personality of every woman is dependent upon her full social equality....
>
> Therefore the professional life of women in socialist society is not the consequence of an increased need for labor power or simply a means by which to raise the living standard of the family. For every individual woman, work entails objectively and subjectively meaningful social activity, the development of her personality, and therefore also growth in her relationship with her husband and children. In other words, the right to a career is a prerequisite for the meeting of equal human beings in partnership and love. (21)

In its characterization of gender parity as a question primarily of equal access to "meaningful social activity," that is, work outside the home, Schnabl's officially sanctioned, state-sponsored treatise explicitly echoes party doctrine. He quotes article 20 of the GDR constitution, which declares: "Men and women have equal rights in all areas of social, political, and personal life. Society and state must strive for the advancement of women, *especially in occupational development*" (22, italics mine). Taken at its word, the GDR might indeed have seemed to be the society of sexless workers envisioned by Beauvoir.[5]

Yet, as we saw in chapter 3, the GDR's declining birthrate highlighted the need to address the tricky question of biology: if *production* enjoys such extravagant pride of place, then how will society *reproduce* itself? Indeed, in practice genderless

---

4. See chapter 2, p. 61.

5. In the popular imagination of the West—and, to some extent, of the East—this stereotype launched a thousand lampoons. One thinks of the satirically unfeminine apparatchik Ninotchka in the eponymous Lubitsch film, Horst Buchholz's fiery but innocent Otto Piffl in Wilder's *One, Two, Three*, the caricature of the "manly" East German female athlete after the 1980 Olympic doping scandal, or the chaste socialist-realist "romance" parodied in the *Stacheltier* episode analyzed in chapter 1 (pp. 38–39).

productionism was tempered by a more pragmatic understanding of sex difference and erotic desire. East German psychologist Heinz Dannhauer's formulation of this view in his 1973 study *Geschlecht und Persönlichkeit* (Gender/Sex and Personality) deserves quotation at some length:

> The relationships between men and women are not simply "natural," but rather are characterized above all by their social content. The sexes are, however, fundamentally destined for completion in partnership. This partnership is not just to be seen in the striving for bodily union, but also in the manifold emotional forms of contact between men and women....Fundamental psychic sex-differentiation can be found in sexual and erotic appetency, as well as in diverse behaviors that are directed toward the opposite sex. A further psychic differentiation exists in the different biological functions of the sexes. (187)

Here the text breaks for a quotation from a previous study by Rolf Borrmann:

> The woman is subject to burdens that no one can take away from her. Pregnancy and motherhood as the consequences of her biological role characterize the realm of her particular burdens and duties. Society must take the particular situation of the respective sex into consideration. (Borrmann, 27; qtd. in Dannhauer, 187)

It is interesting that Dannhauer calls in East German educator and sexologist Borrmann, author of the 1966 *Jugend und Liebe* (Youth and Love), to deliver the crux of this message. Perhaps Dannhauer wants to distance himself from the biological imperative, which is so inconvenient to his previous assertions about social conditioning. Or perhaps Borrmann functions as a kind of reverb effect, amplifying the claim into a chorus of authority. In any case, the accent here on "burdens" (*Belastungen*) and "duties" (*Pflichten*) is meant to be offset by a later emphasis on state support of working mothers:

> Even in our society, women are responsible for much of the care and welfare of children in the first years of life. This societal division of labor between women and men seems sensible and natural. In antagonistic class society, the biological and social role of motherhood leads to the disadvantage of women. Only in socialist society is it possible to configure the living conditions of women in such a way that no social disadvantages arise from her duties as mother. Numerous provisions have been made in our society to aid women in their duties....
>
> Socialist society cannot create all the necessary conditions for the complete equality of women in just a few decades (full-day education for children, places in day care and kindergarten for all children, care for children in cases of sickness, creation of the necessary service industries to assist with housework). Within the objectively

existing possibilities, however, we have to push for the socially optimal version. We must create the objective conditions to help women keep up with all their commitments. (Dannhauser, 187, 193–94)

Such state assistance is necessary if women are to achieve meaningful equality, since, as it is defined here, "the realization of the equality of women demands equal standing in all social sectors, *especially in production*" (193, italics mine). Taken together, these statements present East German women with an ultimatum and a quandary. The message seems to be the following: *Real* meaning may be found in social activity, that is, work outside the home, but your duties also lie elsewhere. Fortunately, the state will help make this necessary nuisance more tolerable.

If this formulation seems extreme, it is less so than the conclusions reached by the narratives examined in this chapter. These stories and novels undertake a radical interrogation of the roles and duties imposed on women (and, as we will see, on men) in East German socialist society. The first set of texts, all taken from the 1975 anthology *Blitz aus heiterm Himmel* (Bolt from the Blue), puts the universalist utopianism of socialist ideology to the test. The anthology's stories of gender turmoil ask, what happens to interpersonal relationships, especially erotic relationships, when the variable of gender difference is changed? The results range from the disastrous to the miraculous.

When one of the stories intended for *Blitz aus heiterm Himmel,* a riotous sex-change fantasy by Irmtraud Morgner, proved too racy for the censor's sensibilities, it found its way into Morgner's extraordinary 1974 montage novel, *Leben und Abenteuer der Trobadora Beatriz* (Life and Adventures of Trobadora Beatrice). This chapter will offer a reading of *Trobadora Beatriz* with particular emphasis on its framing love story: an 800-year search for a man worthy of love. Morgner's *Amanda: Ein Hexenroman* (Amanda: A Witch Novel), the 1983 sequel to *Leben und Abenteuer der Trobadora Beatriz,* radicalizes the social critique of the earlier work to suggest that the problem lies not only in contingent asymmetries in social roles, but also in the fundamentally different needs and desires of men and women. This standpoint underlies the novel's distrustful depiction of heterosexual romantic love, which appears only in its negative instance, as one more weapon of the patriarchy. In the final section of this chapter, I consider Morgner's unfinished (and perhaps unfinishable) novel *Das heroische Testament* (The Heroic Testament), which attempts to answer the open question of the previous two works: is there hope for love in the face of so much injustice and inequality? And if not, why is its lure so irresistible? Knowing the well is poisoned, why does one drink again and again?

Eros and (S)Exchange: *Blitz aus heiterm Himmel*

In 1975, the Hinstorff Verlag in Rostock published a volume of short stories called *Blitz aus heiterm Himmel* (Bolt from the Blue). The anthology, which was edited by

Edith Anderson, contains short stories by three women and four men, all of which revolve around the theme of *Geschlechtertausch:* women becoming men and men becoming women—literally—through scientific or magical means.[6] As Anderson put it in the exposé she wrote to convince first the Aufbau publishing house (unsuccessfully), then Hinstorff, to take on the project, "Let us place ourselves in the skin of the opposite sex and just for once, instead of envying, resenting, despising it—or desiring, loving, worshiping it—picture how we would feel if the positions were reversed. Might this not be a salutary game for the whole of society? . . . It would be an attempt to cast light on regions that have been too long in the dark, first and foremost in ourselves" ("Genesis and Adventures of the Anthology," 4). As Anderson's prospectus illustrates, this project belongs to the pattern identified by Bammer as characteristic of the 1970s in East Germany. In this "game for the whole of society," one cannot speak of an "essential" male or female experience; gender, in Anderson's description, is only skin-deep.

In this light, the publishing history of *Blitz aus heiterm Himmel* has a great deal to say about gender discourse on both sides of the Wall. When the book was republished in the West in 1980 as *Geschlechtertausch* (Sex Change), it had undergone a *Geschlechtertausch* of its own: only three of the stories remained, all by women. At the risk of reading too much into this editorial decision (which may have had as much to do with the vagaries of licensing as anything) we may hypothesize that it reflects the tendency of Western feminism in the 1970s and early 1980s to view the experience of gender as women's experience—one consequence of the "essentialism" discussed in the above-quoted Bammer passage. Whatever its rationale, the decision to publish *Geschlechtertausch* as a volume of women's writings undermined the innovation of the book's original version, which anticipated later developments in gender theory in its insistence on the universal dissemination of gender norms. Four examples from the original volume will illustrate some of the valences of this premise and set the stage for an account of its reappraisal in the literature of the following decade.

Günter de Bruyn's contribution to *Blitz aus heiterm Himmel,* which lent the volume its intended title *Geschlechtertausch,* begins with a scenario that calls attention to a fundamental contradiction within the code of heterosexual romantic love. On the one hand, the distinction between men and women represents the constitutive difference of the heterosexual love story—it is what distinguishes a romantic narrative from, for instance, a story of passionate friendship. On the other hand, the existence of this gap poses a threat to the demands of romantic love for unanimity

---

6. *Geschlechtertausch* can mean "sex change" or "sex exchange." The original volume was to have contributions by four women, but Irmtraud Morgner's story fell through for ideological reasons. See Wolfgang Emmerich's afterword to *Geschlechtertausch: Drei Geschichten über die Umwandlung der Verhältnisse* (Darmstadt: Luchterhand, 1980), 101.

of understanding and emotion. In *Love as Passion*, Niklas Luhmann portrays such epistemological claims as a necessary condition of love's communicative function:

> One would have to participate in the other person's self-referential information pro-
> cessing or at least be able to adequately reconstruct it, in order to be able to "under-
> stand" how input works in him as information and how the person in turn reconnects
> output (what is said, for example) and information processing.
> The communicative medium of love functions to make this seemingly improba-
> ble step possible. (24)

In this light, gender distinction can be a ticklish subject for heterosexual romance: too great a disparity in outlook or experience would endanger the lovers' mutual understanding, while too little difference erodes the texts' heteronormative polarity. The stories in the *Geschlechtertausch* volume take positions all along this spectrum—often with surprising results.

At the outset of "Geschlechtertausch," de Bruyn literalizes love's claim to an absolute transcendence that would effect the "union of two souls" (Anderson, *Blitz*, 8). Lost in passion, Karl and Anna want to "traverse the empty space between them." Karl cries: "Oh, if only I were the woman! Oh, if only you were the man!" (8). The magic formula takes, and both find their bodies transformed into those of the opposite sex.

Overwhelmed by the change, Anna checks into a clinic, but Karl (now Karla) puts on Anna's clothes and heads off to work. After some initial awkwardness, Karla's coworkers come to terms with this new arrangement and eventually begin treating Karla like any other woman at the office—unfortunately for Karla. Predictably, Karl/Karla's crossover reveals inequalities that he had never noticed as a man: Karla feels objectified and patronized at the office, forced to endure unwanted advances and double standards in etiquette and appearance. After being slighted by her male peers at a professional conference, Karla decides she's had enough. She goes to the clinic to trade back with Anna. Here, though, de Bruyn's story takes an unexpected and revealing turn. Adam, it turns out, doesn't want to go back to being Anna. While staying at the clinic, Adam has fallen in love with a nurse named Karin, who explains to the dumbfounded Karl/Karla that she and Adam are looking forward to an egalitarian life together (Anderson, *Blitz*, 44).

What started, then, as a love story between Karl and Anna ends in the happy union of Adam/Anna and Karin. Though Karla is left stranded at the end, Adam/Anna and Karin seem to have resolved the paradox of heterosexual love: one is biologically a man, both are culturally women. Hope may be found in the fluidity of gender, which can be learned and, therefore, unlearned. In the end, magical *Geschlechtertausch* turns out to be less the apogee of romantic love than its only chance for survival.

Though lighter in tone than de Bruyn's, Sarah Kirsch's story "Blitz aus heit-erm Himmel" is no less acute in its critique of the symbiotic relationship between romantic expectations and gender inequality. Kirsch tells the story of Katharina, who works in the research department of a factory. The first five pages of the text follow Katharina as she performs various household chores, cleaning up after her boyfriend, Albert, a long-haul trucker. Waking up one morning, Katharina discovers that she has turned into a man. His first reaction is amusement, which turns into alarm when he thinks of Albert. Ever the optimist, Katharina, who now calls himself Max, decides that he may have lost a lover, but that their friendship might be all the stronger for it (Anderson, *Blitz,* 197). When Albert comes home after an overnight delivery, the two men spend the day together doing household tasks: hauling coal to the basement, cooking, taking out the trash, washing dishes. Max connects the dots: "Now that I'm a man myself, now I'm gettin' the women's lib" (Jetzt, wo ich selbern Kerl bin, jetz kriekich die Ehmannzipatzjon) (204). Though neither says anything about Katharina's new body, Albert seems unperturbed by the change. After stacking coal in the basement, they shower together and laugh at each other's erections.

Kirsch toys with the idea of an inherently gendered psyche: after becoming a man, for instance, Max finds that he suddenly enjoys soccer and knows his way around tools. Ultimately, though, the story's resolution suggests that the warp and woof of socialized gender and sexual identity can be unraveled. Not only are Max and Albert able to share domestic work equitably and harmoniously, but there is even a suggestion that their relationship may go beyond the friendship that Max had predicted. In the story's closing scene, the men go for a drive in Albert's truck and imagine a new kind of utopia:

> Protein and carbohydrates would be produced either synthetically or through hydroculture. Jungles would overgrow city and country. People would hunt in their spare time with crude weapons and wouldn't think about wars and border conflicts. [Albert and Max] were happily inventing things, talking as fast and thinking as harmoniously as they ever had when they were together. They circled the small ugly church, honked a cat out of the street, and stopped in front of the old house. Albert sat in his place. Max turned to him. His hair can stay that way, thought Albert. (Anderson, *Blitz,* 207)

With this conclusion, Kirsch offers a rendition of the parked-car-in-front-of-the-house trope, the moment of truth in the standard date narrative. The moment seems to augur a positive future for Max and Albert: they are getting along as well as ever, and Albert approves of Max's appearance, even as a man. In the intersection of social utopia and personal affirmation rendered by this passage, Kirsch offers a new permutation by which the problem of love and inequality might be solved: both partners are biologically men, one is culturally a woman.

Where Kirsch and de Bruyn discover new possibilities for interpersonal relationships in the fluidity of constructed gender roles, Christa Wolf's story of *Geschlechtertausch* seems to point toward more fixed conceptions of male and female identity. In "Selbstversuch: Traktat zu einem Protokoll" (Self-Experiment: Treatise on a Protocol), a female scientist volunteers to test a new drug designed to turn a woman into a man. The procedure works, and Anders (as the scientist's masculine self is called) discovers that he has become a man, or—in the narrator's telling correction—"runs the risk of becoming a man" (Mann zu werden droht) (Anderson, *Blitz,* 47). As the story goes on, it becomes clear that the narrator's self-experiment was motivated by more than scientific curiosity. Addressing her director at the laboratory, the inventor of "Petersein masculinum 199," the narrator admits that her main goal in making the switch was to discover what she calls his "secret" (53). This desire for knowledge, in turn, seems to be motivated by unrequited love. The narrator describes searching out the director's window in the city lights "with a woman's gaze" (58), once even calling him on the telephone just to hear him breathe (52).[7] And so when Anders does get behind the director's "secret," the shock of this revelation convinces him to return to feminine form: "I suddenly realized …: your artfully constructed rule-systems, your unholy work-ethic, all your maneuvers to escape were nothing more than the attempt to safeguard yourself from discovery: that you are incapable of love and you know it" (81).

When she was asked in an interview about the view of the relationship between the sexes informing "Selbstversuch," Wolf responded:

> As the material conditions allowing the sexes an equal start improve—and this must necessarily be the first step towards emancipation—so we face more acutely the problem of giving the sexes opportunities to be different from each other, to acknowledge that they have different needs, and that men and women, not just men, are the models for human beings. (*The Fourth Dimension,* 34–35; qtd. in Martens, 96)

In this answer, as in "Selbstversuch," Wolf seems to be auditioning the notion of inherent—or at least indelible—gender difference that Bammer identifies in the later novel *Kassandra*. Lorna Martens states the matter more unequivocally, claiming that Wolf's works from the period "tell us not that women are merely as good as, as capable as men; they leave us with the impression that women are better than men, and that femininity is better than masculinity" (74). Later in her study, Martens uses "Selbstversuch" to sum up the nature of this superiority: "Wolf

---

7. In reading these scenes as tokens of romantic longing, I follow Schmitz-Köster's cue, who remarks: "For the subject of the experiment, love toward this man, who is incapable of loving, was…a decisive motivation for her transformation" (78). It would also be interesting to apply Julia Hell's argument in *Post-Fascist Fantasies* to this story, reading the director not as a potential lover, but as a father figure. However compelling, such an interpretation would take us far afield of the current line of reasoning.

takes…stereotypical differences and turns them around into a set of positive attributes for women. Expressed positively, they mean that women see (the truth), while men are partially blind. Women are capable of love, while men are incapable of loving" (95).

This is not the only difference between the sexes, however. As we learn in a brief flashback in "Selbstversuch," the narrator's disappointment with the institute director recapitulates an earlier experience with a romantic partner named Bertram:

> I, Anders, thought back on the former lover of the woman that I had been. My dear Bertram, who three years ago almost to the day told me on the way to the observatory that it just wouldn't work anymore: a woman as a scientist—yes, of course women have the IQ for it, but what doesn't befit a woman is the penchant for absolutes. It wouldn't work, my long nights at the institute.…And it wouldn't work as long as I kept avoiding the main problem. The main problem was a child.…I should know what I wanted. I should want a child. (Anderson, *Blitz,* 56)

Bertram's broadside, while indisputably sexist and patronizing, is also recounted by Anders with a note of ambivalence. Given the negative valuation of masculine patterns of thought in Wolf's text, the narrator's masculinization—of which actually becoming a man is only the tail end—would be highly problematic. Describing her entry into the hypermasculine world of science, the narrator says: "You were right, professor, when you joked that *scientia,* science, may be a lady, but she has a man's brain. It cost me years of my life to learn to subjugate myself to that kind of thinking, the highest virtues of which are noninterference and impassivity" (64). It is no wonder that Anders, the man with a woman's brain with a man's brain, is ambivalent:

> The next morning [after breaking up with Bertram] I took over the leadership of our group, and in my first night as a man I could think about it for the first time without regret. The word "unnatural" had been uttered and could not be conjured away. A woman who rejects the trade-off that had been created especially for her sex, who cannot manage to lower her sights and turn her eyes into a piece of sky or water, who doesn't want to be lived, but wants to live: she will experience what it is to be guilty.…I did feel sorry when Bertram turned away in front of my door. And now all of a sudden as a man in the same place I no longer felt sorry. What I felt was thankfulness. (57)

What does it mean that the narrator has to become a man before she can purge her remorse at having turned down the "trade-off" Bertram had offered her: the loss of her scientific career for the comforts of family and children? If in "Selbstversuch" the masculine perspective is associated with blindness, self-deception, and pathological impassivity, then does this passage validate the narrator's previous regret?

That is, might her second thoughts have been more valid than she originally assumed? Was there some truth to Bertram's construal of her desires? It is no coincidence that the narrator's unresolved question—a feminine parallel, perhaps, to the director's masculine "secret"—revolves around the matter of biological reproduction. As we will see below, the theme of reproduction was one of the most crucial and complex nodes of contention in the evolving discourse of gender difference in the GDR.

In the end, the narrator of "Selbstversuch" presents the director—and the reader—not with a result, but with another experiment: "Now my experiment stands before us: The attempt to love. Which incidentally also leads to fantastical inventions: to the invention of a man that one is able to love" (Anderson, *Blitz,* 82).

The Gospel of Trobadora Beatriz

Perhaps the most radical interrogation of gender roles and relations in the 1980 volume *Geschlechtertausch,* Irmtraud Morgner's "Gute Botschaft der Valeska" (Gospel of Valeska), failed to make the East German censor's cut in the original anthology. Anderson, the original volume's editor, remembers how Hinstorff's head editor objected to the story's frank language and transgressive implications: "When Valeska was not experimenting with other women—this could not be termed lesbian, because she was a man—she was magically assuming her old female form in order to sleep with the husband she loved above all. She could effect this change temporarily by drinking strong coffee" ("Genesis and Adventures of the Anthology," 8). As Anderson's summary indicates, Morgner's story careens through a series of erotic permutations after its protagonist, the professionally and romantically frustrated scientist Valeska Kantus, changes her sex by uttering the magic phrase "One would have to be a man." Having undergone an overnight metamorphosis, Valeska books a flight to Moscow, where she explores the practical and erotic ramifications of her transformation with a Russian friend, a woman named Shenya.

Though Shenya is "absolutely enchanted by the miracle" (*Life and Adventures of Trobadora Beatrice,* trans. Clausen, 463), Valeska finds that after a while her initial excitement cools: "Shenya was too familiar to her.... Valeska was unable, even with supreme effort, to raise narcissism to the stage of passion" (463). On the continuum of sameness and difference considered at the outset of this analysis of *Geschlechtertausch,* Valeska's relationship with Shenya has too much of the former and not enough of the latter. Significantly, the language of this passage leaves ambiguous whether the necessary difference is physical or psychological: it is not Shenya's body that is "too familiar," but Shenya herself. Either way, their uneven investment in the erotic relationship begins to erode their friendship: "I give up," Valeska says. "If I have to pay this dearly for my vision, I don't want it. Being a man isn't much use to me anyway, unless my past and my role socialization are magically removed too. One ought to be a woman with a man's past" (463). Eventually, Valeska decides that she is still in love with Rudolf, her husband, and returns to live with him—still in her male body. "So as not to transgress prevailing concepts of morality," the narrator says archly, "Valeska set aside her masculine body temporarily during love-making" (465). Here, once again, the corporeal specificity of the desired object is ambiguous: is it simply prevailing morality that rules out male-male desire? As the publisher's resistance attests, this concession to the GDR's strictly heteronormative public sphere could not stifle the riot of anarchic sexuality circulating in the text.

And it is not just sexual desire that loosens its ties to the gendered body in the "Gospel of Valeska." For her husband, Rudolf, the phenomenon of sex difference anchors a set of assumptions about domestic roles and interpersonal relationships. And so each time Valeska assumes her female body, he hopes that she will retain it for a while, not because he finds her more desirable that way, but "because he want[s] a break from the egalitarian division of household duties that [is] now taken for granted" (*Life and Adventures of Trobadora Beatrice,* trans. Clausen, 465). Through its fantastical scenario of *Geschlechtertausch,* the story simultaneously highlights the absurdity of the asymmetrical demands of the East German domestic sphere (the uneven expectation disappears with a minor anatomical adjustment) and acknowledges the stubbornness of gender's "little difference."[8]

The designation of this story as a *gute Botschaft*—"good message or news," as in *gódspel* (gospel) or *evangelium*—raises the question "A message to whom?" The story's final paragraph answers this question decisively:

> My teaching, which urges women to believe in themselves and in the transformation just described, is pragmatic. Shenya advised me to work miracles in order to spread word about the teaching. Since then I've learned a few, I can walk on my hair, make rain, multiply loaves of bread. Of course, that won't be enough. Because people believe great truth more readily in unlikely clothing. If I had the prospect of winning over a majority of women to a temporary transformation by having myself nailed to the cross, I might accept even this means. The danger of humanity's self-destruction through war causes me to see as right every means that can extort peace. (*Life and Adventures of Trobadora Beatrice,* trans. Clausen, 465)

This "pragmatic" teaching seems akin to Spivak's "strategic essentialism," in this case a message directed specifically toward women that addresses the specificity of their experience. The recipients of Valeska's "message" are tasked with revolutionizing gender roles; in light of the intractable—perhaps even inherent—warmongering of the patriarchal mind-set, women's personal transformations become tantamount to the survival of humanity. This pragmatic teaching, like the

---

8. *Der kleine Unterschied und seine grossen Folgen* (The Little Difference and Its Big Consequences) was the title of an important book by West German feminist theorist Alice Schwarzer, published in 1975.

metamorphoses involved, is provisional. The next step, the rendering of gender difference equally as men's experience, would fall to the novel of which the "Gute Botschaft" became a part.

After the "Gute Botschaft" was rejected by Hinstorff for *Blitz aus heiterm Himmel,* it joined the likewise-censored manuscript *Rumba auf einen Herbst* (Rumba for an Autumn) in the "intermezzo" sections of Morgner's pastiche novel, *Leben und Abenteuer der Trobadora Beatriz* (Life and Adventures of Trobadora Beatrice).[9] In the framing story of this dazzlingly complex work, the character Irmtraud Morgner is approached on the street by a woman who introduces herself as Laura, minstrel to the renowned Beatriz de Dia. Laura offers to sell the author a manuscript for publication that purports to be the true story of Beatriz, a twelfth-century Provençal "trobadora" who arranges with the goddess Persephone to sleep until conditions are more "sympathetic to her profession" (trans. Clausen, 26). She awakens in France in 1968 and, hearing rumors of a place where "there is equality of citizens of all races and nationalities, equality of women and men in all spheres of political, economic, and cultural life" (70), makes her way to this "promised land" (91): the GDR. The story of what she finds there is combined with asides, anecdotes, interviews, parables, political speeches, excerpts from contemporary and historical texts, and the aforementioned intermezzos to constitute the 172 sections of Morgner's sprawling novel.

Trobadora Beatriz has received a good deal of well-deserved critical attention and forms the centerpiece of a number of studies of 1970s feminist literature.[10] It has been a favorite of feminist critics both for its exuberant millenarianism and for its sweeping critique of gender roles, which in many ways anticipates the most radical concerns of Western feminist theory more than a decade later.[11] As an object of literary analysis, Morgner's novel presents a daunting challenge. Its protean form and plurivocal structure allow it to assume contradictory positions simultaneously, frustrating any effort to shoehorn it into a given theoretical or ideological mold.[12]

---

9. For more on *Rumba auf einen Herbst,* see Westgate, 39–58.

10. See, for instance, Martens's *The Promised Land? Feminist Writing in the German Democratic Republic,* Schmitz-Köster's *Trobadora und Kassandra und——: Weibliches Schreiben in der DDR,* Sonja Hilzinger's *"Als ganzer Mensch zu leben…": Emanzipatorische Tendenzen in der neueren Frauen-Literatur der DDR,* Ilse Braatz's *Zu zweit allein, oder mehr? Liebe und Gesellschaft in der modernen Literatur,* and Beth Linklater's *"Und immer zügelloser wird die Lust": Constructions of Sexuality in East German Literatures.* For a detailed account of the mixed reception of *Trobadora Beatriz* in the GDR, FRG, and United States, see Silke von der Emde's *Entering History: Feminist Dialogues in Irmtraud Morgner's Prose,* 39–74.

11. See Bammer; also von der Emde's chapter (131–76) on *Trobadora Beatriz* as a postmodern feminist novel.

12. In an imaginary interview with the book's potential publisher, Laura advertises this adaptability as a key feature of this "novel form of the future" (trans. Clausen, 175). Obliquely acknowledging the presence of the censor in the East German publishing industry, Laura points out that in the montage novel "all the publisher's requirements in terms of figures, deletions, and additions could be taken into account; all priorities and shadings of day-to-day politics could be incorporated without serious harm to the work. The operative montage novel is an indestructible genre…. An absolutely ideal genre for interventions" (175).

To help untangle this Gordian knot of possible interpretations, the reading below will focus on one narrative strand in the story: the quest for romantic love. In a text as heterogeneous as Morgner's, the framing love story lends a curiously conventional structure to the novel, even if both the opening and the resolution are too ambivalent and open-ended to be mistaken for a traditional romance. At the beginning of the novel, Beatriz goes into hibernation because her conceptions of romance—which are, after all, the tools of her trade as a trobadora—are out of touch with the times. "A passive troubadour," she explains to Laura at one point, "an object that sings of a subject, is logically unthinkable" (114). Here, as in Wolf's "Selbstversuch," the matter is framed according to activity and passivity. Wolf describes a woman "who wants to live, rather than be lived" (die nicht gelebt werden will, sondern leben), while Morgner's Beatriz wants to love rather than simply be loved. Although Beatriz fears that a female troubadour may be "logically unthinkable," Laura articulates a more nuanced view of the matter: "A medieval minnesinger of the female sex is historically conceivable," she explains to the novelist I. M. "A medieval love poet of the female sex is not" (30). While the formal laws of *Minnesang* may have allowed a woman to elevate herself and her poetic object above the social conditions of her day (as Beatriz does in composing songs to "the real [read: imaginary] Raimbaut d'Aurenga, who doesn't correspond to reality" [36]), love, as Laura understands it here, demands an uncompromising equality that would have been unthinkable in the twelfth century—and perhaps in the GDR as well.

Indeed, a central question throughout the novel is whether East German socialism has created circumstances more favorable to "real love": love between equals. The novel does not take a single, succinct position on this, tending instead to oscillate between euphoric reports of political gains (such as the GDR's legalization of abortion in 1972) and dispirited accounts of setbacks and holdovers, especially in the interpersonal sphere. Such peaks and valleys notwithstanding, the narrative gravitates toward the conclusion that the GDR provides better conditions for women than the rest of the world but still has a long way to go. Beatriz observes at one point: "A woman of character today can only be a socialist....Moral relations can only be revolutionized after the revolutionizing of economic relations. One cannot take the second step before the first. In the GDR the first step has long since been taken. Now we are working on the second one, selah" (402).

What might this second step look like? In *Trobadora Beatriz,* as in many of the narratives from this period, the "revolutionizing of moral relations" is framed through the language of heterosexual love, through relationships that break apart under the strain of insurmountable differences or—in keeping with the utopian propensity of Morgner's novel—through the one romantic bond that might have staying power. The framing love story of *Trobadora Beatriz* begins with Beatriz dropping out of history until she can find an object worthy of her love, and ends when Laura, through supernatural means and Beatriz's help, locates one such—or perhaps the only such—worthy object: Benno Pakulat, the younger brother of Laura's (and Beatriz's) onetime lover, Lutz.[13]

In a comically literal dea ex machina, Benno is displayed to Laura via a "celestial vehicle," replete with cardboard clouds, which is lowered squeaking from the heavens as she stands on her balcony. In the celestial vehicle is a sleeping man, identified by a cardboard plaque that also gives key personal information and employment details. She later discovers that this vehicle was sent by the "beautiful Melusine," Beatriz's sister-in-law, a supernatural agent of the goddesses Persephone and Demeter. Melusine sends Benno a few more times for questioning before Laura requests to meet him in person. Both in the somnambulant interrogations and in their face-to-face encounter, Benno proves to be a man unlike the others described in the novel. "When my second daughter started talking," he reveals in the first interview, "she called me and my wife Mama" (267). This makes it particularly galling to him that his ex-girlfriend has denied him visitation rights: "When in hell is our state going to pass laws to protect the interests of our working fathers?" (267). Laura is so startled that she breaks the spell, and the celestial vehicle disappears. In a role reversal worthy of the stories in *Geschlechtertausch,* Benno is so dedicated to parenting that he is thrilled to be called Mama.

In the second interview, Benno explains that his first partner threw him out because he was too interested in parenting and homemaking to "qualify himself out of the working class" (278). His lack of career ambition jarred with her preconceptions about gender relations: "She needs a man to look up to," Benno explains. "Can a master craftsman look up to a carpenter? The whole time we were together, the poor dear had to put her qualification on hold, to maintain the traditional difference" (278). Another facet of the "perfect man" is revealed: Benno does not begrudge his partner her career and social status. On the contrary, he is content—to anticipate the language of the next section—to reproduce her labor power by keeping house for her. Benno also reverses the active–passive dichotomy explored above: in his next nocturnal visit, the sleeping Benno expresses his desire "to be courted seriously for once, publicly. When women's emancipation leads to that, I'm their man" (285). At their first face-to-face meeting, Laura does just that, and within a short time she proposes marriage.

"Judging from what you're saying," Laura says to Benno in one of their interviews, "you must be a man from a picture book. And where's the catch?" (278). A

---

13. The fact that Benno's role in *Trobadora Beatriz* has received little critical attention may be explained in part by Western feminist critics' suspicions toward Morgner's novels' fairly traditional romantic scenario and expectations. On this note, Patricia Herminghouse observes: "In the enthusiasm of feminist critics for Morgner's novels in the 1970s and 1980s there was...a tendency to forget that already in the *Trobadora,* despite the death of Beatrice, Laura's optimism derives from the happy future she expects to enjoy with Benno Pakulat" ("Taking Back the Myth and Magic," 64).

conversation with Melusine just prior to Laura's marriage proposal reveals the fly in the ointment:

LAURA:...You know Benno inside and out. Is he really the way he talks and acts?

MELUSINE: Yes.

LAURA: Does he love [my son] Wesselin?

MELUSINE: Very much.

LAURA: Does he love me as a representative of my gender or personally?

MELUSINE: I believe personally as well. But if you don't love him...

LAURA: My marriage and all subsequent marriagelike situations were based on love. On my side, at any rate, that's certain. And love, which as you know effects a wonderful narrowing of consciousness, always cast the men in such a favorable light that I overlooked their egotism at first: I was building on sand. For me only the opposite route would be possible now, if at all. I feel friendship for Benno. If, in addition to love, he also feels friendship toward me, actively, I mean, I would risk marrying again.

MELUSINE: Without love on your side?

LAURA: It will grow if there is peaceful accommodation. (342)

Here, desire reveals itself in all its contradictions. Having finally found a man worthy of love, Laura discovers that she does not love him, at least not yet. With this conversation, Morgner suggests that desire is not as ductile as politics and ideology. Indeed, it seems to be complicit in the perpetuation of gender inequalities. Laura wants to want an equal relationship; but what if, like Benno's former girlfriend, her desire rests on a difference at odds with her rational self-understanding?[14]

In this light, the "Gute Botschaft der Valeska," placed just a few pages from the end of *Trobadora Beatriz,* takes on added significance. In narrating the "transformation of relations" (as the subtitle of the West German *Geschlechtertausch* anthology put it, connoting East Germanness with the Marx-inflected "Umwandlung der Verhältnisse"), the "Gute Botschaft" imagines not just a realignment of men's expectations, but a recalibration of women's desire. In Lacanian psychoanalytic

---

14. In this light, we may complicate von der Emde's Frankfurt-School-inflected thesis that "the emancipation of women, the main concern in Morgner's novel, figures both thematically and structurally as the emancipation of desire and imagination from the bonds of pragmatism and rationality" (88). I would argue that *Trobadora Beatriz*'s central erotic narrative betrays a suspicion that desire and imagination may in fact be always-already penetrated by patterns of social domination. To the extent that this is the case, Morgner's novel calls for a dialectical interplay between desire and rationality: the former loosening the reins of instrumental reason, the latter interrogating the deeper substrates of fantasy and desire. The novel's misgivings regarding desire, which are only amplified in *Amanda,* relate to an ambivalence in Morgner's work identified by Linklater: on the one hand, the erotic sphere is portrayed as "the domain of men" (*Trobadora Beatriz,* 112; qtd. in Linklater, 101), whose hegemony over erotic norms and imagery render sexuality highly problematic. On the other hand, all three novels appeal to the "productive power of sexuality" as a key motor of their emancipatory agendas (Linklater, 115–30).

terms, we might say that Valeska's *Geschlechtertausch* allows her to traverse the fantasy of phallic desire. In "The Signification of the Phallus," Jacques Lacan claims to "pinpoint the structures which will govern the relations between the sexes" according to "a being" and "a having" that "refer to a signifier, the phallus" (83–84). Since neither sex can actually *be* or *have* this signifier, Lacan posits "an 'appearing' which gets substituted for the 'having' so as to protect it on one side and to mask its lack on the other" (84). In the "Gute Botschaft," Valeska occupies *both* positions in Lacan's model, the impossible "being" and the illusory "having" of the phallus. And so when Rudolf returns to Valeska, who is still in her male body, the sudden discovery of the sameness of their anatomy short-circuits the Lacanian schema:

> 66
> Rudolf stood before her. Came in as usual. Kissed Valeska as usual. Took off his and her clothes as usual.
> 67
> Later it occurred to Valeska that she should be afraid. Later it struck Rudolf that the naked Valeska was disguised.
> 68
> At that, they realized that if necessary they could do without the images that they had made of each other and that others had made for them.
> 69
> Then they knew that they loved each other. Personally—miracle of all miracles. (464)

Faced with the "disguise" of Valeska's masculine body, Rudolf and Valeska decide that they will have to "make do without" the social constructions that define their gendered bodies. Here, our theoretical compass swings from Lacan to Butler, who claims:

> Precisely *because* [the phallus] is an idealization, one which no body can adequately approximate, [it] is a transferable phantasm, and its naturalized link to masculine morphology can be called into question through an aggressive reterritorialization. That complex identificatory fantasies inform morphogenesis, and that they cannot be fully predicted, suggests that morphological idealization is both a necessary and unpredictable ingredient in the constitution of both the bodily ego and the dispositions of desire. (Butler, *Bodies That Matter,* 86–87)

According to Butler, even the body's ineluctable modality is created by internalized cultural and social forces. Such "aggressive reterritorialization" as that prescribed by Butler seems to be at stake in the "Gute Botschaft," as it is in many of the texts from the volume for which Morgner's story was intended. In this "transformation of relations," the reconfiguration of desire involves not simply an alteration of ob-ject-choice, but a revaluation of the love object itself.

If we examine Laura's relationship with Benno according to the psychoanalytic matrix sketched out above, we find that the same traits that establish Benno as a "man from a picture book" also place him on the "wrong" side of the phallic divide: he prefers to be pursued than to pursue; he is apathetic about social status; his daughter calls him Mama. If Laura is indeed embedded within the polarities of phallic desire, then it becomes clear why she can hope at best for "peaceful accom-modation" with Benno (in the Lacanian schema: love), but not desire (which would be ruled by the phallic signifier). In this light, *Trobadora Beatriz* would suggest (in parallel with psychoanalytic theory) that the inequalities that seem again and again to undermine love relationships actually extend deeper, permeating the structure of desire itself. As we will see in the next section, this theme is taken up again in the second novel in Morgner's "Salman" trilogy, *Amanda: Ein Hexenroman* (Amanda: A Witch Novel), which attacks the roots of the problem, reappraising the funda-mental conditions of possibility for a desiring subject.

Benno's eschewal of the phallic position—in plain English, his emasculation—may countervail desire in his relationship with Laura, but it is a necessary precon-dition for the fulfillment of his role in the novel as a whole. In the final chapter, Benno tells Laura the first of his Scheherazadian "thousand and one stories." It begins: "Beatrice de Dia, a beautiful and noble lady, was the wife of Sir Guilhem de Poitiers" (467). This story, a condensed version of Beatriz's slumber and awaken-ing, duplicates long stretches of the novel's first chapter. Benno, we may surmise, has embarked on a renarration of the entire novel. In light of the analysis above, this act of incorporation and retelling signals a shift not only in narrative perspec-tive, but also in ideological consciousness, for, as I mentioned at the outset, one of the salient—and prescient—features of the treatment of gender difference in *Trobadora Beatriz* is the insistence that the experience of gender is universally dis-seminated, and is not just the province of women. As he begins the thousand and one stories, Benno literalizes this insight: he has made the transformative tale of Beatriz's life and adventures his own.

Reclaiming Reproduction: *Amanda: Ein Hexenroman*

Given the importance Morgner assigns to the character of Benno in *Trobadora Beat-riz,* it is all the more startling when she summarily kills him off near the beginning of *Amanda*. Published in 1983, this second volume of the planned Salman trilogy is in structure no less labyrinthine and in scope perhaps even grander than its prede-cessor. *Amanda* continues to tell the story of Laura and Beatriz, enfolding these per-sonal histories within an epic struggle between the primordial forces of matriarchy and patriarchy. After filling in the details of Laura's childhood and student years, *Amanda* picks up the thread of Laura and Benno's life together, where everything seems as we left it. Benno continues to be the "man from the picture book," sharing equally in domestic duties and thrilled by Laura's newfound fame after the publication of *Leben und Abenteuer der Trobadora Beatriz*. Soon, however, his wife's talents and accomplishments begin to chafe. Although Benno declares daily: "I admire and revere you" (122)—an ostentation that Laura finds eerie and repugnant—his envy and jealousy start to show through. In just a few sparse sentences, his part in the story is finished:

> His jealousy of [her son] Wesselin grew. Soon he found himself jealous of other men.
> When he realized that he was jealous of women as well, he began to drink.
> On the 12th of September, 1975, he crashed his car, drunk. He died instantly. (123)

Benno's is no grand Romantic *Liebestod*. It is quick, senseless, and final. The brevity of his appearance in this book, and the violent abruptness of his disappearance, suggest that not only the character but also the ideas and ideals he stands for are being rejected. The exemplary man, whose positioning as the "redeemer" of masculinity played counterpoint to Valeska and her redemptive miracles, turns out to be a fraud. If, in the earlier novel, Benno represented a model "male feminist," assimilating the teachings of Beatriz and her Persephonian comrades to critique his own gendered socialization, we now see how little real transformation actually took place; Benno's incorporation of Beatriz's teachings seems more an arrogation than a tribute. In such chariness toward universalist notions of the tyranny of gender roles—including the big-tent approach adopted by its forerunner—*Amanda* would fit the pattern identified by Bammer in feminist texts from the 1980s. Here, gender may be universal, but the weight of the problem rests solely on the shoulders of women.

If the figure of Benno was the end goal of the love story in *Trobadora Beatriz*, his death also highlights the lack of any comparable romantic narrative in *Amanda*. When romantic love appears in the later novel, it is always in its negative instance, as a false and dangerous ideology that reinforces the patriarchal subjugation of women. Which is not to say that desire is absent from *Amanda*. Martens argues that where *Trobadora Beatriz* depicts a proliferation of possible objects of female desire, from sexualized bodies to abstract ideals like peace or communism, *Amanda* distills desire into a single object—an object, furthermore, that is portrayed as explicitly gendered. In *Amanda*, Martens points out, "Morgner suggests that women's and men's desires have been different from time immemorial. Men have desired, and still desire, to 'lay the world at their feet,' while women have wanted and still want to be undivided, indivisible, and 'have an island at their feet.' Thus in the later novel, Morgner does ascribe a goal, an object of desire" (71). Here I would amend Martens's comment to suggest that, more than an *object* of desire, the "island" in question represents the very possibility of desire at all. In this regard, the notion of desire operative in *Amanda* would dovetail with the argument, outlined in chapter 2, that desire in GDR public culture can best be understood as a "desire to desire." In the face of a prevailing psychological model that acknowledges only determinate, object-driven desire, *Amanda*'s "island" represents a space of radical possibility, of indeterminate motivation and inchoate wants.

The "island" first appears in a passage describing Laura's alchemical pursuits. Laura is looking for the "Philosopher's Stone, Second Order," which is contrasted with the "Philosopher's Stone, First Order," pursued by male alchemists since the beginning of the profession. The First Order stone is said to turn molten metal into gold and "lay the world at one's feet." The Second Order stone, also known as *argentum potabile,* "drinking silver," would turn metals into silver and "lay an island at your feet" (*Amanda,* 113). Laura is particularly taken with the idea of this "island." "The island is a woman's *hinterland*" (114), Laura thinks, echoing an acquaintance's sexist remark that "woman is the soldier's *hinterland*" (112). She imagines the island as "a kind of Orplid" (114).

The mythical island Orplid appears in a number of works by the poet Eduard Mörike, most famously in the poem "Gesang Weylas" (Weyla's Song), which was written in 1831 and later set to music by Hugo Wolf:

You are Orplid, my country!	Du bist Orplid, mein Land!
Gleaming far off;	Das ferne leuchtet;
Sea-fog mists your sunny strand	Vom Meere dampfet dein besonnter Strand
Moistening the cheeks of gods.	Den Nebel, so der Götter Wange feuchtet.
Ancient waters rise	Uralte Wasser steigen
Rejuvenated around your hips, child!	Verjüngt um deine Hüften, Kind!
Before your divinity	Vor deiner Gottheit beugen
Kings bow, who are your attendants.	Sich Könige, die deine Wärter sind.[15]

Mörike's Orplid is a curious mix of elements: it is a country, an island, and a child, ancient and young. Removed from the cares of the world, it still holds sway over earthly concerns; its attendants are kings. Laura's "island" is similarly mixed, combining motifs of escape and rejuvenation, but also of childhood and child care. In one telling passage we learn of her failed relationship with the archivist Konrad Tenner:

> Laura did not want any children without an island as *hinterland*. Tenner read this as a sign of inadequate love. He thought she didn't want children from him, sank into jealousy, and pushed for marriage. Laura didn't want to get married. Since Tenner considered her a "natural" woman, he was suspicious of her refusal of these two "natural" commitments. (*Amanda,* 115–16)

---

15. Mörike, "Gesang Weylas," ed. Baumann and Grosse, 1: 73.

Tenner's thinking here recapitulates the logic of Dannhauer's *Geschlecht und Persön-lichkeit,* where marriage and children are characterized as the "natural" desires of women. Laura, however, has a different understanding of her needs and wants. Significantly, her demand is poetic, not practical. She does not ask for full-day child care, longer sick leave, or laundry service: she wants Orplid. Although practical concerns play a significant role in *Amanda*—the text is filled with critiques of the system's failures to reconcile the requirements of child rearing with the demands of full-time work—the stipulation here is more abstract, more radical, and more puzzling. Why does she consider this "island" a precondition for having children?

A later conversation with Amanda helps fill in the gaps. While they work together on their grand alchemical project, distilling sleep-replacement elixir, Amanda reminds Laura of a key childhood memory, which is recounted in detail in the novel's first chapter. As the adults cower in a bomb shelter, mortally afraid of the advancing Allies, twelve-year-old Laura and her friend Inge live out a lawless idyll, romping in the grass and making a commotion with their wooden shoes on the forbidden metal grates of the courtyard. Somehow these children know instinctively, Laura says, that it is time to come out of hiding. "Ruins all around," Laura says, "the whole city a pile of rubble and it was a sunny May day, just like the calendar said.... High summer and shameless and crashing. But only for Laura and her friend Inge" (18–19).

This formative memory contains potent historical material, for it represents not only the period *after* the devastations of Nazi rule and the World War II, but also the moment *before* "Laura's world was turned on its head by the victory of the Soviet army and their allies" (23). For all its transience, this brief moment of pure potentiality, of anarchic autonomy, returns as a leitmotif throughout the novel and forms the core of its utopian aspirations. It is the prototype for Orplid:

> "Fourteen carefree days in the sun," said Laura.
>
> "Until we were tanned through and through," Amanda said. "Wearing the uniform of a railway worker and black as a Negus and undivided. Whoever has lived through such days is utterly unsuited to obedience. Do you want to conquer Orplid together?"
>
> "Yes, by distilling Orplid," said Laura, gripped by the memory. "The second sphere, where I wouldn't have to wear a uniform to hide from others and myself that I am a woman cut in two; the island where I can throw myself, worn out, as men throw themselves into the arms of a woman; my *hinterland,* where I can retreat with Wesselin, to reproduce my labor power. (223)

Amanda's reference to a Negus, an Ethiopian king, echoes the attending kings in Mörike's poem. Likewise, the "child" apostrophized by Mörike's poem finds echoes in Laura's fantasy of the island: this would be a retreat with her young son, Wesselin. In this passage from *Amanda,* Orplid seems to have two functions: on the one hand, it serves as a *hinterland,* a space of remove where Laura can "reproduce [her] labor power"—a pithy and suggestive formulation that will be unpacked below. On the other hand, it is a space of unmasking and self-knowledge, a place where Laura can reveal to herself and others that she is split in two—literally, as the following analysis will explain. Perhaps it is even a space where the two halves of her divided self might be reconciled. To understand how this reconciliation might take place, we must consider the details of the splitting.

In her reading of *Trobadora Beatriz,* Martens suggests that the characters of Morgner, Laura, and Beatriz may be read as a single individual split into three parts (61). In *Amanda* we discover that this splitting would in fact be a *subdivision* of an already-split Laura. Near the beginning of the novel, as befits a hero's narrative, we receive an account of the unusual circumstances of Laura's birth. No sooner is the newborn bathed and swaddled than a woman in a red robe whisks in on a broom to christen her: "What will the beautiful Amanda be named?" she asks the mother and grandmother. "Amanda Laura," they say involuntarily. Horrified, they exorcise the witch-name Amanda with five baptisms and try to put this odd occurrence out of their heads. Once her mother, father, and grandmother have succeeded in suppressing Laura's preternatural talents and intelligence, her childhood and school years proceed fairly normally. In college she meets a man named Konrad Tenner, who impresses her with his devil-may-care attitude: "No pleasure, no life," he says. As we saw above, however, Tenner proves to be more conventional than his initial self-presentation. His possessiveness convinces Laura that her "island" refuge is all the more imperative. And so she begins her alchemical experiments in the kitchen of their shared apartment, hoping to distill the Philosopher's Stone, Second Order. Since Tenner avoids kitchens, he remains in the dark about her research. One day she receives a visit from a man who introduces himself as Kolbuk. He tells her that she has made herself "liable to prosecution" and begins smashing her laboratory and destroying her books. Kolbuk tells her he needs to "operate": "The half had to be removed. Because the half stood in the way of Laura's happiness. After the operation she would be able to make her husband and children happy and live respectably and contentedly" (*Amanda,* 118). She will be forbidden any future contact with the excised half under penalty of eternal torture. He produces an executioner's sword and cuts her in half, then disappears with the remainder—a tall, thin, red-haired woman: the witch Amanda.

Tenner finds that Laura's new body (short, stout, and brown-haired) and subdued personality no longer hold the appeal of her fiery former self. "Tenner left Laura," the narrator states laconically, "although marriage and children would have been quite welcome to her now" (120). Laura goes on to meet a graduate lecturer named Uwe Parnitzke, settles down, and has children, "as the book *The Life and Adventures of Trobadora Beatrice* describes somewhat accurately" (120).[16] When

---

16. In the present-time action of *Amanda,* Laura has only one child, her son Wesselin. *Trobadora Beatriz* recounts how, when her eleven-year-old daughter dies of pneumonia, Laura blames herself and her

Beatriz, resurrected in *Amanda* as a tongue-tied siren, reads the earlier novel, she bristles at Morgner's unawareness of Laura's exceptionality: "The writer...conventionalized Laura Salman as an exemplum of the typical working woman with an assortment of virtues: hardworking, modest, eager, nondescript, self-abnegating, devoted. [The writer did this] out of ignorance, I assumed" (23). In this way *Amanda* adds a new layer to the already trenchant critique laid out by *Trobadora Beatriz*. Now we learn that to the degree that Laura was able to abide her living conditions at all it was only because a part of her had been removed. Amanda, her witch half, was meanwhile being held captive in the Blocksberg fortress, formerly known as the Brocken, the seat of matriarchal power, now occupied by the head devil Kolbuk and the forces of patriarchy.

Amanda escapes and returns twice in the novel, both times in the wake of Laura's attempts at self-destruction. The first time, overwhelmed by the demands of life as a single mother, Laura poisons herself and her young son Wesselin:

> Once...her shift on the S-Bahn was over she felt exhaustion, vulnerability, a need for protection. And she dragged herself to the second shift.
>
> It took her utmost self-discipline to cope with the second shift, in which she took care of her work as a housewife and mother. She had no energy left to play with Wesselin. Her son dealt with this deficiency by pulling out his hair. His despair consumed the last of her will to live.
>
> She requested medical help.
>
> In the form of assisted suicide for herself and her son. (127–28)

After being turned down by three doctors, Laura brews the lethal potion herself. Amanda's intervention saves her and her son: the witch half, it turns out, has veto power if her counterpart decides to end their shared life. Laura's second near-death may be accidental. In an attempt to brew sleep-replacement elixir—once again in response to the problem of the "second shift"—Laura creates phoenix elixir, which causes her to burst into flames and return in twelve hours (an old formula, Amanda explains later, to escape burning at the stake) (222). These desperate efforts to find relief from the demands of work outside and inside the home raise the stakes of the quest to find Orplid. The initial suicide attempt in particular, which is described with a pathos otherwise foreign to Morgner's ironic tone, elevates the infamous "double burden" to a matter of life and death.[17]

Each time she returns, Amanda insists that there is only one solution: to take back the Brocken and reunite with Laura through the power of drinking silver. In

---

busy academic career and decides to transfer "into production," becoming a trolley-car driver (111). She has divorced Uwe Parnitzke before the action of *Trobadora Beatriz* takes place.

17. For a sociological-historical account of the double burden in the GDR, see Barbara Einhorn, "German Democratic Republic: Emancipated Women or Hardworking Mothers?" in *Superwomen and the Double Burden: Women's Experience of Change in Central and Eastern Europe and the Former Soviet Union.*

this way, she says, "the Brocken could become Orplid" (224). In Amanda's estimation, Laura's alchemical pursuits are a waste of time: "Distilling is impossible," she says. "We have to conquer Orplid" (223). Amanda is not the only witch with these intentions. In one raucous scene, a supernatural television commentator describes the three factions of witches: the Red-Robed Faction, led by Isabel (the same witch who had christened Amanda-Laura), militant man-haters who believe in using military force to take back the Brocken; the Greenrobes, who know only what they don't want, which is to be like men; and the Owl Faction, Amanda's group, who are androgynous and want to spread their "dangerous tendencies" among the forces of the patriarchy (329–30).[18]

This lineup allows us to delve deeper into the status of gender identity in the metaphorical framework of Amanda-Laura's splitting. If Amanda is the "androgynous" half, then what is Laura? To the degree that the novel's descriptions of her daily life focus on her activities as a mother to Wesselin, she would embody the "essentially" feminine gender identification emphasized by Beauvoir and Kristeva and elucidated in the discussion above: her central symbolic role, especially in *Trobadora Beatriz,* revolves around reproduction. Yet we have also seen how, in her "first shift" as an S-Bahn engineer, Laura works "like a man." Within the productionist value-system of the GDR's dominant culture, it is this role that confers dignity and worth. Suspended between these two roles, Laura's center cannot hold: her suicide attempts speak to the untenability of her position.[19]

In *Amanda,* the most salient aspects of gender difference play out as a conflict between modes of work, a polarity congealed in the figure of the opposing philosophers' stones. To this degree, these stones become material answers to the loaded question posed in chapter 2 of this book: Why do we work? The first-order philosopher's stone, the goal of masculine endeavor since time immemorial, creates value—gold from base metal—and "lays the world at one's feet." This is, as well, a description of "productive" labor: the SED's *Kleines politisches Wörterbuch* (Compact Political Dictionary) defines *Arbeit* as "the purposive, conscious activity of the human being. Through the use of the means of production he *[sic]* changes objects and makes them useful for his purposes" ("Arbeit," 47). The second-order philosopher's stone, on the other hand, is concerned less with wealth and domination than with healing, remotion, and recuperation. It will make what is divided whole again,

---

18. As Lorna Martens and Monika Meier point out, these factions seem to represent various strands of feminism in East and West, though the fairness of their characterization here is the source of some dispute (Martens, 121–23; Meier, 226).

19. In this sense, Laura's story would conform to the pattern identified by Cheryl Dueck in her book *Rifts in Time and in the Self.* In a chapter titled "A Matter of Life and Death," Dueck calls attention to the striking number of protagonists of East German novels in the 1980s who die through accident, sickness, suicide, or at the hands of others. In these novels, Dueck points out, "the main character either finds him/herself divided, unable to maintain a single subjecthood, or fails to find a place within the societal order and dies at its hands. This dissection of the subject necessarily implies its death, because, although the separate parts continue to live, the original entity has ceased to exist" (113).

carry one away, and "lay an island at one's feet"—an island, Laura imagines, where she could "reproduce [her] labor power." In this way the second-order philosopher's stone, Laura's "Orplid," becomes not a site of *production,* but of *reproduction.* Importantly, this is not the sex-specific capacity for biological reproduction, but rather the universal need for what Marx called the "reproduction of labor power."

In the first volume of *Capital,* Marx portrays reproduction as a kind of backdoor capitalization. When the capitalist pays out wages, he is really furthering his own ends: "The individual consumption of the worker, whether it occurs inside or outside the workshop, inside or outside the labour process, remains an aspect of the production and reproduction of capital, just as the cleaning of machinery does" (718). Under socialist conditions, reproduction no longer serves the creation of profit, but it is no less necessary to the production process. Workers need to eat, sleep, and stay warm. This requirement partakes of the asymmetry of gender roles, for, in the words of *Amanda*'s "marriage swindler" (who will be described below), wives have long been held responsible for the "reproduction of the labor power of [their husbands]" (264).[20] But when would women reproduce their own labor power? Orplid, as Laura imagines it, would fulfill precisely this function: it becomes "the island where I can throw myself, worn out, as men throw themselves into the arms of a woman" (223).

Here, then, is one of the key valences of the discourse of gender difference in *Amanda.* In focusing attention on the problem of reproduction—all too often the sole province of women—*Amanda* calls attention to a blind spot in socialist ideology: a willful ignorance as profound as that of the capitalists. Significantly, this shift in focus represents a *reorganization*—not a rejection—of Marxist theory, as a key quotation makes clear. As one of a series of mottos attributed to the revolutionary-utopian "Nonsense Council" (*Unsinnskollegium*) of witches and fools, Morgner quotes a rarely cited passage from Marx, an essay collected in the fourth volume of *Capital: Theories of Surplus Value:* "The real wealth of a people will be measured by time which will not be absorbed in direct productive labour, but will be available for enjoyment, for leisure, thus giving scope for free activity and development" (Marx, "Source and Remedy," 390). In Marx's essay, real liberation is cast less as a matter of redistributing wealth than of reallocating time, for, Marx goes on to say, "free time, disposable time, is wealth itself, partly for the enjoyment of the product, partly for free activity which—unlike labour—is not dominated by the pressure of an extraneous purpose which must be fulfilled, and the fulfilment of which is

---

20. In a speech at the Seventh Writers' Congress in 1973, Morgner caused a small scandal by portraying the relationship between men and women in terms of exploiter and exploited: "The largest part of the masculine half of humanity, the powerless men, have had their history expropriated for millennia; but the other half, the female half of humanity, the slaves of the slaves, have in this sense been doubly dispossessed" (qtd. in Baume, 122). Brita Baume points out that the responses to Morgner's speech took vehement exception to the designation of women as "slaves" to men—a condition, after all, that would remain in place even after men had been freed from their bonds by socialism (122).

regarded as a natural necessity or a social duty, according to one's inclination" (391). Leisure, in other words, does not exhaust its value in reproducing labor power. Rather, it is labor that acts in the service of free time by securing the necessities of existence (food, clothing, shelter) and thereby allowing for the free unfolding of one's "faculties."

The feminist implications of this notion are becoming apparent: emancipation, seen from this standpoint, is not just a matter of equal access to the means of production. Instead, the measure of equality would be access to "disposable time"—time allotted in the productionist value-system for the "reproduction of labor power," which includes but is not limited to biological reproduction. Because of what Beauvoir starkly calls their "enslavement to the generative function" (108), women have long been forced to grapple alone with the question of reproduction—both biological (gestation and childbirth) and familial (reproducing the labor power of the family unit). If, with Morgner's *Unsinnskollegium,* we turn the productionist value-system on its head, then the biological "fact" of gender difference—the particularity of women's historical experience—would afford insight into a new understanding of the human. A standpoint that ceases to generalize from the specificity of men's experience—and the resulting overvaluation of "productive" labor—comes closer to Christa Wolf's admonition "that men and women, not just men, are the models for human beings." *Amanda*'s utopian vision proposes that labor does not create the human, as Engels had it, but instead opens a space beyond necessity—an "island," an Orplid—within which the fully human can develop.

Thus it is perhaps fitting that *Amanda*'s one "concrete utopia" (a dubious one at that, as we will see) is a men's community—the Gardening Commune (*Gärtnerische Produktionsgenossenschaft,* or GPG) described in the short interlude "The Marriage Swindler, or Why Must Barbara Wait for Her Day in Court?"[21] The story of the commune's origins is elliptical and puzzling, equal parts acerbic satire, social critique, and redemption story. Tired of working on the assembly line at a lightbulb factory, Barbara, a jaundiced divorcee, places a personal ad in the paper offering her services as a diligent, devoted, indulgent housewife. She receives hundreds of applicants. She chooses one, busies herself with cooking, cleaning, and caring for him, and after he proposes marriage, absconds with all of his money. A series of bogus marriages follow, all fueled by the men's desire for what she calls "nostalgic," uncomplicated inequality. "I was the locus of their unofficial lives," she explains, "where they could recover from their ideological and moral stress" (265): as she puts it at one point, she serves to "reproduce their labor power" (264). In this capacity she is placed on a pedestal by some, humiliated and even beaten by others—for the last, she states drily, she acts as a "valve function." Eventually, Barbara decides to start covering the traces of her sham marriages. She buys a garden cottage at the edge

---

21. "Concrete utopia" is Ernst Bloch's designation for a realized utopian vision, as distinguished from an abstract, as-yet-unmet goal. See chapter 2, pp. 87–89.

of town and installs her most recent husband there. He is joined by a second, and a third, until twenty-seven men are living on the property, enclosed by an invisible fence and camouflaged by a magic hood. To her surprise, the men do not mutiny but instead begin improving the house and tending an ever-larger garden. Each time a new "victim" arrives, they tell him that he has been rewarded for extraordinary service by being allowed to live out his wish to become "a Robinson of the new type" (266). In good Voltairean fashion, they find satisfaction in cultivating the property into a thriving communal garden. Disgusted, Barbara decides to shut the operation down by turning herself in to the police. The case never comes to trial, as none of the men are willing to testify against her; having exchanged their roles as workers and husbands for homesteading and husbandry, the men find that they are happier and more productive.

In this way, the separatist communal society of the GPG seems to be the masculine counterpart of the women's collectives imagined by a number of East German feminist authors in the 1970s. Christa Wolf's eponymous heroine Cassandra, for instance, takes refuge in a women's community hidden in the hills around Troy. A number of commentators have elucidated the utopian qualities of this matriarchal secret society.[22] In a more mundane context, Sarah Kirsch's 1974 poem "The Plot of Land" (Das Grundstück) describes a run-down piece of property that nonetheless serves an invaluable function for the women who own it:

On Sundays the girls come with their children to the plot of land	Sonntags kommen die Mädchen mit ihren Kindern zum Grundstück
That they bought cheap years ago. Still no money for	Das sie vor Jahren billig erwarben. Noch immer kein Geld für
Fences and solid doors; so they go and see and count	Zäune und festere Türen; so gehen sie und sehen und zählen
What has vanished: the pump, the cups, the fluffy quilt—	Was da verschwand: die Pumpe, die Tassen, die flauschige Decke—
....	....
—So Sunday after Sunday the girls See the grounds disappear, lovingly roaming the grass and the pines;	—So sehn sich die Mädchen Sonntag für Sonntag den Grund abgehn, das Gras und die Kiefern
They count and measure and calculate:	Liebevoll streifend; sie zählen und messen und rechnen:
A thousand Marks for a fence, who will put it in? Perhaps the woodpeckers	Eintausend Mark für den Zaun, wer setzt ihn? Etwa die Spechte

22. Sabine Wilke writes: "In contradistinction to the strictly hierarchical social stratification in Greece and Troy, [the women's community on the outskirts of Troy] is not hierarchically organized and therefore free from structural violence. The women who meet in the cave dwellings on Mount Ida live their lives beyond the false choice of living or killing" (94). See also Chiarloni, 139.

Tomtits and jays? And is that the old	Meisen und Häher? Und naht zwischen
woman approaching between the pines	Kiefern die Alte
Whom they, her pension is small, fête with	Die man, die Rente ist klein, mit Wurst und
sausage and pudding?	Pudding bewirtet?
Whom they, good as they are, put up for	Die man, gut wie man ist, herbergt: und hat
the night: and what if they now had	nun drei Wünsche
three wishes	Frei? Wie im Märchen würden sie leben mit
Free? They'd live as in a fairy tale with the	Kindern
children	Und Geliebten in Datschen im Sommer und
And sweethearts in cottages in the summer	sorglos.[23]
and carefree.	

For these women, the poem's *Grundstück* (piece of land) is a place of togetherness and escape, a sovereign space that would allow them and their children to live "carefree," "as in a fairy tale," if they could only prevent incursion from the outside world. It is, in other words, a weekend Orplid, an island of retreat where they can relax and recuperate (or in Marxist terms reproduce their labor power). With the old woman's supernatural help, they could live like this throughout the summer, protected not just from the marauding neighbors, but from the financial worries of "measurement and calculation."

The GPG's *Grundstück* in *Amanda* is protected precisely by such witchery, in the form of Barbara's "magic hood" (*Tarnkappe*). This detail becomes significant when Laura avails herself of the commune's invisibility to hide Wesselin from Kolbuk and his minions. The forces of patriarchy, it turns out, intend to abduct her son in order to force her to marry their leader—a complicated subplot involving a Faustian wager between the head angel Zacharias and the head devil Kolbuk. While living with the men of the GPG, Laura discovers that there is a trade-off for this dubiously utopian sodality:

> One day Dr. Dietrich [the chairman of the GPG] explained to Laura the theory behind the Commandment and thus also their strict rules and regulations. This moral commandment, the prime commandment—the GPG had agreed unanimously upon nine in all—reads: "The garden is your master, your friend, you shall have no women beside it." "A strange commandment, you may well say," Dr. Dietrich admitted. "But isn't the culture of love that prevails beyond our GPG equally strange? There, love means: being in love. Love in itself. Many people, men and women, are preoccupied with this feeling their whole lives. To put a finer point on it: with the production of this feeling. The so-called beloved is just a catalyst. The important thing is the intoxication. When our mens' community here was established—initially without women, for better or worse—the interchangeability of the catalyst got one clever head among us thinking that the role of the catalyst could also be played by a

---

23. Kirsch, "Das Grundstück," 54–55.

nonhuman entity or by a thing or by an idea. Our prime commandment suggests the garden as catalyst. (432)

What is this "utopia," then, that the men of the GPG have created? Work in the garden, Dr. Dietrich suggests, should be so wholly fulfilling, so all-consuming, that it replaces even the need for erotic relationships. This language may seem familiar to the reader. Recalling the argument in chapter 2 of this book, it would seem that the GPG reproduces in miniature the ultraproductionist ethos of 1950s *Aufbau* culture, which imagined that a worker could be entirely satisfied by the process of production. According to this model, a proper cathexis onto work was capable even of slaking the incessant demands of desire. In this light, the GPG represents a throwback to the GDR's early collectivist enthusiasm—a tempting utopian vision, but one that operated on a constitutive exclusion. Like the "men's community" of the GPG, *Aufbau* culture sought value and gratification in the process of production. Yet, as we saw in chapter 3, this culture could not adequately address the question of reproduction—whether biological, social, or the reproduction of labor power in leisure time.

The GPG and Orplid, then, are worlds apart. Where the former apotheosizes productive labor as a means to social, personal, and even sexual fulfillment, the latter represents life-saving flight from labor in and outside the home. Men and women, it seems, dream very different utopias. These two visions, however, share an important trait: both the monkish gardening community and Laura's private *locus amoenus* categorically exclude heterosexual love relationships. *Amanda's* radical interrogation of gender roles uncovers rifts too wide even for the soaring spans of romance.

"A single advantage": *Das heroische Testament*

It is a testament to the intractability of the problem of romantic love that Morgner returns to it again and again through three volumes of the Salman trilogy, despite all evidence of its incommensurability with the social and political aims of the novels. The cast of the final volume of the trilogy, the unfinished *Heroische Testament* (Heroic Testament), teems with archetypal romantic pairs: Hero and Leander, Titania and Oberan, Hanswurst und Grete. Even when the characters' pursuits of romantic fulfillment falter and fail, the novel's very structure seems to compel them into pairs. Throughout the trilogy, the figure of Beatriz de Dia embodies this tenacious attachment to love's utopian potential: she suffers death (real or symbolic) three times, only to be resurrected each time to chase once more after this chimera.

In the *Testament,* Beatriz seems finally to fulfill her 800-year quest. Still trapped in the half-avian, half-human body of a siren, and still without a voice, Beatriz meets a young male prostitute in the red-light district of Paris. Like Benno in the first volume of the trilogy, this man is recommended by his ambiguous gender presentation: he wears makeup, tight jeans, and a ruff. Intrigued by her wings and feathers, he asks her to fly with him over the city. They spend the night together, whereupon Beatriz finds herself featherless, human, and capable of speech. In classic fairy-tale form, the power of love has broken the enchantment that imprisons her in a false body. The man gives his name as Leander, aka Désiré, and calls himself an aspiring harlequin.

Leander/Désiré, it turns out, is the famous "man from the rib," whose unusual origins have occasioned the flurry of letters that constitute the novel's epistolary first chapter. In these letters, various scientists, academics, and concerned laypeople try to make sense of reports that a woman in Düsseldorf has just created a man by cutting him out of her rib. This reversal of biblical precedent seems to some letter writers a salutary event, to others a threat; to some a media hoax, to others an opportunity to earn much-needed foreign currency. The woman, Herta Kowalczik, nicknamed Hero, is a doctoral student at the Humboldt University and intends to submit Leander as her dissertation, having smuggled him across the border after creating him in the FRG.

Because Morgner, who died of cancer in May 1990, never finished the story of Hero and Leander (or any of the other plotlines in the *Heroische Testament*), we can only speculate where it was going. From Morgner's notes, collected and annotated by her literary executor, Rudolf Bussmann, we get a picture of the tremendous symbolic importance she assigned to the metaphor of the "man from the rib": "In the image of the man from the rib is contained the condition: in a world without a future/utopia, one must literally excise the missing element from oneself in order not to get sick. As an individual and as a species.... Every individual must bring something out of themselves to create a future when ideology fails" (124).[24] As Morgner sketches him here, Leander represents an externalization of a lack, a negation of a negation. In order "not to get sick" in the face of ideology's collapse, one must break one's attachment to collective utopian visions. What hope remains, the individual must find within and externalize. In this case, Leander becomes a projection of Hero's vestigial hope: "Hero cuts the future/hope/love—the island she stands on—out of her ribs" (124).

In this way, the process of refashioning a social utopia as an individual one becomes facilitated and symbolized by the trope of love. Revisiting the symbology of

---

24. "Sich (etwas) herausnehmen" means both "to take something out of oneself" and "to undertake to do something." In the world that Morgner describes in the *Heroische Testament,* all hope of a grand future utopia has been extinguished. The world itself is divided into three kingdoms: the DDR, where Beatriz, Leander, Hero, and Laura Salman live; the "Geehrtenrepublik Avalun," the kingdom of the "big shots" (Bonzen), now the home-in-exile of the mythical forces of patriarchy and the witches, who were forced into exile after their failed invasion of the Blocksberg; and Dschinnistan, the "land that doesn't exist," a world of the elemental powers of nature, ruled by Titania and Oberan. Of all the witches, Amanda is the only one who has chosen exile in Dschinnistan.

Amanda, Morgner's notes claim that "in a world of hate, struggle, fear, panic, love is an island (private)" (157). In the *Testament,* love becomes what Patricia Herminghouse describes as "a private utopia," located "not in any socio-political constellation, but in the love between two human beings" ("Taking Back the Myth and Magic," 63).

Especially in post–Cold War hindsight, the collapse of collective utopian hopes as depicted in the *Testament* maps onto the gradual dissolution of the GDR, both as a political entity and as a projection screen for the postwar socialist imagination. For East German Marxist feminists (or parafeminists) like Morgner, this breakdown was doubly laden. The evaporation of socialist aspirations toward transcending class inequality also entailed the loss of utopian socialism as a path toward overcoming patriarchal domination. Morgner's notes for the *Testament* indicate that this double disappointment would have been mirrored in the continuing separation and bodily decline of Laura and Amanda: "Laura = collapse of socialist hope; Amanda = collapse of feminist hope" (39; qtd. in Herminghouse, "Taking Back the Myth and Magic," 67). At the same time, however, Morgner suggests that the troubled relationship between feminism and socialism offers a way out. If women were excluded from socialist history in the first place, then they are also shielded from its implosion: "A chance for woman the outsider. Many disadvantages. A single advantage. It is not my history. So I have no history: There is none. History is a fiction of men. Why would I want to enter into history like Beatriz wanted to?" (*Testament,* 145).

In *Trobadora Beatriz,* the search for love takes place alongside the struggle for political and social power: the attempt to "enter history." These two strands are united dialectically in the figure of the Trobadora Beatriz, whose cultural and political involvement relies on finding an adequate object of her love. In *Amanda,* the quest for romantic fulfillment is subordinate to practical and political concerns. Although the resurrected siren Beatriz, having lost her tongue, cannot spread the word about the looming ecological and nuclear catastrophes, Amanda and her witches have a plan to take back the Brocken—to enter history—by any means necessary. Yet, *Amanda* tells us, even if social conditions were revolutionized, men and women would find themselves occupying very different utopias. Where the one strives to dominate, the other longs for relief from domination. In *Das heroische Testament,* at the end point of the trilogy, the decade, and the socialist experiment, the stakes are just as high, but expectations have plunged. If hope exists at all, it would be found in love's insular utopia, in a retreat from moribund ideology into the personal, the private, the individual: one's own rib.

As we will see, it was not just women who endeavored to "escape from history," abandoning the collective utopian project of the GDR to seek fulfillment within the private sphere. Chapter 5 will track the decline of the East German collective utopia and the ascendancy of "private utopias" like those imagined by Morgner: the private sphere, the underground, the "niche" society. The fact that Hero and

Leander, according to Morgner's notes, had an unspecified tragic fate in store reminds us that society is rarely kind to such private utopias—least of all societies as insistent on collectivity as the GDR. Morgner herself was well aware of the state's efforts to infiltrate private relationships: in 1977 she divorced her husband, the poet Paul Wiens, when she discovered that he had been informing on her to the State Security Agency (Westgate, 186).[25] The following chapter, an analysis of four Stasi narratives from before and after the *Wende,* will investigate the conditions—and even the possibility—of the private sphere in the shadow of state surveillance.

---

25. In *Strategies under Surveillance: Reading Irmtraud Morgner as a GDR Writer,* Geoffrey Westgate offers an intriguing interpretation of *Amanda* as a critique of the SED surveillance state; see esp. Westgate, 206–45.

5

Eye Contact

Surveillance, Perversion, and the Last Days of the GDR

> Corinna hatte die Stirn gerunzelt.
>
> —Ich kann nicht glauben, sagte sie, daß es bei der Stasi liebenswerte Männer gab.
>
> Corinna wrinkled her forehead.
>
> —I can't believe, she said, that there were likable men in the Stasi.
>
> —From a conversation between Marianne, the protagonist of Brigitte Burmeister's 1994 novel, *Unter dem Namen Norma* (Under the Name Norma), and Corinna Kling, a friend of Marianne's boyfriend from Mannheim (in the former FRG)

When public fury and court injunction opened the archives of East Germany's Ministry for State Security in 1991, the Stasi became the most transparent secret police in the history of state repression. Historians, lawyers, and victims raced to uncover the complete catalog of the Stasi's misdeeds, from the banal to the murderous. That the Stasi, that frantic fact collector, would become the object of another such compulsive drive to know suggests a certain historical irony. "One extreme follows another," Timothy Garton Ash observes in his personal history of Stasi surveillance, *The File*. "Probably no dictatorship in modern history has had such an extensive and fanatically thorough secret police as East Germany did. No democracy in modern history has done more to expose the legacy of the preceding dictatorship than the new Germany has" (21). In the turbulence following unification, historical disclosure seemed to supply some sense of moral clarity. No matter how tangled the threads of deception and betrayal pulled from the archives, the important thing was to bring the whole knotted mass to light.

For cultural producers confronting the legacy of the Stasi past, the material is even murkier, even more amorphous. Facts sprawl into feelings, actions into motivations. Fictional accounts of state surveillance leave the fixed moral categories so prevalent in postunification discourse—domination, victimization, and resistance—and enter the crisscrossed and multilayered channels of fantasy and desire. In the examination that follows, four Stasi narratives from the past two decades provide entry points into what might be called the phantasmatic dimension of state surveillance: the place of the Stasi in the collective imagination of the former GDR and in the changing cultural vision of unified Germany.

Positioned between the Stasi's obsessive pursuit of information and the archaeological zeal of postunification Germany, these fictive depictions of surveillance work all evince a zone of tension around the question of certainty. In the ideological configurations of both the pre- and postunification order, uncertainty provokes anxiety; it is not just unknown elements that threaten the system's stability, but rather not-knowing as such that causes concern. This anxiety becomes a structuring feature of these Stasi narratives; the professional inquisitors they portray are all chronically underinformed. Indeed, a great deal of the narrative tension in these texts derives from the disparity between the protagonists' understanding of the events unfolding around them and the historical reality of the GDR's last days.

Formally, these narratives could not be more different. Where two of the texts resolutely withhold narrative certainty, playing intricate shell-games of perspective, the other two provide (or claim to provide) epistemological and moral clarity. Yet despite the differences in their narrative frameworks, these texts share a remarkable assumption about the possibility of real knowledge. In the course of their duties, the protagonists all catch glimpses of another way of being, an always-foreclosed alternate reality that becomes ever more tantalizing the farther it retreats. In this parallel universe, knowledge—specifically knowledge of the other—resides not in secrets unearthed or coerced, but rather in intimacies freely given. By a logic familiar since Plato and Augustine, knowledge and truth correlate with love. Thus my argument will treat these texts not just as police-state thrillers or spy capers, but as love stories—albeit gone awry: narratives of missed connection, ill-fated attraction, and deviant desire. While realized love is always absent in the lives of these Stasi agents, its opposite—what we might call "not-love"—is all the more emphatically present. The most striking instances of not-love in these texts are "perversions": scopophilia, onanism, homosexuality, exhibitionism, and sadism, to name a few of the acts with which these narratives associate Stasi work.

We have come a long way, then, from the programmatic pairings of socialist realism and the (more or less) glamorous romance of the New Course, from the decorous, sublimated "neue Romantik" and the bourgeois domesticity of the 1960s and 1970s *Wohlstandskommunisten*. In the Stasi narratives explored here, romantic love exists only as a distant memory, a wistful longing. The political and narrative clarity of the love story has been replaced by a chaotic tangle of contradictory impulses and desires, an ideological and libidinal pandemonium arising from the implosion of the GDR's framework of legitimation, and its replacement, just as suddenly, by the symbolic order of a unified Germany. What will emerge in the following analysis, then, is not only an outline of the fantasy life of the East German surveillance state, but also an account of the retrospective revision of these fantasies in postunification Germany.

The names of the works under consideration suggest what is at stake in asking such questions here and now. Brigitte Burmeister's 1987 novel, *Anders* (German for "different" or "other than"), brings us into the "other" Germany, where we find that the contemporary Western categories of self and other, of private and public, are not entirely adequate to the alterity of East German public culture. Conversely, the titles of Wolfgang Hilbig's *"Ich"* ("I") and Thomas Brussig's *Helden wie wir* (Heroes like Us), both published in 1995, are constructed around first-person pronouns. The former simultaneously establishes and undermines the unity of the narrating self, destabilizing its emphatic first-person singular with scare quotes. This typographical detail reflects a keynote of epistemological doubt throughout the novel—an uncertainty that doubts even its own uncertainty. *Helden wie wir* (Heroes like Us) seems less existentially dubious. "We" exist definitively: we are "heroes." But who is included in this heroic—or mock-heroic—"us"? Is it the Stasi? The East Germans? Unified Germany? The pointed satire of Brussig's novel both critiques and deploys the categories by which such lines of inclusion and exclusion might be drawn. Finally, Florian Henckel von Donnersmarck's 2006 film *Das Leben der Anderen* (The Lives of Others) returns us to the question of the "otherness" of the GDR. One of the great achievements of the film, as attested by its numerous awards, including a 2007 Oscar, is how it brings this "other" Germany back to life through its fraught emotions and painstaking detail. Yet the urgency of the film's staging of "East Germanness" also attests to an undercurrent of anxiety, a concern that certain aspects of the East German experience are not "other" enough—indeed, that they are all too familiar.

"With life I have only eye contact": *Anders, oder Vom Aufenthalt in der Fremde*

Few critics have failed to point out that Brigitte Burmeister's 1987 debut novel, *Anders,* owes a great debt to the French *nouveau roman,* one of the author's primary research interests in her earlier career at the Institute for Romance Languages and Literatures in East Berlin.[1] Critics' fixation on this intertextual affiliation owes in part to its relative novelty in GDR literature. Even amid the increasing cultural openness of the 1980s, the *nouveau roman*'s modernist experiments seemed an unlikely prototype for East German prose. This was not the GDR literature readers were used to. Eschewing the linear, event-driven narrative of East Germany's

---

1. Colin Grant remarks: "The success of the novel in 'inviting a different kind of reading'...was underlined by the reviews published elsewhere which tended to stress its formal similarities with the *nouveau roman*" (76). See also Gebauer, 91.

still-doctrinal realism, *Anders* confronts the reader with shifting temporality, wavering subjectivity, and epistemological unreliability. In light of such uncertainties, the placement of *Anders* in the context of an established literary tradition may be understood as an attempt to master the novel's cryptic style and form: the *nouveau roman*'s indeterminacy of action is at least a certain uncertainty. At the time of its publication, *Anders*'s indeterminacy, the impossibility of finding out what, if anything, is actually going on in the novel, seemed to provoke a good deal of consternation in critics on both sides of the Wall.[2] Such unsettling ambiguity is not just a matter of perception or perspective; it is built into the pathways along which meaning circulates in this text and its context.

Anders, oder Vom Aufenthalt in der Fremde (Anders, or Of a Foreign Sojourn) is told as a series of fifty-three letters from David Anders to his "loved ones at home," friends and family, perhaps, in his rural hometown. Anders insists that he never intends to send these missives: "I let my letters disappear into the desk drawer," he writes (16). In his letters, Anders describes his experiences in his new home, a large unnamed city, probably Berlin. Despite a wealth of details about his work life, the reader never gets a clear sense of Anders's duties and activities. His job seems to involve observation and reporting but otherwise remains vague.

Always watching from the outside, Anders complains of an *Ereignisarmut,* a "dearth of experience." He has no friends and little interaction with the outside world. "With life I have only eye contact," he says (15). This situation improves, however, when he makes an unusual friend, whom he refers to only as D. Though the impulsive, nonconformist D. is nothing like Anders in temperament or worldview, they seem to hit it off. Eventually D. takes Anders home with him and introduces him to his wife.

Anders's initial encounter with D.'s wife, to whom he will refer throughout the novel as "the Woman" (*die Frau*)—is characteristically visual, even cinematic. Entering D.'s apartment, Anders sees her writing at her desk: "First I saw the Woman. She was encased in a cone of light like an insect in amber. She did not look up as D. and I entered the room. She held her head bent, as though she wore the light like a heavy crown" (19–20).

This ethereal vision of the Woman cues a memory of lost love. Anders describes a riverbank in summer, where he waits for someone addressed only as "you": "I didn't know then that you were coming for the last time" (20). Like the initial sighting of D.'s wife, this scene is conspicuously visual. Even the brief, indirectly reported conversation between Anders and his companion, which concludes several pages of dense landscape description, takes place in a visual register—or, more appropriately, overwhelms the visual register. Anders writes: "Everything around

---

2. For a detailed account of *Anders*'s reception, particularly in the GDR, see Colin Grant's article "Brigitte Burmeister's *Anders, oder Vom Aufenthalt in der Fremde:* Tracing the Texts in a 'New Novel,'" esp. 75–77.

us vanished, and you asked me the question. I've forgotten my answer. I had the sensation of seeing how our words sank into the evening mist that swallowed up the sky's milky color...so that, when we looked up, there was just a pale, empty space" (21).

As he gets to know her, Anders's relationship with D.'s wife carries echoes of this lost love from the past. After she gives him a pile of her writings, Anders writes:

> Why this exactly, why in this way? If you had just asked me the question, one single important question, and not on paper, but up close, so that I could see your face, while everything around us would vanish...as though swallowed by fog, and around us a pale, empty space, and within it clear and indestructible my answer: yes. (68–69)

This time, the question asked of Anders would not collapse the field of vision entirely, but rather would focus it—everything in the scene would vanish except the most important: "your face." Now he would be able to answer: yes. This scenario, however, is hypothetical. The Woman has not recapitulated that question from long ago, that intimate question asked face-to-face, but rather has handed Anders a pile of her writing, ostensibly so that he could use the remaining space on the pages—the backs, the margins, between the lines—to write his own story (40). The writing on the pages, Anders assumes, is intended as a message to him: "My name is nowhere to be seen," he thinks as he reads, "but I know that she means me" (42). Likewise, his letters are increasingly addressed to her: the "you all" (*ihr*) of the "loved ones at home" is replaced by the "you" (*du*) of "the Woman." Communication, however, is not transpiring. His letters are never sent, her messages remain inscrutable: "How can I answer you," he writes, "if I don't understand your message?" (68).

In light of these episodes, we can begin to posit two opposing semiotic regimes in the novel. On the one hand, visuality and the written word, tokens of distance, rupture, and a failure to communicate; on the other, aurality and dialogue, which would signal intimacy, presence, participation. As the novel progresses, Anders becomes increasingly frustrated with his life of distanced observation: "I hate the observer," he says. "It's not enough. What I want is something else [Was ich will, ist anders]" (80). This other—*anders*—that he wants is both the other and himself, Anders.

Anders's growing discontentedness with his position as observer, his desire to replace eye contact with face-to-face encounter, has self-evident professional repercussions: "Unlike my coworkers," he says, "life has awakened in me a desire to become a bad observer, that is, a participant" (134). Eventually, Anders's coworkers notice his inferior output and force him to sign a contract promising to distance himself from his nonconformist friends.

How can we contextualize these rival influences—one, inflected as dissident and libidinal, that pulls Anders toward society, communication, and contact; the other, associated with his job, the state, and propriety, that demands he hold himself above the fray, observing and reporting? Applying a perhaps overly programmatic interpretive schema, we can recast this dichotomy in political terms. As the embodiment of party bureaucracy, Anders in his loneliness would attest to the critical attenuation of the ties between state and society in the GDR of the 1980s, the persistent and widening gulf between party and populace described in the previous four chapters of this book. "Against the will of the SED," Gert-Joachim Glaeßner notes, "society since the beginning of the '60s had attained a certain autonomy. It had emancipated itself from the party" (3).[3] Anders's yearning for approach would signal the desire to overcome this dissociation, to intervene more immediately and effectively in the everyday life of GDR society, "to become a participant." Within this analogy, surveillance—Anders's longing gaze—becomes an expression of the state's unrequited love, a desperate effort to maintain contact with an indifferent beloved: the people.

The latter possibility, that of face-to-face or dialogical relationship, would stand not only for the negative space of the GDR's foreclosed public sphere, but also for East Germany's active counter-public sphere—the so-called *Nischengesellschaft,* or "niche society"—which replaced various dysfunctional social systems, from the aesthetic to the economic.[4] This is the world inhabited by D. and his wife, the world of self-publication and unofficial gatherings, barter and black market.

It is the allure of this world, of the counter-public life shared by D. and his wife, that tempts Anders to trade observation for participation. Yet the more Anders's harmless watching gives way to active intervention, the more his activity looks like the modus operandi of the Stasi. That Anders's attentions might have ominous consequences becomes apparent when D. and his wife suddenly disappear. This section, the dramatic high point of the novel, is also where the narrative's murkiness is most pronounced. In a fever-induced delirium, Anders imagines an interrogation, apparently of D. "Why are you making this so hard for us?" the interrogator asks in classic form. "Twelve hours, and not one sensible word. And you know that we already know everything" (121). "Of course you know everything," says the man being interrogated. "You have his reports, after all" (122). Anders's reports, it seems, have incriminated his friends.

Perhaps seeking answers to the mystery of his friends' disappearance, Anders visits the abandoned apartment of D. and his wife to read "the Woman's" writings. Nowhere in the novel does he more fit the mold of a Stasi snoop than here, breaking into an author's apartment to read her unfinished manuscript. In a way, however, this purloined letter seems to have reached its intended destination. Like the section she gave to Anders, the rest of "the Woman's" novel is addressed to

---

3. I was alerted to Glaeßner's argument by a passage in Charles Maier's *Dissolution* (36).

4. The term *Nischengesellschaft* was coined by Günter Gaus, the Federal Republic's ambassador to the GDR between 1974 and 1981. See Gaus, 156 ff.

an unspecified "you"—a *du,* as a number of wordplays suggest, that in fact refers to Anders. "You're not what I expected," writes "the Woman." "You're different [Anders bist du]" (260).

It is a curious form of communication between Anders and "the Woman," these long letters never sent. Though they are formally addressed to the other, they seem intended less to initiate dialogue than to lament its impossibility. Such skepticism regarding the communicative potential of the written word, I suggest, can be read not only philosophically or poetologically, but also as a fairly direct reflection of the political conditions informing the novel's production. This dynamic comes into focus as Anders reads further in "the Woman's" manuscript, and the novel's Klein-bottle plot turns in on itself. The manuscript that Anders is reading, we may infer, is that of Burmeister's novel. "Now the man who was originally addressed as 'you' is having a say," Anders writes in his letter, describing "the Woman's" manuscript. "He's informing his relatives about this or that detail from his monotonous life" (261). Via this metanarratological switchback, the "authorship" of the text that we are reading changes hands; we are now led to believe that we are reading Anders's account of "the Woman's" account of Anders's account of "the Woman."

This feedback loop offers an apt metaphor for the conditions of cultural produc-tion within the GDR's dysfunctional public sphere. In the system of censorship and self-censorship that ensured the state's control of public discourse, all published texts were, to a degree, palimpsests. As a generic account might have it, the state rewrites the text of the author rewriting the introjected text of the state.[5] With Anders stepping in as an all-purpose surveillance bureaucrat, the drama of the East German publishing industry plays out in miniature. For "the Woman's" manu-script is not simply intended "for the desk drawer"—a phrase used in the GDR to refer to unpublishable texts—but rather for the man who will fetch it out of the drawer, the same man who would literally overwrite her story with his own.

At times, "the Woman's" manuscript is almost a panegyric to her personal snoop and *Lektor,* that uniquely East German hybrid of an editor and a censor.[6] "Neither of us will declare love for the other," she writes, "but to me you are indispensable [*unentbehrlich*]." D., whose marginal notes in the manuscript add another voice to the conversation, sees the matter more straightforwardly: "Admit it," he has scribbled in the margin, "you love him!" (261).

---

5. In "Old Movies: Cinema as Palimpsest in GDR Fiction," Katie Trumpener describes "the often palimpsestic structure of GDR fiction, in which characters find a superimposed veil of memories— voluntary, involuntary, personal, collective, historical, subjective—overlaying, coloring or muffling the world around them" (40–41). I am suggesting here that this superimposition expresses the fraught rela-tionship of GDR cultural products not only with the past, but also with the political present.

6. In the GDR publishing industry, the *Lektor* had a role somewhere between that of an editor and a censor: before a work could be published, it had to pass through the *Lektor's* careful ideological evaluation.

In a 1990 interview, Burmeister described the growing "suspicion" she felt as she wrote *Anders* that its hero might be an agent of the secret police:

> My own suspicion that the "hero" could be a member of the Stasi came about through a verbal association. This character is very lonely, looks out of the window, "observes" a lot. In French the word is "observer"—"observe"—and "observe" is a security service term. Then I said to myself, "This bastard is a member of the Stasi." And I fought against this suspicion for a long time, but finally gave up. I grew to like the character more and more as I went on writing. (von Hallberg, 133)

It is a remarkable testament to the pervasiveness of the East German state security service that an author could find herself wondering whether a character she herself had invented was moonlighting as a Stasi snoop. Burmeister's subsequent discovery seems even more counterintuitive: that despite this suspicion, she "grew to like the character more and more."

What is it that makes Anders likable, *unentbehrlich,* even lovable, within the terms of the novel? And what might this mean for the political-allegorical interpretation we have been pursuing thus far? With Anders as its feckless avatar, the state seems at first to be cast as a star-crossed lover, a pitiable, even likable figure. As much as he longs to make contact with his beloved, he is doomed to helpless observation. Embodied in Anders, this state is a lonely watcher and a loving reader. It can be an interlocutor—indeed, an interrogator—only in its fevered dreams. Unfortunately, the East German state's fever-dream was also a reality: the state within a state of the Stasi. Likewise the state was not just a passive reader. The censor's interventions—and the prophylactic revisions of self-censorship—sapped the communicative potential of the written word, turning authorship into palimpsest, dialogue into feedback.

Yet it is precisely this interference that necessitates the counter-public sphere, that shadow society from which Anders—and the organization he represents—is categorically excluded. In a 1999 interview, Burmeister discussed the loss of this counter-public sphere with the collapse of the GDR, specifically the lamentable disappearance of a certain mode of writing and reading she calls "the conspiratorial" (*das Konspirative*): " 'The conspiratorial' is something that I miss from GDR times. Now it seems like one can say anything, push the limits further and further out.... But that's not always good for the quality of literature. Crudely put, one is going for sensation, not subversion" (Gebauer, 97).

Following this line of argument, we are forced to revise the earlier claim that the overpresence of the state in the public sphere led solely to a designification of public discourse in the GDR. The model of the "conspiratorial" public sphere suggests that the opposite might equally—and concurrently—be the case, for state surveillance also creates the conditions for the "conspiratorial" mode, that intimate confederacy of writer and reader that raises the stakes, heightens the drama, overdetermines the significance of the communication that passes between them. This heightened sense of significance is captured in a passage from Monika Maron's 2004 novel, *Endmoränen,* the story of a writer working on a biography of Wilhelmine Enke, the lover of Friedrich Wilhelm II:

> Fifteen years ago this harmless biography could have been a hammered Morse code from the underground, a pale flare on the horizon, a smoke signal over the pathless forest, and whoever wrote it could be assured of the importance of their activity, indeed of their whole existence. Even those who didn't write the biography but shared in the outrage it triggered, even secretly, could feel important, because their receptivity for messages of this kind made them indispensable [*unentbehrlich*] to the sender. They were initiates, and people like them guaranteed the survival of culture. (40)

Within East Germany's tightly controlled public sphere, dissent was often a matter of a few evocative words, an ambiguous phrase, a coded "smoke signal." For this reason, East German authors could expect conscientious, critical readings from their audience, but also, and especially, from their *Lektoren.* Like Anders—and through agents like Anders—the surveillance state pored over these communications, searching for evidence of obedience or dissent, for signs of love or hate. East German state surveillance hobbled art and ruined lives, but it also considered art important enough to ruin lives for. This apparent incongruity helps to account for the ambivalence attested by the novel's convoluted love story. "Admit it," D. says to his wife, "you love him." Perhaps she worries that at the level of fantasy, of illicit desire, she does.

"What a simulation this reality was!": *"Ich"*

Written in 1995, eight years after Burmeister's novel, Wolfgang Hilbig's *"Ich"* shares *Anders*'s temporal and geographic setting. With the added clarity of hindsight, *"Ich"* captures the heady, even apocalyptic atmosphere in late-'80s Berlin, the look and feel of a society sliding inexorably toward dissolution. Hilbig's novel, which garnered a great deal of critical attention and a number of literary prizes, narrates the day-to-day life of a low-level Stasi agent. "W." has been assigned to observe the underground literary scene in East Berlin, in particular an avant-garde writer known as *Reader.*[7] Much of the novel's present-time action occurs literally underground, in the warren of cellars beneath Berlin. W. uses these tunnels as a means of surreptitious access and movement, but also as a space of contemplation. Alone in his subterranean retreat, he reflects on his peculiar job and tries to

---

7. The protagonist in *"Ich"* is known variously as W., M. W., Cambert, and C. The nomenclature seems to be motivated both temporally and thematically: at some point, W. becomes C. almost exclusively, perhaps indicating a wholesale identification with his Stasi persona.

reconstruct the circumstances that brought him to it. The narrative of *"Ich"* is as labyrinthine as W.'s hideout, a bewildering tangle of past and present tense, third- and first-person narration, direct and indirect discourse. In this redoubled obscurity, narrated and narrational, the reader joins W. in epistemological crisis, in the desperate effort to determine what has taken, is taking, or will take place.

Throughout the novel, W. tries to ascertain which parts of his life constitute "reality" and which are "simulation": "So he had simulated his life before....But when had he awoken to this reality?" (64). The theoretical resonance of such language is not accidental. Like all participants in the Berlin literary scene, W. is an avid reader of contemporary French philosophy, even if he has misgivings about the scene's apotheosis of Foucault, Derrida, and others (22). W.'s fascination with Jean Baudrillard's concept of "simulation" is particularly important. By Baudrillard's account, reality itself has become a simulation—which is not to say it does not exist. Instead, simulated reality is in fact hyperreal, no longer tethered to substance or origin. According to Baudrillard,

> The real is produced from miniaturized cells, matrices, and memory banks, models of control—and it can be reproduced an indefinite number of times from these. It no longer needs to be rational, because it no longer measures itself against either an ideal or a negative instance. It is no longer anything but operational. In fact, it is no longer really the real, because no imaginary envelops it anymore. It is a hyperreal, produced from a radiating synthesis of combinatory models in a hyperspace without atmosphere. (2)

This vision of an irrational reality that has ceased to measure itself against "either an ideal or a negative instance" is an apt description of GDR ideology in the 1980s. By this time, the guiding principles of East German socialism had evaporated. The working class had little use for its ostensible vanguard, the SED, and the egalitarian promises of a Workers' and Peasants' State had borne fruit only as collective privation. For Hilbig and his peers, writers like Baudrillard offered a compelling new way to describe and critique the conditions of the East German public sphere.

Yet, as Sylvie Marie Bordaux points out, Hilbig does not adopt the language of the French structuralists and poststructuralists uncritically: "Baudrillard, like Foucault and Deleuze, is invoked in a negative context in the text and is portrayed as an example of a false and modish world" (180). While recognizing the descriptive power of poststructuralist theory, Hilbig worries that such thinking could lead to a total disavowal of the real—and therefore capitulation to the realities of state power.[8]

---

8. Bordaux quotes a lecture by Hilbig in which he says that Baudrillard's idea of simulation "must have been very attractive to the ideologues of the GDR" since it facilitated their spurious claims to legitimacy (Hilbig, *Abriss der Kritik,* 53; qtd. in Bordaux, 180).

Such uncertainty regarding the reality of reality leads to the deep ambivalence identified by Julia Hell in her article *"Wendebilder:* Neo Rauch and Wolfgang Hilbig."* Hilbig, Hell argues, rejects the "specular realist epistemology" prevalent in the official literary culture of the GDR, the totalizing "view from above" that aims at knowledge and mastery (280). Such a totalizing viewpoint can only operate according to what Hilbig calls *Beschreibungsrituale* (rituals of description), the bankrupt literary practices of East Germany's linguistic dictatorship (284). This critique of official literary culture in the GDR, according to Hell, "testifies to an implicit belief in the 'visibility' and the 'truth' of reality behind the 'Beschreibungsrituale' that distort it." Yet, Hell suggests,

> there is also a more radical strand in Hilbig's writing.... There is 'nothing to see' because reality—that which lies behind the official *Beschreibungsrituale*—has been destroyed by [these rituals of description], or rather, our ability to perceive the reality has been shattered. ("*Wendebilder*," 285)

The following reading of *"Ich"* will address this contradiction, plumbing the depths of the text's apparently bottomless simulation, for there *is* a "reality" in Hilbig's novel, a level of causes, events, and consequences that can break through the otherwise total simulation in the narrative. Such moments of rupture, of reality's incursion into simulation, can be characterized as *catastrophe,* understood both as dénouement and disaster: a sudden turn, a revolution, a calamity. In *"Ich,"* two very different catastrophes prove capable of piercing the membrane between simulation and reality: violence and love.

Despite an undercurrent of imagined or indirectly reported violence throughout the novel, only one act of physical aggression in *"Ich"* is marked for the reader as "really" happening. This incident, long foreshadowed and invested with considerable significance by the novel's symbolic framework, compels a reevaluation of many of the events and circumstances preceding it. While brutality is largely suppressed in *"Ich,"* love is entirely absent, defined only negatively by what it is not. In the novel, we see love solely as a lack, an always-unfulfilled potential for connection, change, and growth. In place of love is a passionless simulation of intimacy, a sadistic attraction to cruelty. W.'s emotional compass allows only desire without attachment, sensation without engagement. In W.'s "perverse" libidinal order the catastrophes of love and violence have been evacuated of their potency. Diluted, they are easily confused; the closer W. comes to real interpersonal contact—to love—the more violent his fantasies become, while thoughts of violence tend to provoke his sexual interest.

In this way, "perversion" shields W. and his coworkers from the consequences of their actions, transforming the scruples of love or the shock of violence into a seemingly meaningless play of fantasy and desire. An investigation of the portrayal of "perversion" in *"Ich,"* in particular the key role of "deviant" sexuality in defining and delimiting the Stasi personality, reveals the missing thread that would lead to the surface of this sunken labyrinth. The novel suggests that if there were a way out of this simulated reality for W.—which there is not—it would be found in heterosexual romantic love.

When he first starts working for "the Firm," W. experiences the psychosexual dimension of his trade—what might be called the erotics of surveillance—in one of its most basic manifestations. Out walking at night, he stops to watch a conversation taking place in a neighbor's house. Soon, such clandestine observation becomes a habit—or perhaps a job, as it is never clear whether W.'s nightly rounds are part of his assignment at the "Firm." Whether business or pleasure, this new activity has a distinct voyeuristic allure: "The organs of speech, as he explored them with his eyes, suddenly took on the character of body parts from the so-called private area" (127–28).

Eventually, voyeuristic tendencies creep into W.'s sex life. After beginning a physical relationship with his landlady, Frau Falbe, he discovers that his imagination is more and more necessary for sexual arousal. Frau Falbe is not surprised to learn of W.'s flights of fantasy. As she explains, her now-absent husband displayed similar proclivities:

> Didn't I tell you, she said, that he was in the security service as well? … My husband talked about it sometimes and said we're all in the service because we can't do it with women. Because we can't do it with people in general. We can only investigate people.… Foreplay, my husband used to say, for him that's the important part, just like at work. There, he said, we just do the foreplay as well, it's much more exciting.… He always wanted to see everything … Watching, he said, that's the thing. (264–65)

Frau Falbe's initial characterization of the Stasi type as a man attracted to the service because he "can't do it with women" is not the first insinuation of a link between homosexuality and Stasi work in the novel. In an earlier conversation, Frau Falbe tells W. how Harry Falbe, who seems to be either her son, nephew, or husband, had been harassed and threatened by the Stasi, apparently in an effort to recruit him. "They said," Frau Falbe explains, "that he's the other way round, that he should admit it!"

> "Homosexual?" W. asked.
>   "Yes, that he's a homo, that he's gay, they told him that. But I know better, because Harry doesn't lie to me." (217)

Frau Falbe goes on to describe how the agents, in particular a man named Feuerbach, who happens to be W.'s current boss in Berlin, escalated their intimidation to abuse:

> "And you know what happened that night? The guy stuck his pistol up his …"
>   "Impossible!" said W.

"Oh, it's possible all right, he stuck it in him, Harry told me exactly how it happened. Harry wasn't wearing anything, just his coat over his pajamas, that's what he was wearing when they put him in the car and took him away. And back at the office the man stuck the pistol in his backside and said: 'Should I pull the trigger? You like that, you queer dog,' he said. 'Admit it, you're a queer, or I'll pull the trigger'..."

"Unbelievable!" said W. (217)

As her story goes on, the "reality" of the violence it describes gives way to a scene of fantasy construction—a simulation of violence. "Really the story was unimportant," W. thinks.

Much more interesting was the inflection with which Frau Falbe told it. She really didn't narrate as much as gasp it out, with a throaty voice, without paying any attention to his interjections. She had propped up her upper body on the desk, twisting halfway out of the armchair, and held one hand on the triangular neckline of her blouse, as though she wasn't getting enough air....He had to admit that he was excited by the woman's discomposure. (219)

Despite its manifest cruelty, Frau Falbe's story occasions not horror but desire in both the teller and the listener. This incident, in fact, begins their erotic relationship. "Excited/infected" (*angesteckt*) by her "discomposure" (*Aufregung*), W. returns the next day to hear the story again. "A moment later," Hilbig writes, this time in the third person, "they were rolling across the double bed" (220).

The play of fantasy—the simulation of reality—at work here is best summed up in a note scrawled idly by W. a short while later:

The game of the idea of the incident with the pistol [das Spiel der Vorstellung der Sache mit der Pistole]...the idea of the game of the woman of the incident with the pistol...the story of the idea of the woman of the game of the incident with the pistol...and so on...the structure of the genitive of the genitive,—that seemed somehow familiar to him!" (231–32)

As W. points out earlier, such a "stringing together of genitives" is a characteristic usage of the Stasi. "Essentially, it was a linguistic form used to destroy one's sense of reality" (23).

In playing "the game of the idea of the incident with the pistol," W. and Frau Falbe begin a relationship within the Stasi's "perverse" libidinal order, for the "incident with the pistol" is a thoroughly transgressive fantasy, simultaneously breaking sexual, moral, and political taboos. W. is oddly pleased by the alleged unscrupulousness of his employer: "W. felt a certain satisfaction in the thought that his superior officer had such a reputation" (218–19). For W., the latent and manifest violence of his profession is just a matter of *Ruf* (reputation)—he has only ever heard about it but never seen or experienced it. It is, in other words, simulated, phantasmatic violence: "just the foreplay," as Frau Falbe's husband had put it.

"Ich" exposes the dangers of this illusion of inconsequence, maintained through such psycholinguistic mechanisms as the Stasi's "reality-destroying" genitive. Thus W.'s split with "the Firm" (though less a decisive repudiation than a kind of "inner exile") is possible only after he has relinquished the erotics of the "rampant genitives," the infinite chain of phantasmatic desire that confuses simulation and reality and binds him to his profession. The "something else" for which he gives it up will be love—or something like it.

In many ways, the love story in *"Ich"* is highly dubious; W.-in-love is not so different from W.-just-doing-his-job. To put it bluntly, he seems less a lover than a stalker. Yet in light of its importance to the novel's conclusion I will hazard a more credulous reading of this subplot than it might at first seem to warrant.

When W. first begins working for Feuerbach and "the Firm's" Berlin branch, it is unclear what his official duty is to be. He is supposed to keep an eye on *Reader* and his circle, and instructed to write detailed descriptions of those involved in the avant-garde literary scene. Eventually, however, a more specific task is assigned to W.: he is told to find a West German "contact" to facilitate work in West Berlin. The contact person Feuerbach has in mind is "the girl that runs after *Reader*" (192), a woman whom W. had already noticed and labeled "the Student" *(die Studentin)*. Essentially, W. thinks he is being groomed to become a "Romeo spy," an East German agent who seduces Western women into spying for the Stasi.[9]

Here, W. balks. Instead of passing on to his superiors the profile he has written of *the Student,* W. decides to keep it for himself. With this small act of defiance, W. begins his "private operation"—to shadow *the Student* on his own initiative (315). Since he is not following her for his job, W. decides that he must have another motivation: "It occurred to me," he thinks, "that I must love *the Student* in a very peculiar way and chased after her for that reason" (322).

Still, W. does intend to give Feuerbach some account of his "private operation"—just not a profile of *the Student.* He decides to invent a character called "the Woman" *(die Frau)*, a wholly superior being due to her origins in the "free West."[10] "Her hands were entirely different hands, her arms were different, her musculature was made of another, much finer material than anyone else I knew…her DNA was

---

9. For more on the Romeo spies, see Elisabeth Pfister's *Unternehmen Romeo: Die Liebeskommandos der Stasi.* In his autobiography *Man without a Face,* Markus Wolf, chief of foreign intelligence at the MfS, boasts: "If I go down in espionage history, it may well be for perfecting the use of sex in spying. My Romeo spies gained notoriety across the world by winning women's hearts in order to obtain the state and political secrets to which their targets had access" (135).

10. It is an intriguing coincidence that both Anders and W. refer to the objects of their affection as "die Frau." Where the word is not distinguished typographically in Burmeister's novel, Hilbig puts it in italics. I have retained this usage, though I chose to capitalize the English word in both cases.

absolute West-DNA" (323). Such magnificent alterity, then, is what W. imagines as corresponding to "the Firm's" conception of a Westerner.

As he allows his invention free rein, it becomes less and less clear whether this is still W.'s projection of "the Firm's" imaginary image or his own increasingly violent fantasy:

> As I saw her, *the Woman* was…an unapproachable being—and for that matter…much stronger than I. I couldn't do otherwise, I had to surround *the Woman* with an obscene thought if I wanted to make her attainable. With the thought, to catch up to her one evening and to throw her down on the cold stones in the dirty half-light of the pedestrian bridge over the train tracks at Storkauer Straße…, to throw her into the Eastern dust of this concrete tunnel so that she would finally lie in reality, and to force apart her legs…
>
> One may *think* anything, my superiors in the security service said, one even *has* to. Maybe they even said, it is the *duty* of the writer to think *everything*…(324)

W.'s rape fantasy seems to combine both a desire for proximity—a brutal, coercive version of Anders's wistful longing for approach—and the distancing effect identified throughout *"Ich"* as characteristic of the Stasi mentality. At the same time as he tries to make *the Woman/Student* "real" and "approachable" through the creation of this rape scenario, W. insists that it is only a fiction (after all, *the Woman* is his invention), and that it is his *duty* as an agent and a writer—roles that are inseparable throughout the novel—to fantasize in this manner. W.'s partition of *the Woman* from *the Student* may best be understood as a kind of object splitting, whereby *the Woman* becomes a "bad object," the object of W.'s violent fantasies and perverse desires. Significantly, *the Woman* is also the "bad object" of the Stasi: a Western provocateur in the Eastern underground who is politically dangerous, tactically desirable, and diplomatically untouchable. In separating *the Woman* from *the Student,* W. attempts to isolate and disavow the part of his personality he has given over to the Stasi. The agent Cambert (his code name) might stalk *the Woman* with violent and lascivious intent, but W. follows *the Student* because he "must love [her] in a very peculiar way" (322).

In a scene near the end of the novel, W. is confronted with the indivisible reality of *the Woman/Student.* While he is following her through the streets one night, she suddenly turns and walks toward him. Eye to eye with his quarry, W. panics and flees. Thinking about the event later, W. concludes: "There was no doubt about it, I fled from her. She turned the tables and became my pursuer just like that!" (330). This scene models the catastrophic potential of love in *"Ich,"* its ability to overturn the perverse order of simulation and allow "reality" to break in. The one-way gaze of W.'s voyeurism becomes reciprocal contact.

Here we might recall Emmanuel Levinas's concept of the face-to-face encounter, the moment he calls the "entrance of the ethical": "The proximity of the other showing me his or her face, in society with me, and the implications of that encounter overturn the logical and ontological play of the same and the other, transforming it into ethics" (76). In a very literal way, the face of *the Student* confronts W. with the ethics of his actions, with the violence, real and imagined, of an "operation" he has adopted as his own. He suddenly realizes that Cambert and W.—his professional and private selves—are one and the same.

Through a number of disclosures by Feuerbach, W. learns that *Reader* is in fact an "unofficial employee" of the MfS and that he has been given the task for which W. was being considered: that of wooing *the Student* as a possible contact in West Berlin. Whether out of jealousy or goodwill, W. decides to warn *the Student* of her entanglement in this spy caper and smuggles a note into her pocketbook revealing a fact he has recently "stumbled across" (358): "It said: she shouldn't get involved, I could tell her some interesting things about the writer S. R. Just by way of example: I happen to know that he is a homosexually inclined person, and this is perhaps significant for a certain ambiguity about him" (360).

W.'s claim is a bald ploy to wrest *the Student*'s affection away from his rival. But why "out" him in this way? When he uses *Reader*'s alleged homosexual tendencies to drive a wedge between the writer and *the Student,* W. proves to be the consummate Stasi man. This, after all, was the tactic that Feuerbach had used to press-gang Harry Falbe into "the Firm." Yet, paradoxically, W. intends his note to signify the opposite. By labeling *Reader* a homosexual, W. hopes to create an ontological distinction between *Reader* and himself. As W. sees it, he may have given himself over to his job—given up his very "Ich"—but he has not relinquished the last trace of his former self, which in the novel's psychosexual shorthand is his heterosexual self. In pursuit of what he takes to be love, W. would turn his back on the Stasi's simulated world. As he thinks back later on this event, W. finds a small consolation in this escape attempt: "I made an effort: I wanted to reveal myself to *the Student*—probably!—myself and the Operation: Reader" (372).

With the qualifier "probably" (*vermutlich*) W. calls his own intentions into doubt. The love story in *"Ich,"* the story of W.'s "private operation," cannot be taken wholly at face value. Within the world of deception and self-deception inhabited by W. and his coworkers, motives are slippery and unreliable. Yet, ultimately, the novel's narrative itself confirms the logic by which sexual deviance—here represented by homosexuality—would become a token of ontological difference, the logic of splitting and disavowal. The essential difference, however, is not between W. and *Reader,* but between "the Firm" and the society around it.

This confirmation can be found in the novel's final catastrophe, a sudden moment of violence that cuts through the layers of fantasy and simulation, revealing the "truth" of Stasi perversion. On the way to his meeting with *the Student,* W. is arrested and thrown in prison. After a few weeks in solitary confinement, W. receives a late-night visit from a highly inebriated, nearly incoherent Feuerbach. Without warning, Feuerbach attacks him:

> In the darkness, Feuerbach threw him against the wall and yanked down his pants; he
> felt a hard cold thrust between his buttocks, it was metal, it was the barrel of Feuer-
> bach's pistol, the muzzle boring painfully into his insides.—Should I, you dog...bel-
> lowed Feuerbach....Should I shoot you in the hole, you queer bugger? (366)

Here "the game of the idea of the incident with the pistol" is visited upon W.—neither
as a game nor as fantasy, but bodily. "As though to prove the reality of the scene
that night," we read a page later, "his anus hurt for a week when he had to relieve
himself" (367). This scene, the novel's only instance of directly reported violence,
offers not only narrative resolution, but, more importantly, moral clarity. Feuerbach's Stasi, it seems, is not just trafficking in fantasies, simulation, "foreplay," but
rather in acts of "real" depravity.

In this light, we can see how the concept of perversion would function in *"Ich"*
as a marker of "the Firm's" alterity, for where there is perversion, there must also
be its opposite, an assumed "normality" that consolidates its identity by disavowing
the abnormal, deviant, perverse. In the libidinal economy of *"Ich,"* this normative
pole is only hinted at because we are trapped, with W., in the labyrinth of the Stasi's
perverse order. The novel suggests that history itself will see to the overturning
of this order and the creation of conditions under which "real" social ties—"real"
love," we could say—might be possible. It is no coincidence, then, that W.'s nearest
approximation of heterosexual romantic love—his "private operation," culminating in the face-to-face confrontation with *the Student*—becomes an "omen" for the
changes that are underway in the GDR: "It was a sign that something was coming
at us in this country" (330).

What he calls a "small event that could get larger" (330) will ultimately become
the 1989 revolution. Near the end of the novel, W. reflects on the atmosphere of
malaise and unrest in the GDR of the late 1980s, a mood he summarizes with the
word *Haß* (hate):

> The reasons for this hate were not the untenable or broken promises of the gov-
> ernment, not the blindness and toadying of its representatives, not the fraudulent
> elections, perhaps not even the Wall, the police, the party hacks with their dou-
> ble standards and cowardice...*we* were the reason for this hate....We, the small
> and low, blurred, tireless shadows that clung to the people of this land: we nour-
> ished this hate....We were the shadows of life, we were death...we were the
> dark side of humanity split off and become flesh, become shadow-flesh. "I" was
> hate...(371–72)

In W.'s lyrical self-abnegation, the Stasi becomes a projection of the "dark side of
humanity"—the "bad object," we might say, of civil society. We see such projection at work as well within Hilbig's novel, in the emphatic assertion and reasser-
tion of the perverse nature of the Stasi mentality, in the logic of disavowal that *"Ich"*
both critiques and upholds. What remains to be seen, however, is why the Stasi in

particular becomes this "bad object"—why this institution is freighted with the disavowed "perversion" of a bygone state.

"Was that what you wanted to know?": *Helden wie wir*

At the hands of satirist Thomas Brussig, the Stasi is treated very differently from what we have just seen. The history of the Ministry for State Security is less a tragedy than a farce as told by Klaus Uhltzscht, the hero of Brussig's comic novel *Helden wie wir* (Heroes like Us). In Brussig's novel the Stasi is ineffective, incompetent, and inconsequential—a far cry from the sinister, formidable organization depicted in *"Ich."* Yet the Stasi in *Helden wie wir* shares a significant characteristic with Hilbig's "Firm": in both texts, the Stasi is manifestly perverse. *Helden wie wir*, however, associates surveillance work with a collection of harmless and humorous kinks, rather than with sadistic depravity, as in *"Ich."*

Helden wie wir is framed as a monologue in which Klaus Uhltzscht tells his life story to Mr. Kitzelstein, a reporter for the *New York Times*. *New York Times* readers should be interested in his story, Klaus opines, on account of his key role in the events of November 9, 1989. "The story of the Wall's end," he declares, "is the story of my penis" (5).

Klaus's exposure to a certain erotics of surveillance begins in the stuffy and repressed atmosphere of his parental home. His mother is an uptight hygiene inspector who teaches young Klaus to be afraid of germs, public toilets, and especially sex. As one might predict, Klaus becomes obsessed with the latter, a process he outlines meticulously for Mr. Kitzelstein. From the eye-opening disquisitions of his more enlightened peers at summer camp to his careful study of Siegfried Schnabl's sex-ed standard *Mann und Frau intim* (Man and Woman Intimately), Klaus's adolescence is a dogged quest to learn more about this mysterious, frightening, thrilling subject. The greater his ignorance, the more obsessive his fascination: "But *Mann und Frau Intim* afforded no clues to the G spot. Did it, or did it not, exist? Did it exist only in the West? Was the G spot peculiar to Western women? Would the solution of this mystery be rewarded with a Nobel Prize? Other people were always privy to information I knew nothing about" (62).

One of the things Klaus knows nothing about is the Stasi, the headquarters of which is across the street from his childhood home. When Klaus learns that the Stasi had been involved in the dismissal of one of his favorite teachers, he puts the pieces together: "I suspected duress of some kind, presumably on the Stasi's part. Such a great big building, and nobody knew what went on there. Everyone spoke of it in whispers. A teacher was fired and no one would tell me why. Ergo, there was something fishy about the Stasi" (63). Klaus makes the Stasi his "secret enemy," staking out the building and writing down what he sees. When his father finds out about Klaus's activities, he is extremely upset: "Writing in mental anguish, he told me that if my activities ever came out, he and my mother would be convicted of espionage and sent to prison" (64).

And his father should know. He is himself, as Klaus soon finds out, an employee of the Stasi. Later, Klaus will describe him as "every inch the man from the Stasi. He was probably an interrogator—the one who switches on the spotlight and shines it in your eyes, who roams the interview room in his shirtsleeves and expects you to earn your glass of water by confessing all" (70). As this description attests, Klaus's father is not a very nice man. He is gruff and indifferent by turns, paranoid, misanthropic, and highly critical of young Klaus. Nonetheless, or perhaps all the more, Klaus looks up to his father with admiration and awe. And when his father suggests that Klaus join the Stasi as well, Klaus jumps at the chance. This career move, however, does nothing to counter Klaus's inferiority complex. On the contrary, his association with the Stasi will ultimately be added to his litany of failures.

Nor does Klaus's new job lessen his sex obsession. In fact, it offers vast new resources for the exploration of his number one hobby. At training camp, Klaus meets Raymund, a self-styled ladies' man and chronic masturbator, who leads his fellow cadets on a moonlight cruise to pick up women. After an alcohol-soaked night aboard the *Wilhelm Pieck,* a young woman named Marina takes Klaus home with her, where he trades his virginity for a case of gonorrhea and a newfound appreciation for the mysteries and delights of the sexual act.

Eventually, Klaus is assigned to his first post: the "Periodicals Postal Subscription Service" in Berlin, which in reality is a Stasi front. Klaus is shocked and dismayed to find that his coworkers are neither suave, competent master spies nor even grim bullies like his father, but rather eccentric, blundering buffoons. "Was I really in the genuine, legendary Stasi," Klaus asks himself, "or in an outfit that only called itself by that name the better to disguise the *genuine* Stasi, which would one day send for me?" (123).

Because of his tendency to assume that everything he doesn't know must be a sexual secret, Klaus's always-inscrutable work assignments become increasingly sexualized—just as his sex life becomes more and more influenced by his Stasi work. Thus, for instance, his misinterpretation of his boss's exhortation to "put ourselves in the enemy's place so as to render his actions predictable":

> I once found, on Grabs's desk, the transcript of a bugged telephone conversation in which AE Individualist [the code name of a dissident under Stasi surveillance] was referred to as "Chicken-fucker." I was intrigued despite myself. *Chicken-fucker?* What did it mean? . . . Would it be easier for me to put myself in the enemy's place and render his actions predictable if I myself became a chicken-fucker?
>
> With this in mind, I bought a whole broiler after work, took it home, and, without consulting higher authority, sexually abused it. (194)

When he checks Schnabl's *Mann und Frau intim* to see if it says anything about sex with a broiled chicken, Klaus becomes aware of the full scope of his deed: "I had done it with an *animal!* A *dead* animal! A dead *young* animal! A headless, i.e. *mutilated,* dead young animal! I had simultaneously indulged in *four* perversions" (195). Suddenly, Klaus realizes his mission and calling, to do his part toward improving the GDR's balance of trade: "What an idea: the invention and exportation, in exchange for foreign currency, of patented perversions!" (199). With Schnabl's book as his guide, Klaus sets out on a twisted path of discovery:

> No, Mr. Kitzelstein, *fucking* was for ordinary folk. *I* aspired to be a disciple of Part III, Chapter 9—to plumb the cavernous depths of *Sexual Aberrations* and illuminate them with the torch of scientific research. I knew what it meant to have a vocation. I would be a historic missionary instead of a Nobel laureate, become a Great Pervert instead of persisting in my potentially lethal, physically injurious, legally hazardous sex life. (245)

Klaus works diligently on his project, inventing such perversions as "mass sodomy," achieved by putting on a condom filled with tadpoles, one for each East German who had defected the previous day.

Klaus's decision to turn his back on what he considers a "normal" sex life and become a "pervert" follows closely on the heels of a pivotal event in the novel: the beginning and abrupt end of what he calls his life's only love story (173). After losing his wallet in a telephone booth, Klaus gets a phone call from a young woman named Yvonne. She has found his wallet and wants to give it back in person. They get along immediately; Yvonne charms Klaus with her spontaneity and joie de vivre, and Klaus—to his surprise—manages to woo Yvonne with dignity, perhaps even panache. When their chaste courtship gives way to physical passion, however, things begin to go wrong:

> She lit some candles and settled herself in my lap, and we kissed. I found myself in a genuine ethicomoral predicament. Why? Because it became clear to me that I wanted—let's not beat about the bush—to *fuck* her. Could my conscience permit me to fuck an *angel*? An angel, what was more, whom I *loved*? (191)

As usual, the prospect of sexual activity sends Klaus spiraling into guilt and self-recrimination. It seems impossible to him that love and sex could coexist.

Suddenly something happens that derails him completely:

> And then she said something she shouldn't have said: two fateful words. "Hurt me!" She whispered. That did it.…What did it mean, *Hurt me?* At that moment…my world disintegrated. Was I supposed to scratch her? Draw blood? Hit her? Bite her? Dislocate her arms and legs? I didn't feel equal to anything of the kind.
>
> I rose, got dressed, and left. (192)

Despite his careful studies of *Mann und Frau intim,* Klaus has no idea what to make of Yvonne's S-M play. Her mild transgression of the boundary between sex and violence magnifies Klaus's confusion on the subject, causing his world to disintegrate. The problem, it seems, is that he has no sense of scale. When Yvonne says, "Hurt me," he doesn't know whether to scratch her or dislocate her arms.

This lack of a sense of scale—one might say moral scale—represents a general characteristic of the Stasi in Brussig's novel: never deliberately cruel, they seem to contemplate or perpetrate horrendous acts almost unwittingly. Klaus's boss Wunderlich, for instance, suggests matter-of-factly that "injured hands were more effective that handcuffs. If only our dissidents could have their bones neatly broken in some way...People with both hands out of action couldn't print leaflets or accompany subversive songs on the guitar, piano, or accordion—they couldn't even pick up a phone" (162). To intimidate one suspected dissident, the Stasi kidnaps her young daughter—a task carried out blithely by Klaus, who seems to feel that his most reprehensible action that day was beating the little girl at Parcheesi and Old Maid. Much of the comedy in *Helden wie wir* springs from these wild oscillations of moral standards, the sheer exuberance with which the narrative hurls Klaus back and forth between utter amorality and moral hairsplitting.

Brussig's comic Stasi is not entirely innocuous, however. Though the narrative requirements of comedy keep Klaus and his colleagues from going too far (the kidnapped girl, for instance, is set free on the same evening), the reader can only imagine what effect their ridiculous capers have offstage—on the owners of the apartments they ransack or on the kidnapped girl's mother. Thus the Stasi of *Helden wie wir,* as embodied in Klaus Uhltzscht and his colleagues, is simultaneously harmless and brutal, naïve and perverse. Indeed, it is to the extent that they refuse to acknowledge how ineffectual they are that Brussig's Stasi men become genuinely dangerous.

In the novel's climactic scene, which takes place at the Bornholmer Straße border checkpoint on the night of November 9, 1989, the East German police-state's combination of impotence and latent menace finds appropriate expression. On that night, thousands of GDR citizens gathered at the Wall all over Berlin, following a remark made by the SED press secretary suggesting that the border might be opened. "It was a pathetic sight," Klaus says of the Bornholmer checkpoint: "Thousands of them confronted by a few dozen border guards, and they didn't dare to make a move" (256). Like the Stasi, the border guards are helpless to staunch the tide of history—though no one knows it yet. It is here that Klaus decides to intervene and does so by showing the border guards, in an idiom they are sure to understand, how inadequate they are: "That was when I had an idea, a kind of inspiration: the border guards might also be sons of mothers of the *Have-you-been-playing-with-it?* type. It *was* an inspiration, there's no other word for it. Slowly and deliberately, I unbuttoned my coat, undid my belt, and unzipped my trousers" (258).

The guards, "as if mesmerized," open the gate. The story of the Wall's end, as Klaus had claimed at the beginning of the novel, does indeed seem to be the story of his penis. Here, some backstory is necessary. Five days earlier, while attending the famous November 4 demonstration at Alexanderplatz, Klaus had decided to respond to Christa Wolf's speech with a speech of his own. As he descends the stairs of an underground passageway leading to the stage, he trips and falls onto a broomstick, skewering himself in an agonizing, if improbable, manner.

Klaus wakes up later in the hospital with a "squashed frog" for genitals. However, he does find one consolation in his misery. Mysteriously, his "squashed frog" undergoes a radical transformation in the days following the accident: "Imagine waking up one day," he says, "and finding that your familiar little dick had been replaced by the biggest *membrum virile* you'd ever seen" (244). This, then, is the irrefutable argument with which Klaus confronts the Bornholmer guards. For "sons of mothers of the *Have-you-been-playing-with-it?* type"—that is, for repressed, perverse, sex-obsessed men, precisely the men who fill the ranks of the East German police state—such a demonstration of penile superiority cannot fail to convince.

What are we to make, then, of the story of Klaus's penis, which happens also to be the story of the Wall's end? Is it simply an elaborate adolescent joke? One interpretive clue can be found in the novel's final passage:

> I've no illusions, Mr. Kitzelstein: no one will believe a social outcast and Stasi pervert, kidnapper and rapist *manqué* like me, but so what? No one who dismisses my story can possibly understand what's wrong with Germany. Why not? Because nothing makes sense without me—because I'm recent German history's *missing link*.
> Was that what you wanted to know? (262)

Here, in this parting question, Brussig's novel reveals the ultimate object of its satire. "Was that what you wanted to know?" Klaus asks Mr. Kitzelstein, the *New York Times* reporter. The whole novel, then, becomes the answer to an implied question: the demand of a Western audience for a "missing link," a Rosetta stone of recent German history. Klaus offers himself as this missing link. As he put it a few pages before, "My own contribution to the debate is the story of my perversions, my little trumpet, my snooping and informing, my impotence, my abnormal masturbatory fantasies, my combination of megalomania and staggering naiveté" (253). Yet how does the story of Klaus's screwball sex life provide the "missing link" required by Mr. Kitzelstein and his readers?

One answer can be found in the trope of perversion, which performs two functions in Brussig's novel. First, it satisfies—with manifest irony—the paradoxical demand of the triumphant West that the history of the Stasi depict an institution that was depraved, corrupt, and decadent, but at the same time ultimately ineffectual. Although Klaus's twisted libido usually lends itself more to light comedy than to moral reproof, it is also characterized by the distorted sense of scale mentioned above, an underlying amorality that makes possible a seamless drift from the droll to the cruel. The trope of perversion allows Brussig to give Mr. Kitzelstein and his readers the Stasi they "want to know": one that is laughably hopeless and casually ruthless, paralyzed by neurotic guilt yet ignorant of the true nature of its crimes.

The Stasi's "inherent perversion" would also satisfy a related, more fundamental ideological demand of postunification discourse: that the East German security state be identifiably, ontologically *different* from the new order. For the German reader in 1995, anchored in postunification reality, the practices of Brussig's Stasi are safely "other," products of a system conspicuously distinct from the present order. The reader is comfortably on the other side of this perverse, deviant state, a state that functions—and falls—according to the logic of *"Have-you-been-playing-with-it?"*

The not-other order, the "normal" according to which Klaus and his coworkers seem "perverse," is played by "the only love story" in Klaus's life, his brief relationship with Yvonne. This truncated romantic subplot is the point at which things could have gone differently for Klaus. Here, with only a touch of the novel's characteristic irony, heterosexual romantic love becomes the normative benchmark against which the distance of deviance is measured. Where *love* incorporates, assimilates, and legitimates, *perversion* disavows, disowns, and abases. The vestigial traces of romantic love in *Helden wie wir* lend potency to its machinery of disavowal, the disintegrative power of its scenario of perversion. The analysis of Florian Henckel von Donnersmarck's 2006 film, *Das Leben der Anderen* (The Lives of Others), that follows will reveal more clearly what is being disavowed in the abrogation—the abjection, in Julia Kristeva's terms—of Stasi surveillance.[11]

"It's for us": *Das Leben der Anderen*

In his review of Florian Henckel von Donnersmarck's *Das Leben der Anderen* for the *New York Review of Books,* Timothy Garton Ash calls attention to another reviewer's modification of the film's closing line:

> One of the finest film critics writing today, Anthony Lane, concludes his admiring review in *The New Yorker* by adapting Wiesler's punch line: Es ist für mich. You might think that the film is aimed solely at modern Germans, Lane writes, but it's not: Es ist für uns—it's for us. He may be more right than he knows. *The Lives of Others* is a film very much intended for others. Like so much else made in Germany, it is designed

---

11. In *Powers of Horror,* Kristeva explores a phenomenon she calls *abjection,* the process by which we separate out and cast off that which "disturbs identity, system, order. What does not respect borders, positions, rules. The in-between, the ambiguous, the composite" (4). In its ambiguity, its blurring of the border between self and other, the abject challenges our very sense of self.

to be exportable. Among its ideal foreign consumers are, precisely, Lane's "us"—the readers of *The New Yorker*. Or, indeed, those of *The New York Review*.

With an eye to the conclusion of Brussig's *Helden wie wir,* we might include the readers of the *New York Times* among the "us" for whom *Das Leben der Anderen* is intended. Donnersmarck, like Klaus Uhltzscht, reproduces the Stasi that Western audiences "want to know": an organization that participates in a distant, defunct, deviant social order. In this, we might say, the film protests too much. Even as it insists on the absolute alterity of the East German surveillance state to its own cultural context, *Das Leben der Anderen* reveals continuities at the level of fantasy. Try as it might to repudiate the social order that it depicts, its fascinated gaze can't look away.

This wavering is evident in the film's ingenious opening sequence, which alternates between Hohenschönhausen Prison, where a prisoner is being cross-examined, and a classroom, where the interrogator, whom we will come to know as the film's main character, Captain Wiesler (Ulrich Mühe), is using a reel-to-reel recording of the interrogation to train Stasi cadets. On the one hand, this lead-in makes every effort to locate us temporally, geographically, and morally: subtitles announce time (1984, fittingly) and place, while the establishing shot of the prison and the depiction of physical and mental torture make it clear that this is not the GDR of recent nostalgia films. "Good-bye Lenin," Donnersmarck seems to say, "hello Stalin." On the other hand, these first few scenes present us with a bewildering proliferation of audiences. In the first shot, we stand behind (and, we might infer, with) the prisoner, then oscillate between the prisoner's and the interrogator's point of view. Suddenly we are sitting in on Wiesler's class, then, in the next scene, watching Wiesler watch a play. These on-screen audiences call our attention to the precarious status of identification in the film. Whose side are we on? And who are "the Others" of the film's title?

Although these positions seem fluid at first, one spectatorial permutation comes to the fore in the course of the film. Having bugged the apartment of Georg Dreyman (Sebastian Koch), a well-respected but party-loyal writer, and his girlfriend, actress Christa-Maria Sieland (Martina Gedeck), Wiesler sits in the attic of their building, listening in on their conversations and quarrels, celebrations and setbacks. As many reviews have pointed out, a large part of the film's appeal lies in watching the subtle play of emotions on the face of Captain Wiesler, portrayed with minimalist intensity by Ulrich Mühe. Like a Greek chorus, he performs audience for us, wincing and thrilling to the melodrama downstairs. Here the emphasis should be on *melos,* "music," the instrument of Wiesler's moral transformation. Garton Ash recounts the story, as told by Donnersmarck on a number of occasions, that the genesis of the film was a remark by Lenin that he could not listen to Beethoven's *Appassionata* because it made him want to do nice things, rather than smash heads for the revolution. How, Donnersmarck wondered, could he make Lenin listen to the *Appassionata?* Hence Wiesler's exquisitely (if improbably) complex audio sur-veillance operation. As viewers, we are in a position to experience the drama even more intensely; through an omniscient camera, we see what Wiesler only hears. If the *sounds* of others are enough to transform this impassive Stasi man, then how much more compelling must be the combined effect of sound and image?

In this sense, *Das Leben der Anderen* seems not to share *Anders*'s distrust of the spectatorial mode—associating spectatorship with distance and rupture—but rather assigns both visuality and aurality a transformative, even redemptive role. Moreover, where *Anders* would look for truly transformative experience outside of the public sphere, within private or counter-public spaces, *Das Leben der Anderen* finds redemption in the making-public of private experience. This redemption is twofold. Through his conversion, Wiesler redeems himself (at least in the eyes of Dreyman and, perhaps, the viewer), while at the same time, his change of heart justifies the audience's identification with him. It redeems, in other words, our par-ticipation in the erotics of surveillance.

As a number of film scholars have argued, the pleasure of cinema can be found largely in the interplay of voyeurism and exhibitionism. In her influential essay "Visual Pleasure and Narrative Cinema," Laura Mulvey states: "The position of the spectators in the cinema is blatantly one of repression of their exhibitionism and projection of the repressed desire onto the performer" (17). In other words, cinema is fueled by fantasies of watching and being watched. Even more explicitly than in many films, *Das Leben der Anderen* puts this vision onto the screen; watching the watcher, we imagine the next link in this spectatorial chain. What if our own suf-fering were so great, our triumphs so profound, as to move the indifferent powers-that-be to tears of sympathy or joy? Yet, as a case like the Stasi makes unavoidably clear, submission to surveillance, even in fantasy, has real-life ramifications for the exercise of power and social control.

For a film like *Das Leben der Anderen,* such an intertwining of cinematic con-ventions with the machinery of social domination represents a significant quan-dary. On the one hand, the film's driving sense of outrage zeroes in on the erosion of privacy in the East German Stasi state. On the other hand, its own erotic economy is backed by voyeuristic pleasure—the pleasure that emerges from the camera's incursion into the characters' most intimate experiences. How can it resolve this contradiction?

Given the adulation and emulation of Bertolt Brecht by Dreyman and his circle, we might expect the film to avail itself of Brechtian alienation effects—calling at-tention to its status as performance, rather than as a mimetic depiction of reality—in order to dismantle the bonds of identification between audience and characters. This critical distance would encourage viewers to reflect on the power dynamics inherent in the very act of spectatorship. Yet, far from following Brecht, Donners-marck's film never strays from the conventions of cinematic realism, combining a straightforward narrative with the emotional guidance of expressive acting and a moving soundtrack. When, in the midst of his transformation process, Wiesler steals a Brecht volume from Dreyman's apartment, he savors a romantic poem from 1920, "Erinnerung an die Marie A." (A Memory of Marie A.)—not coincidentally a poem written by the young pre-Marxist Brecht rather than the Brecht of the radical Epic Theater. Having thus inoculated itself against Brechtian critique, the film is free to enjoy what the later Brecht might have called cinema's "culinary" satisfactions: emotional absorption and vicarious sensation.[12]

With its wholesale investment in the narrative pleasure of cinema, Donnersmarck's film has a lot to lose in the disruption of fantasy projection and character identification. And so, instead of calling attention to the problematic status of spectatorship within its narrative and erotic economies, *Das Leben der Anderen* settles on a strategy of splitting and disavowal. In the course of its plot, the film separates good, redemptive spectacle—the human drama that transforms Captain Wiesler—from bad, perverse surveillance. Like W. in *"Ich"* (albeit with less dubiety), Wiesler must jettison his "perverse" desire in favor of genuine, transformative love. The need to mark this passage helps to account for the otherwise gratuitous scene in which Wiesler engages the services of a prostitute in his dismal apartment. Here, Donnersmarck avails himself of a stock cinematic trope: the prostitute's massive fleshiness, which threatens to engulf Wiesler's slight frame, suggests rampant desire and unchecked carnal appetites. And yet the encounter is all business, mechanical and indifferent. Still seeking the intimacy left unfulfilled by the sexual act, Wiesler implores her to stay a while, but the prostitute has a client waiting in the same building—another Stasi man, we infer. Wiesler's vice, it seems, is also that of his colleagues. In the course of his surveillance operation, however, he exchanges this Stasi desire, this emotionless concupiscence, for empathy and self-sacrifice—in short, for love. And lest the audience find his ardent eavesdropping somehow indecent, Wiesler is provided with the foil of a salacious assistant, who enjoys monitoring libidinous artists because "they're always at it." Wiesler takes no such prurient pleasure in the operation: his is the chaste attachment of idealization.

His first face-to-face meeting with the object of his devotion calls attention to the nature of this attachment.[13] Intercepting Sieland on her way to a liaison with the lecherous minister Bruno Hempf (Thomas Thieme), Wiesler approaches her, claiming to be a fan:

---

12. For more on "culinary" theater, see "The Modern Theatre Is the Epic Theatre," in *Brecht on Theatre: The Development of an Aesthetic*.

13. I have chosen to frame Wiesler's surveillance operation as a heterosexual love plot in order to shed light on the cinematic and narrative conventions informing Christa-Maria's role in the film. An equally strong argument could be made that Wiesler's homosexual desire for Dreyman is the more important affective attachment in the story of his conversion. These readings need not be mutually exclusive, however, particularly if one considers the dynamic in terms of Eve Kosofsky Sedgwick's theory of erotic triangulation, whereby homosocial desire between two male characters is routed through a female figure; see Sedgwick, *Between Men: English Literature and Male Homosocial Desire,* esp. 1–27.

WIESLER: Many people love you because you are who you are.

SIELAND: Actors are never "who they are."

WIESLER: You are. I've seen you on stage. You were more who you are than you are now.

SIELAND: So you know what I'm like?

WIESLER: I'm your audience.

This tribute from the audience to the actress collapses the levels of spectatorship in *Das Leben der Anderen*. On behalf of the viewer, Wiesler pleads with Sieland to be an ideal—a screen for projection and identification, an object of cinematic fantasy—and not "what she is now," a fallible human being degrading herself out of fear and desperation. Having seen her on stage, Wiesler claims to know her "real" self—that is, her ideal self. For "many people," himself perhaps included, such knowledge is tantamount to love—or vice versa, according to the consecution of love at first sight. Wiesler's love, we may assume, is of the first-sight variety. When he glimpses Sieland at the play for the first time, he slowly lowers his opera glasses, a classic cinematic pantomime of spectatorial fascination.

For the film's splitting strategy to succeed, Sieland must be both ideal and abject.[14] She is rendered abject in her dealings with the repugnant Hempf, whose brutal advances remind us how low Sieland has sunk in her professional and pharmaceutical dependency (she relies on him both to ensure her continued employment and to provide a steady supply of barbiturates). Their trysts take place in Hempf's state limousine, a claustrophobic space that renders even more conspicuous the power discrepancy between them, both physical and symbolic.

Thus, as the object of Hempf's obscene attentions, Sieland becomes living proof of the brutal perversity of the East German surveillance state. Inspiring Wiesler's loving regard, however, she represents the transformative potential of cinematic sound and image, catalyzing a miraculous conversion from Stasi snoop to "good man." Ultimately, the split between bad, perverse surveillance and good spectatorship is visited on Sieland's body. Her tragic fate, we might say, is the price of the film's disavowal; to separate good spectatorship from bad surveillance, the link between them must be broken. Sieland's death scene, which references everything from Christian iconography to opera to Rossellini's *Open City,* represents the height of pathos in the film.[15] Dreyman's heartbreaking Pietà embrace of his lover—whose given name, after all, is Christa-Maria—triggers cultural associations of redemption and self-sacrifice, while Wiesler's disconsolate confession to

---

14. Of course, the notion that a female character could embody both the ideal and the abject instance is not a new one: the prevalence of "virgin" and "whore" dichotomies in film, indeed in Western culture, need hardly be mentioned. And like many of her predecessors, Sieland does not fare well at the intersection of the corporeal and the ideal.

15. Matthew H. Bernstein's review of *The Lives of Others* in *Film Quarterly* points out this intertextual allusion to *Open City* (34). In his review Garton Ash calls the staging of Sieland's death "frankly operatic."

the dying actress completes his rehabilitation and secures our sympathies for him. Even as it confirms the transformative power of love—a love born of empathetic watching and listening—the catastrophe of Sieland's death verifies the depravity of the East German surveillance state, a system that serves only the perverse whims of its corrupt rulers.

What is at stake, then, in these narratives of secret police work? Why do *Das Leben der Anderen, Helden wie wir,* and *"Ich"* take pains to recreate a Stasi that is so manifestly and variously perverse? As I argued above, "perversion" always exists in relation to a normative counterpart. In all of these narratives, this "normal" pole is consolidated according to the generic conventions of romantic love. The split between love and perversion allows these texts to isolate and discard part of the symbolic order into which they interpenetrate. How can we account for the urgency of this repudiation, especially when the state apparatus in question has already been annulled by history itself?

I would suggest that this repudiation goes deeper. What is being disavowed in *Das Leben der Anderen, Helden wie wir,* and *"Ich"* (albeit satirically in Brussig's novel) is surveillance as an integral mechanism of social control. Portraying surveillance as the purview of an ontologically corrupt institution—an institution filled with voyeurs, sadists, and perverts—these narratives would deny any continuity between the command-and-control strategies of East and West. In fact, however, as *Anders* reminds us, surveillance—demoscopy, perhaps—is a necessary function of any modern complex society. In a 1999 interview, Burmeister claims that those critics who jumped to label *Anders* a Stasi novel had missed its larger point:

> I really didn't want to write a novel about the Stasi. *Anders* is about something else: a bureaucratic base-function underneath the level of the Stasi, agencies that are there to observe, measure, and collect, for instance how often you go to the doctor, where you move to, and so on. Everything is recorded somewhere. Lives become data. (Gebauer, 93)

There is little in this statement to mark the bureaucratic base-function described in *Anders* as particularly "East German." Far more, it resembles the vision of modern Western society associated with Foucault and his followers: "Our society is one not of spectacle, but of surveillance. Behind the great abstraction of exchange, there continues the meticulous, concrete training of useful forces; the circuits of communication are the supports of an accumulation and a centralization of knowledge" (Foucault, 217).

In this age of linked accounts, instant credit, data mining, and eerily precise demographic marketing, being watched is nothing new. In retrospect, what seems disturbing—indeed, obscene—about the Stasi is not the inhumanity of its methods, but rather their humanity. Stasi agents and informers were real people, tasked with collecting not data, but ideas and memories. The Stasi thrived on human weakness, on greed, betrayal, and cowardice. It targeted one's most intimate personal relationships, driving a wedge of mistrust between friends, family, lovers. Modern surveillance—what we see of it, anyway—seems indifferent to our beliefs and intentions. It just keeps track.

In the narratives discussed in this chapter, we come face-to-face with state surveillance. With varying degrees of sympathy, these characters confront us with the fact that surveillance is not the operation of an impersonal system, indiscriminately sorting zeroes and ones like a fiber-optic Maxwell's Demon, but rather a deliberate strategy of social domination. An ideology that would conceal such domination would disavow surveillance as the perversion of a bygone regime, the brutal tactics of a power-hungry dictatorship. And indeed, the new way seems more moral, or at least less ruthless. There are no secret agents—no human agents at all, in fact. In a sense, though, this might be even more frightening. Perhaps at some level we prefer to be watched than to be ignored. Our watchers might be leering with a voyeur's lascivious gaze, a sadist's obscene intent; or, as even the antiheroes of *Anders, "Ich,"* *Helden wie wir,* and *Das Leben der Anderen* did once, they might be falling in love.

CODA

A Chameleon Wedding

Dennoch ging alles
Wie auf einer
Chamäleon-Hochzeit
Großartig zu

And yet, as if
at a chameleon wedding
everything came
together splendidly

—SARAH KIRSCH, from the poem "Langer Winter"

If the most satisfying ending to a love story is a wedding, then it might be meta-phorically apt to end this historical account on November 9, 1989, with the images seen around the world of people dancing in the streets and atop the Wall. At the conclusion of the German-German love story, this could be a restorative celebra-tion like those that end the comedies of Plautus and Shakespeare. Of such finales, Northrop Frye observes: "As the final society reached by comedy is the one that the audience has recognized all along to be the proper and desirable state of affairs, an act of communion with the audience is in order.... The resolution of comedy comes, so to speak, from the audience's side of the stage" (164). And indeed, when the Wall came down, the world celebrated along with the ecstatic Berliners. In the West, this moment seemed to be the culmination of a long and concerted courtship. The years of patient détente, of wooing and waiting, had finally paid off. Chan-cellor Willy Brandt's "Wandel durch Annäherung" (Change through Approach/ Rapprochement) had had just that as its intended goal. In his "Report on the State of the Nation," delivered on January 14, 1970, Brandt had offered the following reasons for the new *Ostpolitik,* or foreign policy toward East Germany:

Because there will be less fear, because the burdens will become lighter, because peo-ple who have not seen each other for years will be able to meet again, because it will perhaps be possible for two people from the two German states, which are now so in-humanely divided, to marry one another. Those are the objectives, both large and small, but always concerned with human beings. (Qtd. in Freund, 82)

As if in fulfillment of Brandt's prophecy, the initial accounts of the *Wende* (Turn-ing Point—the name given to the unification period, 1989–90) were filled with sto-ries of newfound love and love regained, of couples playing out in miniature the *WiederVereinigung*—(re)unification—of their respective states. Such stories are col-lected, for instance, in a volume entitled *Liebeswende/Wendeliebe* (Turning Point of Love/Love at the Turning Point), published by Morgenbuch Verlag in 1992. "When the Wall fell," we read in the introduction, "people fell into each other's arms. Drunk with happiness. Only on the second look did they see whose arms they fell into, and whose arms they fell out of. The catchphrase of those days: *Madness (Wahnsinn)*. The collective sentiment: Everything goes. Did everything go?" (Mauer, 5).

A note of apprehension like the one at the end of this passage seems almost obligatory in the otherwise euphoric discourse of the *Wende*. Describing the in-toxication of those first days, one also intimated the hangover to come. A collection of political cartoons about the *Wendezeit,* for instance, is ironically entitled *Flitter-wochen: Karikaturisten sehen das Jahr nach der deutsch-deutschen Hochzeit* (Honey-moon: Cartoonists Look at the Year after the German-German Wedding). Here, it seems that the honeymoon was over before it began. The political cartoonists, by vocation naysayers, bring out any and all possible roadblocks to the harmonious merger of East and West. As the title suggests, a number of these cartoons portray unification through the metaphor of marriage. A drawing by Klaus Böhle for *Die Welt,* for instance, shows West German chancellor Helmut Kohl walking arm-in-arm with his bride, East German CDU chairman (and newly elected GDR *Minis-terpresident)* Lothar de Maizière. Maizière is carrying a bouquet of Deutschmarks and along with his train is towing a massive safe, on which sits Gregor Gysi with a PDS flag.[1] The caption reads: "One always marries the whole clan" (Man heiratet immer die ganze Sippe).

In an article on representations of the GDR in political cartoons from the year 1989–90, Susan Morrison investigates the patterned gendering of East and West in the metaphors of marriage and romance so prevalent at the time. The GDR is almost always female, Morrison points out, and the FRG male. Based on the content of the cartoons she has analyzed, Morrison offers an explanation for these standardized gender roles:

Obviously the West has the economic power the East lacks. The East economically plays a role not unlike that of the woman in a patriarchal society....

---

1. After 1989, the SED changed its name to Partei des Demokratischen Sozialismus (PDS). Gysi was the PDS chairman.

Feminist discourse has exposed the role of the "other" played by women. And the GDR was also depicted as "other." The "other" is doomed to definition and marginalization only in terms of the "dominant."…As we know from the political events of 1990, the GDR has indeed lost its independent status and its identity is rapidly becoming blurred—at least officially—into that of the FRG. (49)

For the purposes of the present discussion, what is most interesting about both Morrison's survey and Böhle's cartoon is the centrality of financial concerns as a self-evident component of the marriage metaphor. Consider the 1993 poem "Zweitehe" (Second Marriage) by Kay Hoff, a former citizen of the FRG:

My—no, preferably not a love letter,	Meine—nein, lieber kein Liebesbrief
Not a love poem, why would it be,	kein Liebesgedicht, warum auch,
No flattering words, please:	keine schmeichelden Worte, bitte:
We are, finally, together, decked out	Wir sind, endlich, beisammen, grau
In gray at the registry-office, all business,	gebügelt zum Standesamt, sachlich,
No wafting veil, reasonable….	kein Schleierwehen, vernünftig….
………………	………………
…Mine becomes yours,	…Mein wird Dein,
Henceforth, by law, you	künftig, gesetzlich geregelt, Du
Are mine, that's how it always was with us.	bist mein, so war das immer bei uns.
Once we both knew, back then,	Einmal wussten wir beide, damals,
What joy is—Yours, mine,	was Glück ist—Deines, meines,
Two joys. Now we know,	zweierlei Glück. Jetzt wissen wir,
Of all things, what's what.	ausgerechnet, was Sache ist.[2]

As the poet says, this is "not a love poem." Far more, it seems to be an expression of property relations: "Mine becomes yours, /…You are mine.…" If the West were the "I" and the East the "you" of this poem, then the implicit economy of the political cartoons would apply here as well. The East gains the buying power of the West ("Mine becomes yours") but loses its autonomy and identity ("you are mine"). On the occasion of the German "second marriage," Hoff's poem implies, sentimental gestures would only hide the real nature of this union: "Now we know /… what's what."

It is a self-help cliché that money plays a major role in the success or collapse of marriage partnerships. Even the East German marriage handbook *Unsere Ehe* (Our Marriage) contains a chapter titled "Ehe mit Rechenschieber" (Marriage with a Slide Rule), which begins: "To establish and uphold a household the partners need, along with any number of good qualities, money. The sooner they understand that, the better" (Polte, 97). The historical circumstances of the connection

---

2. Hoff, "Zweitehe," ed. Conrady.

between marriage and money hardly need to be pointed out: until the eighteenth century, marriage was usually a matter of property, rather than of love.[3] These associations can be derived from the other side as well: the word *economy* comes from the Greek *oikos,* "house," and refers to the management of a household. The economy, in other words, begins at home.

Throughout this book, we have been exploring connections between the precepts of romantic love and those of the economy writ large. I have argued that, by definition (at least self-definition), romantic love spurns the consideration of economic factors, insisting on a kind of narrative autarky. Marriage, in its cultural articulation, seems to do the opposite: it is the point at which the romantic couple is recognized as linking up to broader networks of exchange. Thus, for instance, the works analyzed in chapter 3 begin within the connubial sphere: if these marriages are embedded in an increasingly problematic political economy, then the extramarital affair that sets each plot in motion extends the promise—however fleeting or illusory—of escaping, or even transforming, this unsatisfactory status quo.

In light of these considerations we can see why, searching for a metaphor appropriate to the reorganizations of a rapidly unifying Germany, so many commentators looked to marriage—not as the close of a romantic comedy, however, but as the beginning of a domestic drama. Here, true to form, the main conflict seems to be about money. It was immediately clear that it would be a Herculean task to bring these two systems together. If the West saw itself as a garden of golden apples (to stretch the metaphor), then the economy of the East was an Augean stable.

Yet from another perspective—as we will see, from a largely East German perspective—the metaphor of marriage would draw attention to another difficulty involved in the merger. If love and marriage go together, as the old song has it, like a horse and carriage, it seems that the *Wende* may have put the cart before the horse. Jutta Gysi has characterized unification as an "overhasty marriage" which might have benefited from a longer engagement (qtd. in Morrison, 40). And so as economists, politicians, and pundits (the political cartoonists of *Flitterwochen* included) hashed out the financial ramifications of the new German union, cultural producers began working on a task no less pressing—indeed, as Gysi points out, already overdue—that of bringing together what I have been calling the "libidinal economies" of East and West.

In the preceding analysis, I have claimed that romantic narratives, with their inherent impulse toward harmony and closure, often constitute an attempt to mitigate ideological aporias or reconcile incommensurable value-systems. It is no wonder, then, that the *Wende* period saw so many narratives of East-West romance: the *Liebeswende* stories, for instance, or Brigitte Burmeister's 1994 novel, *Unter dem Namen Norma.* Such accounts represent an explicit attempt to navigate the

---

3. See, for instance, the chapter "Love and Marriage" in Luhmann's *Love as Passion,* 145–54.

transformed erotic landscape of unified Germany, to make sense of the sudden proliferation of desires, possibilities, and alternatives.

Sonnenallee, the film with which my investigation began, takes part in this effort. In the introduction, I suggested that Haußmann's film may be understood in part as an attempt to vindicate the ways of the East to a Western audience. *Sonnenallee*'s love story, I argued, is integral to this goal: when Michael declares himself "young and in love," our generic understanding fills in the gaps. "When a boy sees a girl for the first time," remarked Haußmann in an interview, "that's something that everyone understands" (Haußmann et al., 21).[4] We are now in a position, however, to take this analysis a step further, for Michael does indeed seem to be in love—but not just with Miriam, the girl next door. Instead, the film's passionate attachments appear to embrace all the objects of his erstwhile homeland: a battered cassette player, a keenly anticipated telephone, a protean *Multifunktionstisch* (multifunctional table), a homemade T-shirt promoting "Rock & Pop." *Sonnenallee* is, in its way, a paean to the beloved lost objects of the GDR.

In "Performing 'Ostalgie,'" a thought-provoking article on *Sonnenallee,* Paul Cooke draws attention to the film's "fetishistic" focus on certain artifacts of the former GDR, a kind of "'ostalgic' product placement" that allows East German viewers "a celebratory moment of *jouissance* as they recognize a now forgotten object" (163). Further along in the article, Cooke links this romanticization of *Ostprodukte* (East German products) to the film's overall romantic scenario. Drawing on Helen Cafferty's work on *Sonnenallee,* Cooke calls attention to the film's generic "overcoding," its hyperproduction of romantic couples. As Cafferty points out, heterosexual couples proliferate in *Sonnenallee,* from Michael and Miriam to Mario and the existentialist Sabrina, from the rekindled passion of Michael's parents to his sister's serial love affairs (258). "This overloading of the film's generic features," Cooke notes, "which highlights *Sonnenallee*'s light-hearted romantic element, mirrors the film's overtly over-indulgent nostalgia towards the paraphernalia of the GDR." From this, however, Cooke draws a completely different conclusion from the one the analysis in this book would teach us to expect: "This, in turn, suggests that East German spectators are not to take the film at face value, but are rather being invited to explore critically their relationship to their pre-unification experience" (164). As we have seen throughout this book, however, love stories rarely invite "critical exploration," at least on the surface. Invoking the generic privilege of love's ineffability, they resist analytical interpretation, or at least suggest that the price of too much prying is a loss of narrative pleasure. Cooke is right in pointing out a certain amount of exaggeration in *Sonnenallee*'s romantic scenes, perhaps even a touch of Brechtian alienation effect. This light irony, however, never comes between the viewer and his

---

4. I was directed to this quote by Cooke, "Performing 'Ostalgie'" (162).

or her *jouissance*—it neither disturbs the vicarious pleasure of the film's romantic happy ending nor interrupts the delight of ostalgic brand-recognition.

Instead, *Sonnenallee* uses the generic markers of romance to instill and convey a particular affective stance toward the consumer universe of the GDR: not one of critical distance, but of warm affinity. This stance is more than just an exercise in nostalgic reminiscence. Its intentions pertain to the present: namely to the project of finding or forging a connection between East and West, of locating the common denominator of their libidinal economies. In a scenario of triangulation like that of so many romantic narratives, East and West Germany are brought together by a shared love object: the fetishized commodity.

Here one might be tempted to apply to *Sonnenallee* an argument that Cooke makes in a later essay on GDR-nostalgia television shows. The "real purpose" of these commercial entertainment ventures, Cooke claims, is "neither to present an authentic, nor a revisionist, representation of life in the GDR, but to attract viewers— that is, to make the GDR entertaining and, more importantly, saleable" ("*Ostalgie's* Not What It Used to Be," 137). From a marketing perspective, too much friction between the old and new *Bundesländern* (the "old" German states being the former FRG, the "new" the erstwhile GDR) represents a lamentable constriction of the available customer base. Thus, Cooke argues, a formerly defiant *Ostalgie* has become reappropriated as a tool of commodification:

> Rather than viewing nostalgia for the GDR as a barrier to the long-awaited "inner unification" of the German people, as it has been previously represented in some western discourses, it is now used as a means of *achieving* unity. Within the context of the recent television programs, the representation of *Ostalgie* necessarily implies the existence of a unified "community of consumers," in which East German experience appears to have been brought into the cultural mainstream. (137–38)

Cooke, who earlier in this article cited Haußmann's critique of such *Ostalgie* shows, goes on to implicate the director in the creation of this "community of consumers": "The shows," Cooke observes, "appear to be the end product of a process that figures such as Haußmann wished to set in motion" (138).

In fact, however, the effort to triangulate between East and West through a shared attachment to consumer goods might reveal the opposite, for the commodity fetishes that evolved in the two Germanys were fundamentally and qualitatively different. In his article "The Twilight of the Idols: East German Memory and Material Culture," Paul Betts describes the changes in the symbolic valence of consumer goods in the former East. After an initial rush on previously unavailable Western goods, East German consumers discovered that this brave new marketplace left something to be desired:

> East German nostalgia was also fueled by the actual consumption of Western goods. Once purchased, many of these coveted articles lost their nimbus of symbolic capital

and political magic and returned to the "disenchanted" world of hyped exchange-value, credit payments, and planned obsolescence. The point is that the historical aura of German goods had been radically reversed: the former longing for the emblems of a glamorous Western present had now been replaced by those from a fading Eastern past. (742)

Nostalgia for the East German commodity was not just the product of post-*Wende* disillusionment, but also an ex post facto recognition of conditions already in place before the fall of the Wall. These conditions are intriguingly illustrated in a scene near the end of *Sonnenallee*. Having miraculously acquired a copy of the coveted, forbidden Rolling Stones album *Exile on Main Street,* Michael's friend Wuschel brings the record to Michael's house for a listening. When they play the record, it turns out to be an East-bloc knockoff with a false label. It is at this moment, though, that the album reveals its true worth. "Listen carefully," Michael tells the distraught Wuschel. "This is the greatest Stones song I've ever heard!" The friends plug in their air guitars, and the music changes and thickens; it begins to rock. Soon the whole cast is dancing in the street. They boogie into the border zone, past the nonplussed guards, and through the opened gates into the West.

This scene is interesting less for its all-too-quaint rendition of the fall of the GDR—here, a revolution more vinyl than velvet—than for its telling account of East German commodity culture. Throughout the film, *Exile on Main Street* represents a kind of *über*-commodity, its astronomical black-market exchange value created by a combination of Western cool and Eastern taboo. Yet the song that has hippies and burghers, Stasi men, construction workers, and border guards dancing together in the streets is in fact a worthless forgery, an *Ostprodukt*. It is only the boys' investment, their willingness to listen creatively, to consume actively—in short, to improvise—that makes "Schnuk–Schnuk–Schnuk" into the greatest Stones song of all time.

In such consumer investment we see the lasting success of the SED's failed efforts to create a socialist commodity fetish, a material trace of the transformed social order under socialism. Instead of acquiring a fetish quality from the conditions of their production, as the party had hoped, East German commodities were enriched by the circumstances of their *distribution*. The negotiation and cooperation, tips and trades, of the GDR's unofficial niche economy lent—and continue to lend—the East German object-world a unique social character.[5] In *Utopie und Bedürfnis,* Ina Merkel describes how the involved process of acquisition created a "satisfying"

---

5. See, for instance, Evelin Grohnert's fascinating conversation with a former HO department store manager about the complex network of barter and *Beziehungen* (connections) that augmented the GDR's feeble retail sphere: "'Es gab nichts, aber jeder hatte alles.' Renate Z., Verkaufsstellenleiterin, erzählt" ("There Was Nothing, but Everyone Had Everything": A Conversation with Renate Z., Department Store Manager). See also Torben Müller's article on the East German DIY magazine *Guter Rat* (Good Advice), which offered its readers creative solutions to the retail system's constant *Engpässe,* or "shortages of consumer goods": "Vom Westen lernen, heißt improvisieren lernen: *Guter Rat*—eine sozialistische Verbraucherzeitschrift" (Learning from the West Means Learning to Improvise: *Good Advice*—A Socialist Consumer Magazine). From miniature-golf courses made of old tires to recipes

quality that seemed to inhere in the objects themselves: "The extra effort put into obtaining these objects also made their eventual acquisition more deeply satisfying than if one could simply go into a store and buy them. This deep satisfaction, many consumers lament, cannot be found amidst today's overabundance of consumer choices" (387).

If Western commodities obtain much of their fetish quality from their "branding," the distinctive mark of their derivation, then East German goods were subject to the opposite dynamic. As Martin Blum argues, "In the absence of the powerful corporate branding of the West, Eastern consumers frequently had to write their products' biographies themselves—biographies that were often closely related to the actual biographies of their customers' everyday lives" (241). Such "biographies," records of the objects' provenance, uses, and peculiarities, are also expressions of the objects' fetish quality, concretizations of the social ties that governed these object-histories.

The GDR's unique consumer culture, characterized by what Merkel calls "intense personal connections to objects" (364), is now a fading memory, and one that Westernized consumers, whose contrasting fetish would locate an object's value solely in its cost, will never fully understand. The stubborn material existence of East German commodities bears witness to another way of relating to the objects of commerce, another standard of value, another community of exchange. The consumer goods of the former GDR were usually inferior to those of the West, and they were never cutting-edge or state-of-the-art. Yet they were, in their way, precious: not owing to any qualities of their design or manufacture, nor on account of their surplus-value or luxury appeal, but rather because of the consumers' own investment—the time and effort spent to acquire, adapt, and maintain them. And now, unlike the objects of capitalist consumption, they cannot be replaced.

This is what *Sonnenallee* would tell us about its leading props—its truculent tables and hard-won telephones, hand-drawn T-shirts and phony Stones tunes—and why it draws on the tools of romance to get its point across. Looking beyond the obscene overpresence of the East German state, beyond the iniquity and absurdity of its dysfunctional public sphere, we find ourselves in love's temporary utopia, a world of invaluable, irreplaceable objects.

As we have seen, as much as they address the intangible play of emotion and inclination, love stories are also a means of managing objects. This, in fact, is the primary site of their ideological effectivity. Indeed, what love stories legitimize is not so much a symbolic order—most ideological constructions do that, and some more efficiently—as what could be called an object order: the dynamics of attraction and repulsion, of investment and disavowal, that determine the relative desirability of objects in a given sociocultural environment.

---

with substitutions for scarce ingredients, *Guter Rat* was an official version of what GDR consumers had been doing all along: improvising.

As cultural producers have been doing for hundreds of years, East German writers and filmmakers enlisted the love story to help organize the complex, contradictory object order of the GDR. And in the transformed public imagination of unified Germany, the codes of romance will continue to strive for reconciliation; but they will also bear witness to the irreconcilable alterity of forty years' separation. Forty years, that is, of loving another way.

Works Cited

Anderson, Edith. *Blitz aus heiterm Himmel.* Rostock: Hinstorff, 1975.

——. "Genesis and Adventures of the Anthology *Blitz aus heiterm Himmel.*" In *Studies in GDR Culture and Society,* vol. 4, *Selected Papers from the Ninth New Hampshire Symposium on the German Democratic Republic,* ed. Margy Gerber, 1–14. Lanham, MD: University Press of America, 1984.

"An euch alle, die ihr Jung seid." *Junge Welt,* 9 February 1956.

Anz, Thomas. *"Es geht nicht um Christa Wolf": Der Literaturstreit im vereinten Deutschland.* Munich: Edition Spangenberg, 1991.

Apitz, Renate. *Evastöchter: Ein Dutzend Dutzendgeschichten.* Rostock: Hinstorff, 1988.

"Arbeit." In *Kleines Politisches Wörterbuch,* ed. Waltraud Böhme et al., 47–50. Berlin: Dietz, 1973.

Austen, Jane. *Pride and Prejudice.* Oxford and New York: Oxford University Press, 1990.

Baldwin, James. *Another Country.* New York: Dial Press, 1962.

Bammer, Angelika. "The American Feminist Reception of GDR Literature (with a Glance at West Germany)." *GDR Bulletin* 16.2 (1990): 18–24.

Barrett, Michèle. *Women's Oppression Today: The Marxist/Feminist Encounter.* Rev. ed. London and New York: Verso, 1988.

Barthes, Roland. *A Lover's Discourse: Fragments.* Trans. Richard Howard. New York: Hill and Wang, 1978.

Bartsch, Kurt. "Sozialistischer Biedermeier." *Zugluft.* Berlin, Weimar: Aufbau, 1968.

Baske, Siegfried. *Bildungspolitik in der DDR 1963–1976: Dokumente.* Erziehungswissenschaftliche Veröffentlichungen 11. Berlin and Wiesbaden: Osteuropa-Institut; In Kommission bei O. Harrassowitz, 1979.

Bathrick, David. *The Powers of Speech: The Politics of Culture in the GDR.* Lincoln and London: University of Nebraska Press, 1995.

Baudrillard, Jean. *Simulacra and Simulation.* Trans. Sheila Faria Glaser. Ann Arbor: University of Michigan Press, 1995.

Baume, Brita. "Heldinnen nach Plan: Zur literarischen Sozialisation und zum Umgang mit der Frauenfrage in der DDR." In *Der weibliche multikulturelle Blick: Ergebnisse eines Symposiums,* ed. Hannelore Scholz and Brita Baume, 113–24. Berlin: Trafo, 1995.

Beauvoir, Simone de. *The Second Sex.* Trans. and ed. H. M. Parshley. 1953. New York: Vintage Books, 1989.

Becker, Astrid. "USA, Paris, Neukoelln." Interview. *Süddeutsche Zeitung,* 7 October 1999, sec. Berlin-Seite, 14.

Behrends, Rolf. "Gegen den Kitsch im Film." *Neue Filmwelt,* July 1952, 28.

Bernstein, Matthew H. Review of *The Lives of Others,* dir. Florian Henckel von Donnersmarck. *Film Quarterly* 61.1 (2007): 30–36.

Betts, Paul. "The Twilight of the Idols: East German Memory and Material Culture." *The Journal of Modern History* 72 (2000): 731–65.

Beyer, Frank, dir. *Das Versteck.* Perf. Jutta Hoffmann, Manfred Krug. 1977. DVD. Icestorm, 2007.

Biermann, Wolf. *Deutschland: Ein Wintermärchen.* Berlin: K. Wagenbach, 1972.

Bloch, Ernst. *The Principle of Hope.* Cambridge, MA: MIT Press, 1986.

Blum, Martin. "Remaking the East German Past: Ostalgie, Identity, and Material Culture." *Journal of Popular Culture* 34.3 (2000): 229–53.

Blumer, Herbert. *Movies and Conduct.* New York: The Macmillan Company, 1933.

Bondanella, Peter. *Italian Cinema from Neorealism to the Present.* New York: Ungar, 1983.

Bondy, Curt, et al. *Jügendliche stören die Ordnung: Bericht und Stellungnahme zu den Halbstarkenkrawallen.* Munich: Juventa, 1957.

Bordaux, Sylvie Marie. "Literatur als Subversion: Eine Untersuchung des Prosawerkes von Wolfgang Hilbig." Diss., Freie Universität Berlin, 1999. Cuvillier, 2000.

Bordwell, David, Kristin Thompson, and Janet Staiger. *The Classical Hollywood Cinema: Film Style and Mode of Production to 1960.* New York: Columbia University Press, 1985.

Borrmann, Rolf. *Jugend und Liebe: Die Beziehungen der Jugendlichen zum anderen Geschlecht.* Leipzig, Jena, and Berlin: Urania-Verlag, 1966.

Bourdieu, Pierre. *Distinction: A Social Critique of the Judgement of Taste.* Trans. Richard Nice. Cambridge, MA: Harvard University Press, 1984.

Bourdieu, Pierre, and Jean-Claude Passeron. *Reproduction in Education, Society, and Culture.* London, Thousand Oaks, and New Delhi: Sage Publications in association with Theory, Culture & Society, 1990.

Braatz, Ilse. *Zu zweit allein, oder mehr? Liebe und Gesellschaft in der modernen Literatur.* Münster: Verlag Frauenpolitik, 1980.

Braun, Volker. *Das ungezwungene Leben Kasts.* Berlin, Weimar: Aufbau-Verlag, 1973.

Brecht, Bertolt. "The Modern Theatre Is the Epic Theatre." Trans. John Willett. In *Brecht on Theatre: The Development of an Aesthetic,* 33–42. New York: Hill and Wang, 1964.

——. "Remembering Marie A." Trans. John Willett. In *Bertolt Brecht: Poetry and Prose,* ed. Reinhold Grimm and Caroline Molina y Vedia. The German Library 75. New York: Continuum, 2003.

Brussig, Thomas. *Helden wie wir.* Berlin: Verlag Volk und Welt, 1996.

——. *Heroes like Us.* Trans. John Brownjohn. New York: Farrar, Straus and Giroux, 1997.

de Bruyn, Günter. *Buridans Esel.* 1968. Frankfurt am Main: Fischer, 1988.

——. "Geschlechtertausch." In *Blitz aus heiterm Himmel,* ed. Edith Anderson, 7–46. Rostock: Hinstorff, 1975.

——. *Der Hohlweg.* Halle: Mitteldeutscher Verlag, 1963.

——. *Preisverleihung.* Halle: Mitteldeutscher Verlag, 1972.

Bundesvorstand des DFD. "'Frauenschicksale' wird diskutiert: Eine Stellungnahme des Bundesvorstandes des DFD." *Neues Deutschland,* 29 August 1952, 4.

Buridan, Jean, and G. E. Hughes. *John Buridan on Self-Reference: Chapter Eight of Buridan's Sophismata.* Trans. G. E. Hughes. Cambridge and New York: Cambridge University Press, 1982.

Burmeister, Brigitte. *Anders, oder Vom Aufenthalt in der Fremde.* Berlin, DDR: Verlag der Nation, 1987; Darmstadt: Luchterhand, 1988.

——. *Unter dem Namen Norma.* Stuttgart: Klett-Cotta, 1994.

Butler, Judith. *Bodies That Matter: On the Discursive Limits of "Sex."* New York: Routledge, 1993.

——. *Gender Trouble: Feminism and the Subversion of Identity.* New York: Routledge, 1990.

Cafferty, Helen. "*Sonnenallee:* Taking Comedy Seriously in Unified Germany." In *Textual Responses to German Unification: Processing Historical and Social Change in Literature and Film,* ed. Carol Anne Costabile-Heming, Rachel J. Halverson, and Kristie A. Foell, 253–71. Berlin and New York: Walter de Gruyter, 2001.

Carow, Heiner, dir. *The Legend of Paul and Paula [Die Legende von Paul und Paula].* Screenplay by Ulrich Plenzdorf. Perf. Angelica Domröse, Winfried Glatzeder. 1973. DVD. Icestorm International, 1999.

Carter, Erica. *How German Is She? Postwar West German Reconstruction and the Consuming Woman.* Ann Arbor: University of Michigan Press, 1997.

Cavell, Stanley. *Pursuits of Happiness: The Hollywood Comedy of Remarriage.* Harvard Film Studies. Cambridge, MA: Harvard University Press, 1981.

Cerny, Jochen, ed. *Brüche, Krisen, Wendepunkte: Neubefragung von DDR-Geschichte.* Leipzig: Urania, 1990.

Chiarloni, Anna. "Nachdenken über Christa Wolf." In *Rückblicke auf die Literatur der DDR,* ed. Hans-Christian Stillmark and Christoph Lehker, 115–54. Amsterdam: Rodopi, 2002.

Claudius, Eduard. *Menschen an unserer Seite.* Stuttgart: Verlag Neuer Weg, 1984.

Claus, Horst. "Rebels with a Cause: The Development of the *'Berlin-Filme'* by Gerhard Klein and Wolfgang Kohlhaase." In *DEFA: East German Cinema, 1946–1992,* ed. Séan Allan and John Sandford, 93–116. New York: Berghahn Books.

Conrady, Karl Otto, ed. *Von einem Land und vom andern: Gedichte zur deutschen Wende.* Leipzig: Suhrkamp, 1992.

Cooke, Paul. "*Ostalgie*'s Not What It Used to Be." *German Politics and Society* 22.4 (2004): 134–50.

——. "Performing 'Ostalgie': Leander Haußmann's *Sonnenallee.*" *German Life and Letters* 56.2 (2003): 157–67.

Dannhauer, Heinz. *Geschlecht und Persönlichkeit.* Berlin: Deutscher Verlag der Wissenschaften, 1973.

Davis, Lydia. *Break It Down.* New York: Serpent's Tail High Risk Books, 1996.

Decker, Kerstin, and Gunnar Decker. *Gefühlsausbrüche oder Ewig pubertiert der Ostdeutsche: Reportagen, Polemiken, Porträts.* Berlin: Das Neue Berlin, 2000.

Der Handel im Siebenjahrplan der DDR und seine Aufgaben zur weiteren Verbesserung der Versorgung der Bevölkerung. Berlin, 1959.

Deutsches Historisches Museum. *Auftrag: Kunst 1949–1990; Eine Ausstellung des Deutschen Historischen Museums.* 1995. http://www.dhm.de/ausstellungen/auftrag/61.htm.

"Die DEFA zu einem schöpferischen Kollektiv entwickeln! Der zweite Tag der Filmkonferenz in Berlin." *Neues Deutschland,* 21 September 1952, 6.

Doane, Mary Ann. *The Desire to Desire: The Woman's Film of the 1940s.* Bloomington: Indiana University Press, 1987.

Donnersmarck, Florian Henckel von, dir. *The Lives of Others [Das Leben der Anderen].* Perf. Martina Gedeck, Ulrich Mühe, Sebastian Koch. 2006. DVD. Sony Pictures Home Entertainment, 2007.

Dudow, Slatan, dir. *Destinies of Women [Frauenschicksale].* Perf. Sonja Sutter, Hanns Groth, Lotte Loebinger, Anneliese Book, Susanne Düllmann. 1952. DVD. Icestorm International, 2000.

———, dir. *Verwirrung der Liebe.* Perf. Annekathrin Bürger, Angelica Domröse, Willi Schrade, Stefan Lisewski. 1959. VHS. Icestorm Entertainment, 2002.

Dueck, Cheryl. *Rifts in Time and in the Self: The Female Subject in Two Generations of East German Women Writers.* Amsterdam: Rodopi, 2004.

Dyer, Richard. *Stars.* London: BFI Pub., 1998.

Eagleton, Terry. *Ideology: An Introduction.* London and New York: Verso, 1991.

Ebner-Eschenbach, Marie von. *Gesammelte Schriften von Marie von Ebner-Eschenbach.* Vol. 1. Berlin: Paetel, 1893.

Edwards, G. E. *GDR Society and Social Institutions.* New York: St. Martin's Press, 1985.

Ehrenburg, Ilya. *The Second Day: A Novel.* Moscow: Raduga Publishers, 1984.

Einhorn, Barbara. "German Democratic Republic: Emancipated Women or Hardworking Mothers?" In *Superwomen and the Double Burden: Women's Experience of Change in Central and Eastern Europe and the Former Soviet Union,* ed. Chris Corrin, 125–54. Toronto: Second Story Press, 1992.

Eliot, George. *The Mill on the Floss.* New York: Penguin, 1994.

Emde, Silke von der. *Entering History: Feminist Dialogues in Irmtraud Morgner's Prose.* Oxford: Peter Lang, 2004.

Emmerich, Wolfgang. *Kleine Literaturgeschichte der DDR.* Berlin: Aufbau, 2000.

Engels, Friedrich. *The Origin of the Family, Private Property, and the State.* New York: International, 1972.

———. "The Part Played by Labour in the Transition from Ape to Man." Trans. Clemens Dutt. Moscow: Progress Publishers, 1934. http://www.marxists.org/archive/marx/works/1876/part-played-labour/index.htm.

Engler, Wolfgang. "Eine arbeiterliche Gesellschaft." In *Die Ostdeutschen: Kunde von einem verlorenen Land.* 173–208. Berlin: Aufbau, 1999.

"Evenstochter." In *Deutsches Wörterbuch,* ed. Jacob Grimm and Wilhelm Grimm et al. 16 vols. Leipzig: S. Hirzel, 1854–1960. http://www.woerterbuchnetz.de/woerterbuecher/dwb/wbgui?lemid=GE10102.

Eyck, Rüdiger. "Immer dieselbe Frage: Warum dreht die DEFA keine Lustspiele?" *Neues Deutschland,* 19 August 1953, 4.

Fast, Piotr. *Ideology, Aesthetics, Literary History: Socialist Realism and Its Others.* Frankfurt am Main and New York: P. Lang, 1999.

Feinstein, Joshua. *The Triumph of the Ordinary: Depictions of Daily Life in the East German Cinema.* Chapel Hill and London: University of North Carolina Press, 2002.

Foucault, Michel. *Discipline and Punish: The Birth of the Prison.* Trans. Allen Lane. London and New York: Penguin, 1977.

Freud, Sigmund. *Beyond the Pleasure Principle.* Trans. James Strachey. New York: Norton, 1961.

Freund, Michael. *From Cold War to Ostpolitik: Germany and the New Europe.* London: Wolff, 1972.

Fricke, Karl Wilhelm. *MfS Intern: Macht, Strukturen, Auflösung der DDR-Staatssicherheit: Analyse und Dokumentation.* Bielefeld: Verlag Wissenschaft und Politik, 1991.

Fromm, Erich. *The Art of Loving.* New York: Bantam, 1956.

Frye, Northrop. *Anatomy of Criticism: Four Essays.* New York: Atheneum, 1957.

Fulbrook, Mary. *Anatomy of a Dictatorship: Inside the GDR, 1949–1989.* New York: Oxford University Press, 1995.

Garton Ash, Timothy. *The File: A Personal History.* New York: Random House, 1997.

——. "The Stasi on Our Minds." Review of *The Lives of Others,* dir. Florian Henckel von Donnersmarck. *The New York Review of Books,* 31 May 2007. http://www.nybooks.com/articles/20210.

Gaus, Günter. *Wo Deutschland liegt: Eine Ortsbestimmung.* Hamburg: Hoffmann und Campe, 1983.

Gebauer, Mirjam. "Erzählen als Sujet: Über Anders, Arends und Sander." *ndl: neue deutsche literatur* 47.1 (1999): 90–106.

Gebhardt, Manfred. *Die Nackte unterm Ladentisch: Das Magazin in der DDR.* Berlin: Nora, 2002.

Gerlach, Ingeborg. *Bitterfeld: Arbeiterliteratur und Literatur der Arbeitswelt in der DDR.* Kronberg/Ts: Scriptor-Verlag, 1974.

Giddens, Anthony. *The Constitution of Society: Outline of the Theory of Structuration.* Berkeley: University of California Press, 1984.

Gladkov, Fyodor Vasilievich. *Cement.* Trans. A. S. Arthur and C. Ashleigh. New York: Frederick Ungar, 1966.

Glaeßner, Gert-Joachim. "Vom 'realen Sozialismus' zur Selbstbestimmung: Ursachen und Konsequenzen der Systemkrise in der DDR." *Aus Politik und Zeitgeschichte* 1–2 (1990): 3–20.

"Glück—groß und klein." *Die Zeit,* 24 December 1953. http://www.zeit.de/1953/52/Glueck-gross-und-klein.

Goethe, Johann Wolfgang von. *Die Wahlverwandschaften.* Stuttgart: Philipp Reclam, 1956.

Goux, Jean-Joseph. *Symbolic Economies: After Marx and Freud.* Trans. Jennifer Curtiss Gage. Ithaca, NY: Cornell University Press, 1990.

Grant, Colin. "Brigitte Burmeister's *Anders, oder Vom Aufenthalt in der Fremde:* Tracing the Texts in a 'New Novel.'" In *Retrospect and Review: Aspects of the Literature of the GDR, 1976–1990,* ed. Robert Atkins and Martin Kane, 75–91. German Monitor 40. Amsterdam: Rodopi, 1997.

Greiner, Bernhard. *Von der Allegorie zur Idylle: Die Literatur der Arbeitswelt in der DDR.* Heidelberg: Quelle und Meyer, 1974.

Grohnert, Evelin. "'Es gab nichts, aber jeder hatte alles.' Renate Z., Verkaufsstellenleiterin, erzählt." In *Fortschritt, Norm und Eigensinn: Erkundungen im Alltag der DDR,* ed. Dokumentationszentrum Alltagskultur der DDR, 113–28. Berlin: Ch. Links, 1999.

Groschopp, Richard, dir. "Eine Liebesgeschichte." *Die Stacheltierparade, Teil 1.* Screenplay by Richard Groschopp and Günter Kunert. 1953. VHS. Progress Film-Verleih, 2002.

Gundle, Stephen. "Hollywood Glamour and Mass Consumption in Postwar Italy." In *Histories of Leisure,* ed. Rudy Koshar, 337–59. Oxford and New York: Berg, 2002.

Günther, Egon, dir. *Her Third [Der Dritte].* Perf. Jutta Hoffmann, Rolf Ludwig. 1972. DVD. First Run Features, 2006.

von Hallberg, Robert. *Literary Intellectuals and the Dissolution of the State: Professionalism and Conformity in the GDR.* Trans. Kenneth J Northcott. Chicago: University of Chicago Press, 1996.

Haußmann, Leander, dir. *Sonnenallee.* Perf. Alexander Scheer, Alexander Beyer, Katharina Thalbach, Teresa Weißbach, Detlev Buck, Henry Hübchen, Ignatz Kirchner. 1999. DVD. Highlight Communications, 2002.

Haußmann, Leander, et al. "*Sonnenallee,* eine Mauerkomödie: Interview mit Leander Haußmann und Thomas Brussig, geführt von Sandra Maischberger." In *Sonnenallee: Das Buch zum Film,* 8–24. Berlin: Quadriga, 1999.

Heimann, Thomas. *DEFA, Künstler und SED-Kulturpolitik: Zum Verhältnis von Kulturpolitik und Filmproduktion in der SBZ/DDR 1945 bis 1959.* Beitrage zur Film- und Fernsehwissenschaft 46. Berlin: VISTAS, 1994.

Heine, Heinrich. *Französische Zustände.* In *Historisch-kritische Gesamtausgabe der Werke,* ed. Manfred Windfuhr, vol. 12. Hamburg: Hoffmann und Campe, 1973.

Hell, Julia. *Post-Fascist Fantasies: Psychoanalysis, History, and the Literature of East Germany.* Durham, NC: Duke University Press, 1997.

——. "*Wendebilder:* Neo Rauch and Wolfgang Hilbig." *Germanic Review* 77.4 (2002): 279–303.

Herminghouse, Patricia. "New Contexts for GDR Literature: An American Perspective." In *Cultural Transformations in the New Germany: American and German Perspectives,* ed. Friederike Eigler and Peter C. Pfeiffer, 93–101. Columbia, SC: Camden House, 1993.

——. "Schreiben in gewendeten Verhältnissen: Ostdeutsche Autorinnen in historischer Sicht." In *Frauen, Literatur, Geschichte: Schreibende Frauen vom Mittelalter bis zur Gegenwart,* ed. Hiltrud Gnüg and Renate Möhrmann, 477–95. Stuttgart: Metzler, 1999.

——. "Taking Back the Myth and Magic: The *Heroic Testament* of Irmtraud Morgner." *German Life and Letters* 57.1 (2004): 58–68.

Hilbig, Wolfgang. *Abriss der Kritik: Frankfurter Poetikvorlesungen.* Frankfurt am Main: S. Fischer, 1995.

——. "*Ich": Roman.* Frankfurt am Main: S. Fischer, 1993.

Hilzinger, Sonja. "*Als ganzer Mensch zu leben...": Emanzipatorische Tendenzen in der neueren Frauen-Literatur der DDR.* Frankfurt am Main and New York: P. Lang, 1985.

Hirdina, Karin. "Ein Gegenwartsroman: Glück im Hinterhaus? Buridans Esel." In *Günter de Bruyn: Leben und Werk,* 163. Verlag Volk und Wissen, 1983. Westberlin: Verlag Das Europäische Buch, 1983.

Hoff, Kay. "Zweitehe." *Von einem Land und vom andern: Gedichte zur deutschen Wende,* ed. Karl Otto Conrady. Leipzig: Suhrkamp, 1992.

Hohlfeld, Brigitte. *Die Neulehrer in der SBZ/DDR 1945–1953: Ihre Rolle bei der Umgestaltung von Gesellschaft und Staat.* Weinheim: Deutscher Studien Verlag, 1992.

Holmes, Jack. "Blacksmith Blues." http://www.oldielyrics.com/lyrics/ella_mae_morse/the_blacksmith_blues.html.

Höppner, Joachim. "Über die deutsche Sprache und die beiden deutschen Staaten." *Weimarer Beiträge* 9.3 (1963): 576–85.

Hübner, Lilo. "Mehr heitere Filme." *Neues Deutschland,* 23 September 1952, sec. Leser schreiben zu Fragen der Filmkunst, 4.

Illouz, Eva. *Consuming the Romantic Utopia: Love and the Cultural Contradictions of Capitalism.* Berkeley, Los Angeles, and London: University of California Press, 1997.

Jahnke, Karl Heinz, et al., eds. *Partei und Jugend: Dokumente marxistisch-leninistischer Jugendpolitik.* Berlin: Dietz, 1980.

Jakobs, Karl Heinz. *Beschreibung eines Sommers: Roman.* 1961. Berlin: Verlag neues Leben, 1979.

———. *Die Interviewer.* Berlin: Verlag neues Leben, 1973.

James, Henry. *The Art of the Novel.* New York: C. Scribner's Sons, 1934.

Jameson, Fredric. "Authentic *Ressentiment:* Generic Discontinuities and Ideologemes in the 'Experimental' Novels of George Gissing." In *The Political Unconscious: Narrative as a Socially Symbolic Act,* 185–205. Ithaca, NY: Cornell University Press, 1981.

Kaminsky, Annette. *Wohlstand, Schönheit, Glück: Kleine Konsumgeschichte der DDR.* Munich: C. H. Beck, 2001.

Kant, Hermann. *Die Aula.* Berlin: Rütten & Loening, 1965.

Kanzlei des Staatsrates, ed. *Ein glückliches Familienleben, Anliegen des Familiengesetzbuches der DDR: Familiengesetzbuch der DDR und Einführungsgesetz zum Familiengesetzbuch der DDR, sowie Auszüge aus der Begründung und der Diskussion zum Familiengesetzbuch in der 17. Sitzung der Volkskammer der DDR vom 20. Dezember 1965 und der 22. Sitzung des Staatsrates der DDR vom 26. November 1965.* Berlin: Staatsverlag ver Deutschen Demokratischen Republik, 1965.

Karau, Gisela. *Stasiprotokolle: Gespräche mit ehemaligen Mitarbeitern des Ministeriums für Staatssicherheit der DDR.* Frankfurt am Main: Dipa, 1992.

Kaufmann, Eva. "Adieu Kassandra? Schriftstellerinnen aus der DDR vor, in und nach der Wende: Brigitte Burmeister, Helga Königsdorf, Helga Schütz, Brigitte Struzyk, Rosmarie Zeplin." In *Women and the Wende: Social Effects and Cultural Reflections of the German Unification Process,* ed. Elizabeth Boa and Janet Wharton, 216–25. Amsterdam: Rodopi, 1994.

Keaton, Buster, dir. *Sherlock Jr.* 1924. The Art of Buster Keaton, vol. 1. DVD. Kino on Video, 1995.

Keim, Walther, and Hans Dollinger. *Flitterwochen: Karikaturisten sehen das Jahr nach der deutsch-deutschen Hochzeit.* Munich: Süddeutscher Verlag, 1991.

Kersten, Heinz. *Das Filmwesen in der sowjetischen Besatzungszone Deutschland.* Bonner Berichte aus Mittel- und Ostdeutschland. Bonn/Berlin: Bundesministerium für gesamtdeutsche Fragen, 1963.

Kirsch, Sarah. "Blitz aus heiterm Himmel." In *Blitz aus heiterm Himmel,* ed. Edith Anderson, 189–208. Rostock: Hinstorff, 1975.

———. "Das Grundstück." *Zaubersprüche.* Ebenhausen (bei München): Langewiesche-Brandt, 1974.

———. "Langer Winter." *Erlkönigs Tochter.* Stuttgart: Deutsche Verlags-Anstalt, 1992.

Kirsch, Sarah, Irmtraud Morgner, and Christa Wolf. *Geschlechtertausch: Drei Geschichten über die Umwandlung der Verhältnisse.* Darmstadt: Luchterhand, 1980.

"Klasse." In *Kleines politisches Wörterbuch,* ed. G. König, G. Schütz, and K. Zeisler, 402–4. Berlin: Dietz, 1967.

Klaus [Klaus Bartho]. "Star Schnuppen." *Das Magazin,* April 1954, 36–37.

Klein, Gerhard, dir. *A Berlin Romance [Eine Berliner Romanze].* Screenplay by Wolfgang Kohlhaase. Perf. Annekathrin Bürger, Ulrich Thein, Uwe-Jens Pape. 1956. VHS. Icestorm International, 2000.

——, dir. *Berlin—Schönhauser Corner [Berlin, Ecke Schönhauser]*. Screenplay by Wolfgang Kohlhaase. Perf. Ekkehard Schall, Ilse Pagé, Ernst-Georg Schwill, Harry Engel, Raimund Schelcher. 1957. DVD. Icestorm International, 2007.

——, dir. *Berlin um die Ecke*. Screenplay by Wolfgang Kohlhaase. Perf. Dieter Mann, Monika Gabriel, Erwin Geschonneck, Hans Hardt-Hardtloff, Kaspar Eichel. 1965.

——, dir. *Geschichten jener Nacht*. Perf. Hans Hardt-Hardtloff, Peter Reusse, Dieter Mann, Jenny Gröllmann, Ulrich Thein, Angelika Waller, Erwin Geschonneck. 1967.

Klemm, Peter, und Christa Klemm. "Warum nicht einmal die Liebe im Mittelpunkt?" *Neues Deutschland*, 13 March 1953, 4.

Klötzer, Sylvia. *Satire und Macht: Film, Zeitung, Kabarett in der DDR*. Cologne: Böhlau, 2005.

——. "Über den Umgang mit heißen Eisen: Eulenspiegel(eien)." In *Zwischen "Mosaik" und "Einheit": Zeitschriften in der DDR*, ed. Simone Barck, Martina Langermann, and Siegfried Lokatis, 105–15. Berlin: Ch. Links, 1999.

Knappe, Joachim. *Mein namenloses Land: Zwölf Kapitel einer Jugend im Dickicht der Jahrhundertmitte*. Halle (Saale): Mitteldeutscher Verlag, 1965.

Kock, Sabine. "Irmtraud Morgners *Amanda*: Intertextualität und kulturelles Erbe im Spannungsfeld zwischen produktionsästhetischem, politischem und feministischem Diskurs in der DDR der 80er Jahre." In *Frauen in Kultur und Gesellschaft*, ed. Renate von Bardeleben et al., 229–41. Tübingen: Stauffenburg, 2000.

Kohlhaase, Wolfgang. "DEFA: A Personal View." In *DEFA: East German Cinema, 1946–1992*, ed. Seán Allan and John Sandford, 117–30. Oxford: Berghahn Books, 1999.

Kollontai, Alexandra. *Sexual Relations and the Class Struggle; Love and the New Morality*. Trans. Alix Holt. Bristol, Eng.: Falling Water Press, 1972.

Kopstein, Jeffrey. *The Politics of Economic Decline in East Germany, 1945–1989*. Chapel Hill: University of North Carolina Press, 1997.

Krenzlin, Leonore. *Hermann Kant: Leben und Werk*. Westberlin: DEB Verl. Das Europäische Buch, 1979.

Kristeva, Julia. *Powers of Horror: An Essay on Abjection*. Trans. Leon S. Roudiez. New York: Columbia University Press, 1982.

——. "Women's Time." Trans. Ross Guberman. In *New Maladies of the Soul*, 201–24. New York: Columbia University Press, 1995.

Kuehl, Christiane. "Sex und Substitutionsdrogen." *taz, die tageszeitung*, 7 October 1999, 15.

Lacan, Jacques. *Feminine Sexuality: Jacques Lacan and the École Freudienne*. Ed. Juliet Mitchell and Jacqueline Rose. Trans. Jacqueline Rose. New York: W. W. Norton, 1982.

Lenin, Vladimir Il'ich. *Essential Works of Lenin: "What Is to Be Done?" and Other Writings*. Ed. Henry M. Christman. New York: Dover Publications, 1987.

Lennox, Sara. "'Nun ja! Das nächste Leben geht aber heute an': Prosa von Frauen und Frauenbefreiung in der DDR." In *Literatur der DDR in den siebziger Jahren*, ed. Peter Uwe Hohendahl and Patricia Herminghouse, 224–58. Frankfurt am Main: Suhrkamp, 1983.

Lessing, Gotthold Ephraim. *Minna von Barnhelm*. Trans. Kenneth J. Northcott. In *Nathan the Wise, Minna Von Barnhelm, and Other Plays and Writings*, ed. Peter Demetz, 1–74. The German Library 12. New York: Continuum, 1991.

Levinas, Emmanuel. *Alterity and Transcendence*. Trans. Michael B. Smith. New York: Columbia University Press, 1999.

Lewis, Alison. *Die Kunst des Verrats: Der Prenzlauer Berg und die Staatssicherheit*. Würzburg: Königshausen & Neumann, 2003.

"Liebe." In *Kulturpolitisches Wörterbuch,* ed. Harald Bühl et al., 342–44. Berlin: Dietz, 1970.

Linklater, Beth. *"Und immer zügelloser wird die Lust": Constructions of Sexuality in East German Literatures, with Special Reference to Irmtraud Morgner and Gabriele Stötzer-Kachold.* Bern: P. Lang, 1998.

Liszt, Franz. "Biterolf und der Schmied von Ruhla." In *Franz Liszts musikalische Werke,* 7: 126–48. Farnborough Hants, Eng.: Gregg Press, 1966.

Livers, Keith A. *Constructing the Stalinist Body: Fictional Representations of Corporeality in the Stalinist 1930s.* Lanham: Lexington Books, 2004.

Loest, Erich. *Es geht seinen Gang, oder Mühe in unserer Ebene.* 1978. Munich: DTV, 1994.

Lowenthal, Leo. *Literature, Popular Culture, and Society.* Englewood Cliffs, NJ: Prentice-Hall, 1961.

Lubitsch, Ernst, dir. *Ninotchka.* Perf. Greta Garbo, Melvyn Douglas, Ina Claire, Bela Lugosi. 1939. VHS. MGM Home Entertainment, 1999.

Luhmann, Niklas. *Love as Passion: The Codification of Intimacy.* Trans. Jeremy Gaines and Doris L. Jones. Stanford: Stanford University Press, 1998.

Lukens, Nancy, and Dorothy Rosenberg, eds. *Daughters of Eve: Women's Writing from the German Democratic Republic.* Lincoln: University of Nebraska Press, 1993.

M.P. "Berlin- Ecke Schönhauser: Ein neuer DEFA-Film." Review of *Berlin—Schönhauser Corner,* dir. Gerhard Klein. *Junge Welt,* 1 January 1958, 8.

Maetzig, Kurt, dir. *Marriage in the Shadows [Ehe im Schatten].* Perf. Paul Klinger, Ilse Steppat, Alfred Balthoff, Claus Holm. 1947. VHS. Icestorm International, n.d.

——, dir. *Story of a Young Couple [Roman einer jungen Ehe].* Perf. Yvonne Merin, Hans-Peter Thielen. 1952. VHS. Icestorm International, 1999.

——. "Warum gibt es keine Liebe in unseren Filmen? Ein Diskussionsbeitrag von Dr. Kurt Maetzig." *Neues Deutschland,* 1 February 1953, 4.

Maier, Charles A. *Dissolution: The Crisis of Communism and the End of East Germany.* Princeton, NJ: Princeton University Press, 1997.

Mann, Thomas. *Doctor Faustus.* Trans. H. T. Lowe-Porter. New York: Vintage, 1992.

Maron, Monika. *Endmoränen: Roman.* Frankfurt am Main: Fischer, 2004.

Martens, Lorna. *The Promised Land? Feminist Writing in the German Democratic Republic.* Albany: SUNY Press, 2001.

Marvell, Andrew. "The Definition of Love." 1681. In *The Complete English Poems,* ed. Elizabeth Story Donno, 49–50. New York: St. Martin's.

Marx, Karl. *Capital: A Critique of Political Economy.* Trans. Ben Fowkes. Vol. 1. New York: Vintage, 1977.

——. *Early Writings.* Trans. Gregor Benton. London: Penguin Classics, 1992.

——. "The Source and Remedy of the National Difficulties etc.: A Letter to Lord John Russell, London, 1821 (Anonymous)." Trans. Emile Burns, Renate Simpson, and Jack Cohen. In Karl Marx and Frederick Engels, *Collected Works,* vol. 32, *Karl Marx, 1861–63,* edited by Larisa Miskievich, 374–91. Moscow: Progress Publishers, 1989.

Marx, Karl, and Friedrich Engels. *The German Ideology.* Trans. C. Dutt and C. P. Magill. London: Lawrence & Wishart, 1974.

——. *Heroes of the Exile.* Trans. Rodney Livingstone. In *The Cologne Communist Trial,* 135–230. New York: International Publishers, 1971.

——. *Karl Marx, Friedrich Engels Gesamtausgabe (MEGA).* Ed. Institut für Marxismus-Leninismus beim ZK der SED and Institut marksizma-leninizma (Moscow, Russia). Vol. 11 Apparat. Berlin: Dietz, 1985.

Mauer, Charly, ed. *Liebeswende/Wendeliebe.* Berlin: Morgenbuch, 1992.

Meier, Monika. "Konzerte der Redevielfalt: Die Walpurgisnacht-Darstellung in der *Amanda* Irmtraud Morgners." *Literatur für Leser 4* (1990): 213–27.

Meisel-Hess, Grete. *The Sexual Crisis: A Critique of Our Sex Life.* 1917. Eastbourne, UK: Gardners Books, 2007.

Merkel, Ina. *Utopie und Bedürfnis: Die Geschichte der Konsumkultur in der DDR.* Cologne: Böhlau, 1999.

Meuschel, Sigrid. *Legitimation und Parteiherrschaft: Zum Paradox von Stabilität und Revolution in der DDR 1945–1989.* Frankfurt am Main: Suhrkamp, 1992.

Miller, Barbara. *Narratives of Guilt and Compliance in Unified Germany: Stasi Informers and Their Impact on Society.* London: Routledge, 1999.

Molyneux, Maxine. "Beyond the Domestic Labour Debate." *New Left Review* 116 (1979): 3–27. http://www.newleftreview.org/?view=1014

Morgner, Irmtraud. *Amanda: Ein Hexenroman.* 1983. Darmstadt: Luchterhand, 1984.

———. *Das heroische Testament: Roman in Fragmenten.* Ed. Rudolf Bussmann. Munich: Luchterhand, 1998.

———. *Leben und Abenteuer der Trobadora Beatriz nach Zeugnissen ihrer Spielfrau Laura: Roman in dreizehn Büchern und sieben Intermezzos.* 1974. Munich: Deutscher Taschenbuch Verlag, 1994.

———. *The Life and Adventures of Trobadora Beatrice as Chronicled by Her Minstrel Laura: A Novel in Thirteen Books and Seven Intermezzos.* Trans. Jeanette Clausen. Lincoln: University of Nebraska Press, 2000.

Mörike, Eduard Friedrich, "Gesang Weylas." 1831. In *Sämtliche Werke: Briefe,* ed. Gerhart Baumann and Siegfried Grosse, 1: 73. Stuttgart: J. G. Cotta, 1959.

Morin, Edgar. *The Stars.* Trans. Richard Howard. New York: Grove, 1960.

Morrison, Susan S. "The Feminization of the German Democratic Republic in Political Cartoons, 1989–1990." *Journal of Popular Culture* 25.4 (1992): 35–51.

Müller, Torben. "Vom Westen lernen, heißt improvisieren lernen: *Guter Rat*—eine sozialistische Verbraucherzeitschrift." In *Zwischen "Mosaik" und "Einheit": Zeitschriften in der DDR,* ed. Simone Barck, Martina Langermann, and Siegfried Lokatis, 69–76. Berlin: Ch. Links, 1999.

Mulvey, Laura. "Visual Pleasure and Narrative Cinema." 1975. In *Visual and Other Pleasures,* 14–30. Bloomington: Indiana University Press, 1989.

Neutsch, Erik. *Spur der Steine: Roman.* Halle (Saale): Mitteldeutscher Verlag, 1964.

Noll, Dieter. *Die Abenteuer des Werner Holt: Roman einer Jugend.* 1960. Berlin: Aufbau, 2008.

———. *Kippenberg: Roman.* Berlin: Aufbau-Verlag, 1979.

Noll, Hans. "Innenleben eines Spitzels: Brigitte Burmeisters trüber Agententhriller aus der 'DDR.'" Review of *Anders, oder Vom Aufenthalt in der Fremde. Die Welt,* 24 September 1988, sec. Welt des Buches: V.

O'Brien, Mary. *Reproducing the World: Essays in Feminist Theory.* Boulder, CO: Westview Press, 1989.

Parteihochschule "Karl Marx" beim ZK der SED. *Zur Entwicklung der Klassen und Schichten in der DDR.* Ed. Wolfgang Schneider et al. Berlin: Dietz, 1977.

Peynet, Raymond. *Verliebte Welt: Ein Bilderbuch für Liebende und andere Optimisten.* Hamburg: Rowohlt, 1949.

Pfeifer, Martin. *Der Schmied von Ruhla: Ein Dorfstück in drei Aufzügen und einem Vorspiel.* Altenburg: Oskar Bonde, 1894.

Pfeifer, Werner. "Filmbesuch Mangelhaft." *Neue Filmwelt,* June 1952, 29.

Pfister, Elisabeth. *Unternehmen Romeo: Die Liebeskommandos der Stasi.* Berlin: Aufbau, 1999.

Plenzdorf, Ulrich. *Die Legende von Paul und Paula: Filmerzählung.* 1974. Frankfurt: Suhrkamp, 1989.

Poiger, Uta. *Jazz, Rock, and Rebels: Cold War Politics and American Culture in a Divided Germany.* Berkeley: University of California Press, 2000.

Polte, Wolfgang, ed. *Unsere Ehe.* Leipzig: Verlag für die Frau, 1968.

Rauhut, Michael. "Beat in der DDR 1964 bis 1972: Politische Koordinaten und alltägliche Dimensionen; Vol. 2: Dokumente." Diss., Humboldt-Universität zu Berlin, 1993.

——. "DDR Beatmusik zwischen Engagement und Repression." In *Kahlschlag: Das 11. Plenum des ZK der SED 1965,* ed. Günter Agde, 122–33. Berlin: Aufbau 2000.

Redaktionskollegium *Neues Deutschland.* "Über die Liebe in unseren Filmen." *Neues Deutschland,* 5 June 1953, 4.

Reimann, Brigitte. *Ankunft im Alltag.* Munich: Deutscher Taschenbuch, 1986.

——. *Franziska Linkerhand: Roman.* Munich: Deutscher Taschenbuch Verlag, 1986.

Reinecke, Horst. "Ideologische Klarheit und künstlerische Meisterschaft gehören zusammen." *Neues Deutschland,* 13 March 1953, 4.

"Reproduktion." In *Kleines politisches Wörterbuch,* ed. G. König, G. Schütz, and K. Zeisler, 554–55. Berlin: Dietz, 1967.

Riecker, Ariane, Annett Schwarz, and Dirk Schneider, eds. *Stasi intim: Gespräche mit ehemaligen MfS-Angehörigen.* Leipzig: Forum, 1990.

Rimbaud, Arthur. "Une saison en enfer / A season in hell." 1873. In *Rimbaud: Complete Works, Selected Letters: A Bilingual Edition,* trans. and ed. Wallace Fowlie and Seth Adam Whidden. Chicago: University of Chicago Press, 2005.

Robin, Régine. *Socialist Realism: An Impossible Aesthetic.* Stanford, CA: Stanford University Press, 1992.

Room, Abram, dir. *Bed and Sofa.* 1927. DVD. Image Entertainment, 2004.

Rougemont, Denis de. *Love in the Western World.* Trans. Montgomery Belgion. Princeton, NJ: Princeton University Press, 1983.

Rowbotham, Sheila. "If You Like Tobogganing." In *Women, Resistance, and Revolution,* 134–69. New York: Vintage, 1972.

Rubinfeld, Mark D. *Bound to Bond: Gender, Genre, and the Hollywood Romantic Comedy.* London: Praeger, 2001.

Rubinstein, S. L. *Grundlagen der allgemeine Psychologie.* Moscow, 1935. Trans. H. Hartmann. 4th ed. Berlin: Volk und Wissen, 1961.

sander, h., and r. schlesier. "'die legende von paul und paula': eine frauenverachtende schnulze aus der ddr." *frauen und film* 2 (1974): 8–47.

Schiller, Friedrich. *Cabal and Love* [Kabale und Liebe]. In *Plays,* ed. Walter Hinderer. The German Library 15. New York: Continuum, 1983.

Schlenstedt, Dieter. "Ankunft und Anspruch: Zum neueren Roman in der DDR." *Sinn und Form* 18.3 (1966): 814–35.

Schmidt, Heinz H. "Die Geburt des Magazins." *Das Magazin,* January 1954, 1.

Schmitz, Dorothee. *Weibliche Selbstentwürfe und männliche Bilder: Zur Darstellung der Frau in DDR-Romanen der siebziger Jahre.* Frankfurt am Main: P. Lang, 1983.

Schmitz-Köster, Dorothee. *Trobadora und Kassandra und—: Weibliches Schreiben in der DDR.* Cologne: Pahl-Rugenstein, 1989.

Schnabl, Siegfried. *Mann und Frau intim: Fragen des gesunden und des gestörten Geschlechtslebens.* Berlin: Verl. Volk und Gesundheit, 1977.

Scholze, Jana. "Ausgezeichnete Höchstleistungen: Leistungsstimulierungen in der DDR." In *Fortschritt, Norm und Eigensinn: Erkundungen im Alltag der DDR,* ed. Andreas Ludwig, 85–104. Berlin: Ch. Links, 1999.

Schubbe, Elimar, ed. *Dokument zur Kunst-, Literatur- und Kulturpolitik der SED.* Stuttgart: Seewald, 1972.

Schulz, Max Walter. *Wir sind nicht Staub im Wind: Roman einer unverlorenen Generation.* Halle (Saale): Mitteldeutscher Verlag, 1965.

Schwarz, C. "Nachgetragene Liebe." *Neue Zürcher Zeitung,* 29 December 2003, sec. Feuilleton, 21.

Schwarzer, Alice. *Der kleine Unterschied und seine grossen Folgen: Frauen über sich; Beginn einer Befreiung.* Frankfurt am Main: S. Fischer, 1975.

Scott, H. G., ed. *Problems in Soviet Literature: Reports and Speeches at the First Soviet Writers' Congress.* Westport, CT: Hyperion, 1935.

Sedgwick, Eve Kosofsky. *Between Men: English Literature and Male Homosocial Desire.* New York: Columbia University Press, 1985.

Seghers, Anna. *Die Entscheidung.* 1959. Berlin: Aufbau-Verlag, 2003.

Severn, David. *Waldferien: Ein Jugendbuch* [Forest Holiday: A Book for Young Adults]. 1946. Trans. Karl Hellwig. Flensburg: Wolff, 1949.

Shakespeare, William. "Sonnet XXI: So it is not with me as with that Muse." In *The Complete Oxford Shakespeare,* ed. Stanley W. Wells and Gary Taylor, 781. 2nd ed. Oxford: Oxford University Press, 2005.

Silberman, Marc D. *Literature of the Working World: A Study of the Industrial Novel in East Germany.* Bern/Frankfurt: H. Lang, 1976.

Skyba, Peter. *Von Hoffnungsträger zum Sicherheitsrisiko: Jugend in der DDR und Jugendpolitik der SED 1949–1961.* Cologne: Böhlau, 2000.

"Sozialistischer Realismus." In *Kleines politisches Wörterbuch,* Ed. Waltraud Böhme et al., 790–92. 1967. Berlin: Dietz, 1973.

Spivak, Gayatri Chakravorty. *In Other Worlds: Essays in Cultural Politics.* New York: Methuen, 1987.

Staadt, Jochen. *Konfliktbewusstsein und sozialistischer Anspruch in der DDR-Literatur: Zur Darstellung gesellschaftlicher Widersprüche in Romanen nach dem VII Parteitag der SED 1971.* Berlin: Volker Spiess, 1977.

Stern, Kurt. "Kunst ist Menschengestaltung." *Neues Deutschland,* 10 February 1953, 4.

"Strafanzeige gegen Film *Sonnenallee.*" *Frankfurter Allgemeine Zeitung,* 27 January 2000, sec. Berliner Seiten, BS3.

T.N. "Der Alptraum." *Das Magazin* 1.2 (1954): 48–49.

Tetzner, Gerti. *Karen W.: Roman.* Halle (Saale): Mitteldeutscher Verlag, 1974; Darmstadt und Neuwied: Luchterhand, 1975.

Thiel, Heinz, dir. *Der Kinnhaken.* Perf. Manfred Krug, Dietlinde Greiff. 1962. DVD. Icestorm Entertainment, 2007.

Thorp, Margaret Farrand. *America at the Movies.* New Haven, CT: Yale University Press, 1939.

Timasheff, Nicholas S. *The Great Retreat: The Growth and Decline of Communism in Russia.* New York: E. P. Dutton, 1946.

Trumpener, Katie. *The Divided Screen: The Cold War and the Cinemas of Postwar Germany.* Princeton, NJ: Princeton University Press, forthcoming.

——. "Old Movies: Cinema as Palimpsest in GDR Fiction." *New German Critique* 82 (2001): 39–75.

Uhlig, Gottfried, Karl-Heinz Günther, and Christine Lost, eds. *Dokumente zur Geschichte des Schulwesens in der Deutschen Demokratischen Republik.* Vol. 2. Berlin: Volk und Wissen, 1969.

Ulbricht, Walter. "Über die Entwicklung einer volksverbundenen sozialistischen Nationalkultur." In *Zweite Bitterfelder Konferenz, 1964: Protokoll der von der Ideologischen Kommission beim Politbüro des ZK der SED und dem Ministerium für Kultur am 24. und 25. April im Kulturpalast des Elektrochemischen Kombinats Bitterfeld abgehaltenen Konferenz,* ed. Sozialistische Einheitspartei Deutschlands, Zentralkomitee, Politbüro and Ministerium für Kultur, 71–149. 2nd ed. Berlin: Dietz, 1964.

Vogel, Frank, dir. *Das siebente Jahr.* Film. DEFA, 1969.

"Vom Verfall der Kunst und Kultur in Westdeutschland: 'Bonn—Totengräber des Westdeutschen Films': Die Zerstörung der westdeutschen Filmindustrie durch Bonn und den USA-Imperialismus im Spiegel der Presse." *Neues Deutschland,* 23 June 1953, 4.

Weber, Hermann. *Die DDR 1945–1990.* Oldenbourg Grundriss der Geschichte 20. Munich: Oldenbourg, 2000.

Welk, Ehm. "Mehr realistische Dichtung!" *Neues Deutschland,* 19 February 1953, 4.

Wellershoff, Marianne. "Musik der Freiheit." *Der Spiegel,* 4 October 1999: 288.

Westgate, Geoffrey. *Strategies under Surveillance: Reading Irmtraud Morgner as a GDR Writer.* Amsterdam: Rodopi, 2002.

Wexman, Virginia Wright. *Creating the Couple: Love, Marriage, and Hollywood Performance.* Princeton, NJ: Princeton University Press, 1993.

"Wie soll das nur ohne 'Die Legende von Paul und Paula' weitergehen? Abschied von der Börse." *taz, die tageszeitung,* 27 August 2003, sec. cinemataz, 23.

Wierling, Dorothee. "Die Jugend als innerer Feind: Konflikte in der Erziehungsdiktatur der sechziger Jahre." In *Sozialgeschichte der DDR,* ed. Hartmut Kaelble, Jürgen Kocka, and Hartmut Zwahr. Stuttgart: Klett-Cotta, 1994.

Wilder, Billy, dir. *One, Two, Three.* Perf. James Cagney, Horst Buchholz, Pamela Tiffin, Arlene Francis. 1961. VHS. MGM/UA Home Video, 1996.

Wilke, Sabine. *Ausgraben und Erinnern: Zur Funktion von Geschichte, Subjekt und geschlechtlicher Identität in den Texten Christa Wolfs.* Würzburg: Königshausen & Neumann, 1993.

Wilkening, Christina. *Staat im Staate: Auskünfte ehemaliger Stasi-Mitarbeiter.* Berlin: Aufbau-Verlag, 1990.

Wohlgemuth, Joachim. *Egon und das achte Weltwunder.* Berlin: Verlag Neues Leben, 1962.

Wolf, Christa. *Cassandra: A Novel and Four Essays.* Trans. Jan van Heurck. New York: Farrar, Straus and Giroux, 1984.

——. *Der geteilte Himmel: Erzählung.* Frankfurt am Main: Suhrkamp, 2008.

——. *Divided Heaven.* Trans. Joan Becker. New York: Adler's Foreign Books, 1976.

——. *The Fourth Dimension: Interviews with Christa Wolf.* Trans. Hilary Pilkington. London: Verso, 1988.

——. *Kassandra: Erzählung.* Darmstadt: Luchterhand, 1983.

——. "Selbstversuch: Traktat zu einem Protokoll." In *Blitz aus heiterm Himmel,* ed. Edith Anderson, 47–82. Rostock: Hinstorff, 1975.

Wolf, Hugo. "Gesang Weylas." In *The Complete Mörike Songs,* 160. New York: Dover, 1982.

Wolf, Konrad, dir. *Sun Seekers [Sonnensucher].* Screenplay by Karl-Georg Egel and Paul Wiens. Perf. Ulrike Germer, Günther Simon, Erwin Geschonneck, Manja Behrens, Viktor Avdyushko, Willi Schrade. 1958, 1972. DVD. Icestorm International, 2004.

Wolf, Markus, and Anne McElvoy. *Man without a Face: The Autobiography of Communism's Greatest Spymaster.* New York: PublicAffairs, 1999.

Zentralkomitee der Sozialistischen Einheitspartei Deutschlands, ed. *Dokumente der Sozialistischen Einheitspartei Deutschlands.* Vol. 4. Berlin: Dietz, 1954.

——, ed. *Dokumente der Sozialistischen Einheitspartei Deutschlands.* Vol. 9. Berlin: Dietz, 1965.

——, ed. "Für den Aufschwung der fortschrittlichen deutschen Filmkunst." Berlin: Dietz, 1952.

Zimmermann, Peter. *Industrieliteratur der DDR: Vom Helden der Arbeit zum Planer und Leiter.* Stuttgart: Metzler, 1984.

Zinner, Hedda. "Ein Film muß zunächst unterhaltend sein." *Neues Deutschland,* 12 February 1953, 4.

Žižek, Slavoj. *The Sublime Object of Ideology.* London, New York: Verso, 1989.

Index